Ram Gopal

Ram Gopal

Interweaving Histories of Indian Dance

Ann R. David

methuen | drama
LONDON • NEW YORK • OXFORD • NEW DELHI • SYDNEY

METHUEN DRAMA
Bloomsbury Publishing Plc
50 Bedford Square, London, WC1B 3DP, UK
1385 Broadway, New York, NY 10018, USA
29 Earlsfort Terrace, Dublin 2, Ireland

BLOOMSBURY, METHUEN DRAMA and the Methuen Drama logo
are trademarks of Bloomsbury Publishing Plc

First published in Great Britain 2024

Cover design: Charlotte Daniels
Cover image: Ram Gopal, 1944 (© Cecil Beaton / Chronicle / Alamy Stock Photo)

A catalogue record for this book is available from the British Library.

Library of Congress Cataloging-in-Publication Data
Names: David, Ann R., author.
Title: Ram Gopal : interweaving histories of Indian dance / Ann R. David.
Description: [New York] : [Bloomsbury Academic], [2023] | Includes
bibliographical references and index.
Identifiers: LCCN 2023020498 (print) | LCCN 2023020499 (ebook) | ISBN
9781350367197 (pbk) | ISBN 9781350166196 (hbk) | ISBN 9781350166202
(epub) | ISBN 9781350166219 (pdf)
Subjects: LCSH: Ram Gopal, 1917-2003. | Dancers–India–Biography. |
Ethnology–India–Methodology.
Classification: LCC GV1785.G638 D38 2023 (print) | LCC GV1785.G638 (ebook) |
DDC 792.802/8092 [B]–dc23/eng/20230705
LC record available at https://lccn.loc.gov/2023020498
LC ebook record available at https://lccn.loc.gov/2023020499

ISBN: HB: 978-1-3501-6619-6
PB: 978-1-3503-6719-7
ePDF: 978-1-3501-6621-9
eBook: 978-1-3501-6620-2

Typeset by Integra Software Services Pvt. Ltd.
Printed and bound in Great Britain

Contents

Plates

Figures

Acknowledgements

Writing a book is never an easy, speedy or straightforward process. The research for this manuscript on Ram Gopal commenced many years ago and has taken a decade to come to fruition (whilst engaging in other writing and publications) and owes a debt of gratitude to numerous friends, colleagues, acquaintances, dancers and fellow academics for its final appearance. Without this support, the journey of such a delightful, fascinating and at times frustrating project would not have survived. The world pandemic (2020–22) created by the appearance and devastation of Covid-19 did not help. Journeys to many archive collections in Europe and the United States were cancelled allowing only minimal online access and leaving much rich material not consulted. Thankfully, I had accumulated substantial papers, artefacts and other material over the years and had made visits to several national and international archives. I offer a huge vote of thanks to the archivists and staff of the following collections and centres worldwide for their time and expertise in finding material and guiding me through their collections: in India, the Music Academy, Chennai; the Sangeet Natak Akademi and the Indira Gandhi National Centre for the Arts, Delhi; Kerala Kalamandalam, Cheruthuruthy; and to the staff and artistes of the beautiful setting of the Adishakti Laboratory for Theatre Art Research, Tamil Nadu, where I stayed to write and research. Although unable to make further visits to the United States, time spent at the New York Public Library Jerome Robbins Dance Division in previous years yielded fertile material, and I am indebted to curator Norton Own at Jacob's Pillow, Massachusetts, for locating film from Gopal's 1950s performance and allowing me online access. Visits to archives in Europe included the Centre National de la Danse (CND) and the Bibliothèque National de France in Paris, and online consultations with Digitaltmuseum and the Carina Ari Library in Stockholm. My thanks to archivists Satu Mariia Harjanne and Peter Bohlin for their detailed online assistance when Covid-19 prevented the planned visit to Sweden.

In the UK extensive thanks are due to Helen Roberts and her team at the National Resource Centre for Dance (NRCD), University of Surrey; to Jane Pritchard of the V&A collections, London; and to archivist Barnaby Bryan of the Middle Temple, London, all who provided important information in helping piece together some of the narratives of the book. London visits to the British Museum, where curator Richard Blurton granted me private access to paintings of Ram Gopal not on public display; to the National War Museum; to the National Portrait Gallery; and to the British Film Institute have proved invaluable in locating material relating to Ram Gopal. Additionally, online access to the South Asian Diaspora Arts Archive (SADAA), now housed at Birmingham Museum and Gallery, was very useful, and for a short, personal visit to their private archives, I thank Richard Gough in the UK and Ashish Khokar in India. Support for writing during a sabbatical term was provided by the University of Roehampton, London, and by Angela Hobart with two extended research/writing fellowships at her Fondazione Centro Incontri Umani, Ascona, Switzerland. I am indebted to Dr Hobart for her continued, generous support for this book project.

During research visits to India, friends and fellow dancers offered much warmth, hospitality, connections, advice, as well as conversations and more formal interviews, and for all of this I wish to offer deepest thanks to Pushkala Gopal for conversations and generous hospitality, Anita Ratnam, the late M. K. Saroja, Kumudini Lakhia, Alarmel Valli, Abraham Chacko, Thomas Chacko, Sunita Panjabi, Veejay Sai, the late Sunil Kothari, Ashish Khokar, Ayisha Abraham and K. K. Gopalakrishnan, as well as dancers and friends in the UK and others parts of the world: Chitra Sundaram, Anusha Subramanyan, Shane Shambu, Shala Mattingly and Tara Rajkumar. Other dear friends involved in dance and writing on cultural, anthropological and artistic issues have offered unfailing support and advice over many years in a variety of ways: Ananya Jahanara Kabir, the late Andrée Grau, Sarah Whatley, Geoffrey Samuel, Joe Kelleher (in particular for a very fruitful discussion in the early days about the book's structure), Nirmala Seshadri, Rajyashree Ramesh, Priyanka Basu, Mats Merlin, Hari Krishnan, Thomas Kampe, Kusum and Lalit Joshi: I offer them all my warmest thanks as well as to Michal Garapich and Renata Zajdel-Woźniak for information and translations from Polish documents. A very special vote of thanks goes to close friends and fellow academics Stacey Prickett and Magdalen Gorringe for reading through the completed manuscript and bringing their expert attention to the writing. I thank for their time and support other international writers and dancers with whom I have corresponded; these include Nancy Lee Ruyter, Ajay Sinha, the late Naseem Khan, the late Marianne Balchin and her son, Adrian Hindle-Briscall, Reginald Massey and Shala Mattingly. In order to furnish the book with the images it deserves, I am extremely grateful to have been awarded a small grant for additional photos by the Ivor Guest Research Grant facilitated by the Society of Dance Research. My thanks additionally go to editor Anna Brewer and her team at Bloomsbury for their continued support, encouragement and advice.

Finally, a very deep and warm gratitude goes to Gopal's family and closest friends who have again offered their time and support for this book project, graciously putting up with my many questions and detailed checking: dear friends of Ram Gopal – Pamela Cullen and for the many effects of Gopal's gifted to me including photos, books and costumes, the late Denise Iredell, and the late Nani Bhatt and her daughter Leena Kapadia, Jenny Casperson and Peter Hartley; Gopal's family – Joy Jones for the many delightful conversations and access to family photos, Peter Ramgopal, Arjun Nath for all his helpful research and Susan Nath – a very special thank you to all of you. Without you this book would not have contained the wonderful detail of your family and reminiscences that give it life and breadth.

Beginnings: Multiple histories and modernities

> *Which of Mr Ram Gopal's gifts is most to be praised? Is it the enthusiasm that fired him to reveal the glories of Indian dancing to the western world, to instruct European audiences in the appreciation of Kathakali's subtleties ... Is it the marvellous coordination of eye and finger and trunk and foot, the instinct for angle and line, the unsleeping grace of carriage?*
>
> (*The Times* 1950: n.p.)

This book pays homage to one of the early pioneers and public stars of Indian dance, Ram Gopal (1912–2003), examining the cultural, social and political milieu in which he lived and worked. It charts his family background and early introduction to dance, following many of his journeys touring the Far East, the UK, the United States and Europe and tracing his legacy in the dances of India. Although well known in his day, Gopal effectively outlived his fame, residing for his last years in relatively obscure circumstances in a south London nursing home. The book sets out his especially important role in transforming the Indian dance that Westerners witnessed from the late 1930s to the period following the Second World War and the subsequent change in perceptions of the classical Indian dancer.[1] It expounds the significant part that Gopal himself played in bringing Indian dance to international audiences from the 1930s to the late 1960s, a process of transnationalization and the context in which this took place. Part biography, part interweaving histories of Indian dance, the book engages with the use of historical imagination, employing an ethnographic approach through interviews with Gopal's remaining family members, his costume-makers, close friends, dance partners, other dancers and audience members. Using archival material and critical reviews, it covers his early life and brief career in India, the first international tours that saw

1 'Classical' is of course a contested, colonial term and is used with care here. Certain styles of Indian dance were denoted as 'classical' by the Sangeet Natak Academy (set up in 1952) over the period of the 1950s and 1960s. This important, imposed nomenclature is discussed later in this Introduction.

sell-out performances in the United States in 1938 and in London in 1939, his settlement in India during the Second World War and his subsequent performances/tours, weaving together the multi-layered histories that create his story and his legacy.

In the light of encroaching modernism, the early part of the twentieth century saw some major fissures appearing in the spectatorship and understanding of dance performance. Using the metaphor of historical and cultural *interweaving*, a terminology and theoretical paradigm that nods to Roland Barthes's use of the concept of 'weaving' of text and textuality (Barthes 1975) and Erika Fischer-Lichte's coining of the notion of 'interweaving cultures in performance' (Fischer-Lichte 2009: 393), I examine Gopal's extraordinary and pioneering intercultural performance work and the cultural production of modernism through the history of interweaving cultures.[2] In the 1930s, Gopal created a new, modern, international concert dance, based on classical Indian technique, and established an innovative aesthetic through his culturally and historically woven material, disrupting perceived notions of fixed identities, origins, gender, styles and geographies. I argue that Gopal interrupted and challenged European orientalism whilst simultaneously and consciously utilizing tropes of oriental thought in his performances. This analysis reveals how Gopal's dance concerts interwove a myriad of cultures and histories without erasing difference (Fischer-Lichte 2009).

Gopal changed the perception of Indian dance outside of India, providing a taste of classical and folkdance genres to audiences who, up to that point, had mainly been exposed to 'oriental, interpretive' dancers, often (ballet-trained) Westerners with no specific Indian training. The movement vocabulary of these dancers was created through an imagined and impressionistic vision of Eastern forms and included such well-known names as Ruth St Dennis, Anna Pavlova, Nyota Inyoka[3] and Roshanara.[4] Dancer Uday Shankar's performances preceded Gopal's concerts by a few years although Shankar's work was at that time

[2] In using this term, I take note of Emily Wilcox's warnings regarding the loaded dance terminology of 'modern' and 'postmodern'. She argues how they are not 'neutral mediators' and come with a 'cultural context and political history that require critical reflection' (2017: 166).

[3] Inyoka was born in 1896 in Pondicherry and developed a passionate interest for India and its culture as she grew up in Paris, presumably imbibing the Orientalist fascination of the time. Her mother was French and her father Indian. She frequented the Musée Guimet in Paris and its Eastern arts collection, read and studied widely, and became friends with Uday and Ravi Shankar in the 1930s. Performing in the 1920s and 1930s in New York, Paris and London, she was billed as a 'famous oriental dancer'. See also https://project-nyota-inyoka.sbg.ac.at (accessed 2 March 2021).

[4] Roshanara was born Olive Cruddock in Calcutta in 1894 and spent her early years in India. Daughter of an English mother and Irish father, she studied ballet and watched local folk dancers in India. She performed in London in 1911 dancing oriental roles in productions such as *Schéhérazade* and *Kismet*, travelling to perform in Paris and New York with her own productions of what she termed 'Indian dances' (see David 2001a for further detail of these and other interpretive dancers).

mainly imaginative and creative, as I discuss later. Gopal brought specificity and an artistic aesthetic based on Indian imagery and temple sculpture. His performances featured trained dancers from India, Java and Britain, professional musicians, and costumes based on Indian iconography, in contrast with the recorded Western music and makeshift costumes of the early orientalist dancers.[5] But he was also an innovator, using theatricalizing techniques and introducing a mixture of styles of dance from India – including folk as well as classical dance – and performances from Java and Bali. To understand his impact on international audiences I investigate the sumptuous imagery of him taken by well-known society photographers, for example, Cecil Beaton and Carl Van Vechten, and those drawn and painted by artists Feliks Topolski, Milein Cosman and Kay Ambrose.

In addition to the professional photos capturing him Gopal carefully controlled his image off- and onstage. Like most dancers, he maintained a heightened sensitivity to his own physical presence and his performance persona, as it was the tool of his trade. His care for the details of costumes, make-up, ornaments and lighting was renowned. Offstage, he was known for presenting a certain flamboyance in his dress – colourful silk turbans, dramatic caftans, and expensive jewellery, as also the use of make-up, hair dye, and later a toupee – and he always had an eye for the camera, even in his older years (David 2006). Dancer Kumudini Lakhia who worked with him for many years remembers that 'he took great care of himself, paying close attention to his hair, plucking his eyebrows and wearing nice clothes' (quoted in Shah 2005: 47). As a closet gay dancer at a time when homosexuality was illegal, how did Gopal deal with issues of sexuality and perceptions of gender in his historical and cultural interweavings onstage and offstage? Did he knowingly play with the homo-erotic undertones of his photo portraits created by Van Vechten in 1938? These issues are discussed using theoretical approaches to the representation of racialized, exoticized and Othered bodies onstage. The varied, multi-layered and intertwined cultures and histories are embedded in a spectrum of political and social thought, moving as they do through the pre- and post-war years, traversing nationalist movements, the reconstruction of dances, the demise of empire, gender and race equalities, and the subsequent changes in world thinking. Against this backdrop, Gopal's

[5] During the period 1918–20, London's dance monthly, the *Dancing Times*, featured several dancers of this genre, supported by articles entitled *Hindu Dancing* (January 1920, November 1923) and *Impressional Eastern Dancing* (August 1925). A three-page feature in March 1919 described the dancer Dacia who had 'made a special study of the dances of India' (1919: 197) but who had never visited India.

story brings a fresh lens to the conceived category of Indian dance and allows a re-thinking of the classifications of the perception of modernity in dance. The narrative of his life reflects how views of empire changed from Gopal being feted as India's 'jewel in the crown' and taking tea with Queen Mary in 1939, and perhaps somewhat ironically, years after the demise of empire, being awarded an Officer of the Order of the British Empire (OBE) for his services to dance in 1999.

The story I tell examines the lineage from which he came, and the legacy he left, interrogating the cultural, social and political milieu in which he lived and worked and acknowledging the multi-layered tropes of race, gender, colonialist thought and the rise of nationalism in a turbulent global period. Themes addressed include the problematic politics of nomenclature of Indian dance forms (e.g. South Asian dance, Indian classical dance, *Sadir*), the dancing body weighted with colonialist, nationalist and orientalist discourses, and the influence of dance styles such as ballet and modern dance on the new development of Indian dance. In strict terms, Gopal could be considered an outsider: he was from North Indian and Burmese parentage and therefore not fully Indian; he was a non-native Tamil speaker. He grew up with an English Catholic education and spoke some Burmese and later some Polish. Gopal was outside of the *devadasi* system; that is, he was a non-hereditary dancer, as well as outside of the frames offered by the reformers.[6] This meant as a middle-class, educated man Gopal clearly was not of *devadasi* lineage and was not learning and performing dance as a nationalist reformer. As a gay man, he was outside the cultural Indian norms and living at a time when homosexuality was prohibited. Yet he was also partially an insider as he had trained with canonical teachers and became world renowned as an exponent of the south Indian classical dance styles of kathakali and bharatanatyam. It is maybe this outsider/insider status that made him want to explore dance more broadly and to interweave many new and creative ideas into his work, as well as challenging the status quo through acts of resistance that I go on to explore.

Whilst much has been written on the legacy of the female dancers glossed as *devadasi* (Coolawarla 1992, Kersenboom 2010, Meduri 1996, Soneji 2008, 2012, Srinivasan 1983), and on contemporary, historical and global issues relating to the classical dance style of bharatanatyam (Meduri 2004, O'Shea 2007, Soneji 2010, Srinivasan 2012), little writing has focused on Indian male dancers of

[6] As Saskia Kersenboom describes, '[i]t seems probable that the right to become a devadasi was hereditary, although not exclusively so since girls could be adopted and made eligible for the position' (2010: 54). See also Gaston (1996).

the early period. What writing exists has engaged mainly with Indian dancer Uday Shankar, who preceded Gopal in his international performances and who brought a very different kind of approach and style to staged dance concerts, as I have noted earlier (see also Allen 2010 [1997], Erdman 1987, 1996, Munsi 2011). Several writers discuss Shankar and Gopal briefly but without distinguishing between them, conjoining their work simply as pioneers of the 1930s and 1940s. Significantly, Priya Srinivasan argues how the presence of male Indian dancers such as Shankar and Gopal changed the orientalist narrative. 'They were seen as more authentic and traditional than the white female dancers like Ruth St Denis who created and performed Eastern dances.' (2012: 108). Ruth St Denis has variously been seen in the narratives on Indian dance as a dancer who embraced orientalist modes from the early 1900s and who famously and problematically performed a creative dance piece on the Indian goddess *Radha* in 1906, dressed in an Indian sari (2012).[7]

There is no doubt that both Shankar and Gopal challenged the perceptions of Indian dance by Western audiences. Shankar had toured to the United States and Europe before Gopal in the early 1930s to packed, appreciative audiences and produced a modernist, creative style of performance. Both Gopal's debuts in the United States in 1938 and London in 1939 and Shankar's performances brought into reality the breadth, colour, depth and range of the dance forms and music of the subcontinent. Although many similarities exist, the two dancers emerged from different backgrounds in dance as already indicated – Gopal with his strict training in kathakali, bharatanatyam and kathak, and Shankar evolving his own style from careful observation in childhood of folk and kathak dancers. Shankar's study of classical art forms and his later study of kathakali supported this. The fact that both men created short items of music and dance for their Western audiences indicates an awareness of the Western perception of long Indian dances as boring and the music as repetitive and monotonous. They understood the short attention span of these audiences who had no knowledge of the dance form and were aware of the conventions of staging and production on a Western proscenium stage, with the need for creative lighting, accurate sound and an interval in the programme. The necessity for variety in the dance form and the costuming was also understood.

[7] American modern dancer Ruth St Denis (born Ruthie Denis in 1879) was originally trained in Delsarte technique and began her career as a vaudeville dancer. Working with dancer Ted Shawn, they together established a company and training centre in modern dance, called Denishawn, training many of the next generation of modern dancers such as Martha Graham, Doris Humphrey and Charles Weidman.

An imaginative historiography

Using an imaginative historiography to bridge together the rich fragments of evidence from Gopal's life that include scattered excerpts of film, filmed documentaries, photographic imagery from societal and arts photographers of the day, costumes, critical performance reviews and anecdotes from Gopal's friends, work colleagues and family, I attempt to recount/recreate the story of the interweaving cultures and histories of Indian dance in which Gopal was, and remains, a central figure. Larraine Nicholas notes that a researcher must be guided by 'academic rigour and empirical data' (2013: 243) whilst yet being selective with data to produce a coherent account. She acknowledges that the fragments of information must be bridged by what is implied from potential isolated pieces of evidence, and this requires the tool of an historical imagination. These disparate parts are collated from both inside and outside the official documentation and in Gopal's case include the traces that remain of the dancing body. Put succinctly, '[t]he body … cannot escape being a vehicle of history, a metaphor and metonym of being-in-time', argue John and Jean Comaroff (1992: 79). Although events may dominate the historical record, the processes in and through which performances emerge need imaginative analysis too. Dancing is notoriously ephemeral, appearing and then disappearing, although as Diana Taylor points out, a performance's disappearance or sustainability is 'profoundly political' (2003: 5) acknowledging how some traditions are permitted to last and others left to erode. Dancing bodies, and dancing performances, do 'not leave behind … material objects, which remain "relatively" stable in the sense they can be touched, felt or looked at in their extant context' (Thomas 2018: 70).

The book does not set out to be a full biography, although it introduces certain newly discovered biographical detail of Gopal's life, giving context and historical accuracy to the narrative and the weaving of the issues considered – of modernity and diaspora, of colonialism and nationalism, and of homoerotic and celebrity culture. I take heed of Pierre Bourdieu's critical analysis of biographical status (2004 [1987]) where he condemns common approaches to the concept of life history and a person's biography. Bourdieu's post-modern approach rejects the use of the metaphor that life is a journey, that it has a linear, coherent narrative, suggesting that such biographies are in fact an illusion. Life as it is experienced is not necessarily a coherent whole, but full of contradictions, confusions and unclear beginnings and endings. Historical accounts that use a normative biographical approach try to bring order and meaning into life histories; instead, Bourdieu posits that such histories are social constructions and illusory. He notes that 'trying to understand a life as a unique and self-sufficient series of successive events ... and without ties other than the association to a "subject" whose constancy is probably just that of a proper name, is nearly as absurd as trying to make sense out of a subway route without taking in to account the network structure' (2004 [1987]: 304). It is the complex interweaving of networks of social relations that should interest the biographer rather than the identity carried simply by the name that creates 'a constant and durable social identity' (2004 [1987]: 300) of an individual.

Gopal's fame and celebrity status were carried by his name and talent as a performer and such construction of a star image or a celebrity is well documented in film theory (see Turner 2006 [1988], Williams 1995, for example). Graeme Turner illustrates how 'a star has a signifying function which may be separate or different from the written character within the film script' (Turner 2006 [1988]: 139). Through this signification, an audience knows a star both in his/her screen persona and in what appears to be an ordinary, life-like mode, through the various representations in film, press, TV, fan magazines, and in current times, through social media. This star phenomenon is created by the information that is publicly available – the performances, the publicity material, film and TV, press promotion, interviews and critical reviews, as well as audience reception – and is always complex. Gopal's fame was not only constructed by his dance performances and through the wealthy circles he frequented but through a certain presence in popular culture; in 1950 a racehorse, owned by Mr T. Lowry, named Ram Gopal, ran in Britain at the races at Newmarket, Birmingham and Worcester in the spring of that year and was acknowledged in *The Times* newspaper's racing selections. TV appearances in the late 1940s and early 1950s, as well as a central London film premiere and invitations to exclusive receptions all added to his star persona.

The celebrity status of a subject necessarily needs a multi-layered approach to their lives, events, professional colleagues and social circles, especially in the arts. Joan L. Erdman states: 'Writing dance history is a complex project, since the field encompasses not only dances and artists – choreographers, dancers, designers, and composers – but also contexts, contacts, and colleagues of these artists' (2008: 306). Historical ethnography, according to Margaret E. Walker (2014), helps reveal how the past remains operative in the present. This is a pressing question when working with the historical events of a dancer's life and archival material to bring the past to life once more. Immersion in the archives can lead to a strong sense of past realities, a useful historical perspective, but without necessarily leading to an understanding of present practices. The materialities

Figure 1 Ram Gopal in Warsaw, 1938. Photographer unknown. Courtesy of National Digital Archives, Poland.

of the past – the programme notes, written reviews, archival film footage, photographs, human memories, costumes, music – are not simply passive items. They act back in an affective mode with a vibrancy, revealing not just one past but complex, multi-layered pasts which, in the present, create something new. I question here how Gopal's dance productions and the ambassadorial role he played lean persuasively into today's world of Indian dance performance. As Prarthana Purkayastha questions, '[w]hat makes the past of dance so important to our present?' (2014: 123). By working with past effects and memories in discussion and in the written form, they are brought into the here and now and understood as fresh cognitions. These discoveries reveal the minor, hidden relational stories, not just the dominant major ones. Pasts are being created now, giving a less linear view of time, a sort of 'contemporary archaeology', Oliver Harris notes. He argues how in creating pasts, 'we fold past, present and future together' (2019: n.p.).[8]

Employing a sense of historical imagination that creatively finds new ways of looking at the past, using an interpretive technique to fill gaps and produce meanings (Carter 2018) from the plethora of source material derived from witnesses, critics and contemporary accounts that do not arrive without bias and selectivity, is one way forward. I question what are the relationships between the disparate pockets of information; between transnational movements of people, artefacts and dance languages; between journeys of specific dancers and what meaning might be constructed from them. Lena Hammergren (2004) argues that a writer creates a micro-history when looking at the life of an individual dancer but also necessarily must consider the macro-history in examining the context and historical period. Meaning is made through considering 'history's multiple voices', she states (2004: 27). What weaving of cultures took place in this historical period, with movements of people all over the globe, due to war, persecution or economic migration or the ending of empire? What were the interweaving histories of the Indian dance forms? And who were the managers and the impresarios that followed the wealthy patrons of dance in India who supported dance performance? These questions are discussed as the book unfolds.

To reconstruct reception, I have thoroughly researched certain primary sources. Physical archives in India, the United States, Europe and the UK as well as those online have been invaluable treasure troves and have yielded fertile seams of material in their collections of contemporary programmes, sketches, photos, articles and critical reviews from magazines and newspapers. Primary archival material has its limitations, however, as what remains of programmes, reviews and articles from the past is already selective. There is clear evidence of some dance performances, and no data remaining from others. Facts in written programmes may be misleading as there is only recorded the intention to perform particular works and the expected cast, not necessarily the changes that may have taken place on the night of performance. Yet these archival libraries in different parts of the globe have additionally been a valuable source of secondary material in the form of reference books and film and have allowed an historical ethnography to be created. Information gleaned from these source

8 'Archaeology and the creation of past'. Unpublished talk given for the annual Curl Lecture, Royal Anthropological Institute (RAI), September 2019.

materials similarly must be evaluated with care, as June Layson reminds the researcher, 'Source materials in themselves do not constitute dance history but as the remnants of and commentaries upon the past they provide the basic starting point for study' (1995 [1983]: 29). Further, some of these archive collections have been established on the back of colonial power and colonial exhibitionism so are neither silent nor uncompromised partners in the setting out of histories. Renewed care and awareness of these factors are essential in this process, making sure to check for unconscious biases and colonial-infused thinking. In this light, Taylor (2003) reminds the reader how *both* archive and repertoire are essentially mediated. Underscoring this point, Colin Counsell cites Taylor (2009: 8) and her laying out of a clear distinction between the archive and the repertoire and notes that documented archival material as an official record may depend on hegemonic structures, whereas the unofficial, ephemeral material of repertoire is 'the domain of cultural processes' and thus allows for acts of resistance where new meanings can be made. There are several examples of Gopal creating such acts of resistance in his performative career: he and Shankar for example, through their global concerts as previously noted, disrupted the hegemony of the white, interpretive dancers (Srinivasan 2012) who had brought their own forms of ethnic dance to audience goers (see David 2001a); Gopal and dancers such as Ragini Devi were the first to start using the term 'bharatanatyam' more widely – Devi in 1938, Gopal in 1948 – with Gopal identifying the different styles of each dance piece in his programmes.[9] His performances brought detailed knowledge, training and appreciation of the variety and background of Indian classical and folk dance that creatively and culturally challenged the performances by 'orientalist' dancers lacking in such specificity. I argue that Gopal challenged and resisted the reformulation and reinstitution of bharatanatyam by the social reformers, distancing himself from Rukmini Devi's work, for example, by not placing the Siva icon onstage and by embracing the *devadasi* repertoire. In this way, he created pioneering intercultural performance work and demonstrated a cultural production of modernism in his innovative performances and staging.

And I acknowledge here the limits of a work of this kind in that it cannot provide the definitive, comprehensive listing of all performances, all critical reviews, all company details and Gopal's extensive world travels. An imaginative historiography, however, weaves together the available threads of

[9] The term was first used in the Madras Music Academy programmes in 1931 (see Chapter 2).

the multifaceted aspects of a performative career and life, allowing riches to emerge from sources that can be accessed. Significant in the book is a focus on Gopal's embodied practice, allowing him to emerge dancing with energy and charisma out from the archive, bringing back a sense of the lived movement and his bodily dancing presence. The bodily presence is abundantly replete with knowledge, more powerful than the written fragments in dusty libraries and boxed archives, and rightly needs to be privileged. I examine Gopal's living dance expression using several mediums: through analysis of the few films that exist; through a close perusal of his own dance notebooks; by using artist Ambrose's notation of his dances; through the many photographic images of him taken throughout his life; and through careful reading of the critical reviews of his concerts. Taylor reiterates the point, stating that '[e]mbodied and performed acts generate, record, and transmit knowledge' (2003: 21).

'Ram Gopal … is one of the most resplendent figures who have ever appeared on the London stage and one of the loveliest of dancers', noted *The Daily Telegraph*'s critic (1939: n.p.) after watching Gopal in July 1939 at the Aldwych theatre in London, where dance-lovers and theatregoers witnessed an extraordinary phenomenon. A young Gopal, making his British debut performance, played each evening to captivated, packed houses. Such was his impact that audiences queued to buy tickets and the scheduled two-week season was extended to four. In that early programme, Gopal's kathakali-based solo items, *Dance of Siva, Indra, Cobra Devil Dance, Glory of Spring, Deevali Puja* and his famous golden eagle dance, *Garuda*, together with two items of mimed storytelling, made up eight of the eighteen dance pieces of the full evening's performance. He also enacted dances from Java such as the story of King Klarna. As the mythical eagle *Garuda*, Gopal leapt out from the side of the stage, wearing gold leather wings and a beautiful bird headdress with beak. His swooping, grandiose arm movements coupled with huge, vigorous jumps crossing the stage and bird-like movements of head, neck and eyes provoked gasps of wonder in the audiences. Not only is archival material in this way enlivened with Gopal's presence but costume artefacts that remain, such as *Garuda*'s wings and *Siva*'s ornate headdress, now in the Victoria and Albert Museum (V&A) collection in London, are an existing and present testament to the lived, ephemeral, danced form. Engagement with critical reviews of the time and audience response, however, requires an objective and theoretical enquiry using notions of rapture, affect and reception theory, which I undertake in Chapter 4.

Figure 2 Ram Gopal in Javanese costume as King Klarna, 1938. © Hulton Deutsch, Getty Collection.

Terminologies

The term 'South Asian dance' was brought into use in the UK in the 1980s to supersede the existing terminology 'Asian dance' and 'Indian dance' and was designed to include dance traditions from the whole of the subcontinent, regardless of political subdivisions.[10] But the label remains a problematic one. In North America, it refers to the geographical region of the Pacific Rim and includes Indonesia, Thailand, Cambodia, the Philippines and Malaysia, and to British Asian dancers it can appear somewhat reductive. USA-based dancer/scholar Uttara Asha Coorlawala argued 'from my perspective, the phrase "South Asian Dance" is repeatedly embedded within a discourse of pain and anger, a discourse that interrogates whiteness, and negotiates a place for itself in a white driven power structure' (2002: 32). Indeed, the Arts Council Review on South Asian Dance in England admitted that some

[10] Much has already been written on this descriptor (see Grau 2001, Lopez y Rojo 2004, Meduri 2008a).

artists 'feel completely alienated by the term "South Asian Dance", asserting that "Indian Dance or Classical Indian Dance" is a more appropriate term for their work' and go on to state that in the 'development of the field, dissonance is also present' (Jarrett-Macauley 1997: 13–14). The *ADiTi* dance teacher's handbook explained that '[i]n Britain, the term South Asian dance embraces the classical, folk, creative, contemporary and other popular dance styles and genres originating from the countries of Bangladesh, India, Pakistan, and Sri Lanka' (Gordziejko 1996: 6). In 2013, the Imperial Society of Teachers of Dancing (ISTD) made the decision to change the name of their faculty of South Asian Dance, established in 1999, to Classical Indian Dance, after fourteen years usage of the former terminology (see David 2013). This decision arose out of intensive discussions with teachers and practitioners who believed that the new name was more indicative of the actual teaching taking place within the ISTD faculty – that of classical bharatanatyam and kathak. Some also 'commented that the name Classical Indian Dance Faculty has brought a more classic and dignified approach and is more elegant on the tongue as well as creating a more unique identity' (David 2013: 59).

Although now in widespread use in South Asian dance in Britain, distinctions between 'classical' and 'folk' remain challenging. Originally, as Alessandra Iyer argues, these binary classifications were 'not indigenous to the sub-continent' (1997: 5), and the original categorization of *margi* and *desi* (often incorrectly glossed as 'classical' and 'folk') was not as straightforward as our modern distinction of these same terms.[11] *Margi* is described in the *Natyasastra* (a codified Sanskrit treatise dealing with dance, drama, music, poetics and aesthetics and thought to have been composed in the first centuries CE) as the movement forms for dance and drama which were pan-Indian and referred to different geographical areas, languages and tribes. The word *margi* in Sanskrit means a 'high or proper course' and *desi* translates as 'of the country, provincial', although modern colloquial usage of the term means a 'fellow Indian' or anything related to India, i.e. *desi* food, dance or friends. *Desi* dance practices developed in the regional, local traditions as variants of *margi* but were also sophisticated forms in themselves and not analogous to folk dances, as is assumed today. Both *margi*

[11] Various writers and commentators have made their own distinctions between the two forms. Reginald Massey describes *margi* as dance sacred to the gods, or danced for the gods, whereas *desi* is dance for human pleasure (Singha & Massey 1967: 22). Padma Subrahmanyam's detailed study of the sculptural dance poses in Indian temples led her to articulate a theory that *margi* was the original base technique of all Indian dance, out of which developed *desi* or regional styles such as bharatanatyam, kathakali and kathak (Subrahmanyam 1988). See also Indira Viswanathan Peterson's discussion on the distinction between *margi* and *desi* where she notes that *desi* is a more complex concept than perhaps usually thought, stating, 'Definitions and descriptions of dance and music forms classified as *desi* suggest that the term has a very wide provenance, encompassing a variety of phenomena whose origins lie in popular, non-canonical, regional and tribal milieux' (1998: 41).

and *desi* contained aspects of religious practice, as also solo and group forms, dance-dramas and storytelling. Kapila Vatsyayan notes how the twin concepts of *margi* and *desi* extend over the fields of music, drama, dance, aesthetics and language, stressing how the two categories are distinct yet related (1987). She argues that they were not applied with any hierarchical connotation, as they are qualitative artistic terms, not sociological categories, stating, 'Indeed a continuum between the two is evident, in most spheres of Indian art … the *margi* and the *desi* cannot be equated simply to sacred and mundane, because in a single "performance" or piece of work both may be contained' (1987: 16).

There remain further historical dilemmas with these categories. The bifurcation into distinct and weighted binary views of what is considered classical and folk still resonates today, influencing policies of arts funding, performance publicity and political issues. The term 'classical' carries notions of permanence, of an unbroken continuity as well as the accepted features of classicism, such as formality, symmetry, harmony, restraint, order and codified forms. This establishes a binary opposition that sees the folk forms as informal, unordered, unrestrained, implying a sense of inferiority and simplicity. Theresa J. Buckland (1983) notes six ideal characteristics of classical music which can adequately be applied to the classical dance context (these follow A. E. Green's lectures on folk music). They compose a prescriptive written body of literature accompanying the form (c.f. the *Natyasastra* for South Asian dance); formal institutions of learning; distinction between the performer and a passive audience; support from wealthy patrons; and a continuity of transmission supported by accredited standards, such as examination systems and a taught syllabus. Coorlawala argues how in the 1970s in India, 'almost every dance form claiming antiquity and sophistication, noted references within the canonized *Natyasastra*' (2004: 54).

Using ethnography

The research for the book leans towards an ethnographic approach, as noted, using interview sources as primary resources where they exist. Oral histories through interview can simultaneously provide rich seams of data and unrecorded narratives and facts and so provide excellent material for the weaving of cultural histories, despite at times, being potentially unreliable in terms of personal preference and the selectiveness of memory. The how's and why's of memory production are as important as any details of events recalled, so the researcher can note how personal memories and the social world experienced by the person interviewed are mediated. Certain friends and older members of Gopal's family are present at this point of writing (2019–21), as well as some audience members, costume makers and fellow dancers; most however are elderly and the majority of his main dance partners are no longer with us.[12] Interviews carried out with this group of remaining contacts furnish the text with lively personal narratives relating to Gopal and his dancing, but they also contribute an understanding of the wider cultural context in which they are embedded (Abrams 2016). Through detailed archival research and these oral histories, new understanding and knowledge of Gopal's family are uncovered, none of which has been recorded up till now.

As a practice, ethnography has a wide range of methods and far-reaching applications that have formed the backbone of classical anthropology and social and cultural anthropology from the early twentieth century to the present day. Indeed, ethnography's 'centrality to social or cultural anthropology is unquestionable' (Atkinson et al. 2001: 2). Ethnography involves research that is based on direct observation of and participation in a community's way of life. Deirdre Sklar states, '[A]n ethnographer seeks not only to describe but to understand what constitutes a people's cultural knowledge' (1991: 6), and therefore the ethnographer will question how a group of people make or find meaning. But 'the fluidity of the ethnographic enterprise' (Buckland 1999: 8) remains the most compelling element of the whole process, allowing for a comprehensive engagement with the people studied, and it is this adaptable aspect which is particularly relevant for research into dance practices.

Developments in the literature dealing with ethnographic methodology have impacted on the practice of dance ethnography and resulted in a move away from a positivist stance whose main ideas relate to the world being essentially knowable, logical and governed by universal laws, to a more post-modern, reflexive position. These developments are characterized by 'reflexivity, self-criticism, and increasing eclecticism' (Brettell 1993: 1), in which ethnographic techniques have come under a new spotlight and increasing attention and interest has been given to both the fieldwork experience and the written product. Charlotte Aull Davies argues for the importance of issues of reflexivity in ethnographic research 'in which the involvement of the researcher in the society and culture being studied is particularly close' (1999: 4). The participation of the ethnographer in the field and the subsequent construction of data and the written text necessitates a position of self-examination or 'a process of self-reference' (1999: 4). This practice of reflexivity remains a particularly significant factor

12 As well as younger members of the family who had not met him but are deeply interested in knowing of his work and impact. Memories however are mixed and contrasting remembered details of older family members cannot be verified. This is also due to the lack of recording of births and marriages at that time in India and Burma.

for the researcher as an awareness of the power of one's own preconceptions, ethical background, gender, education and beliefs is essential in approaching work in the field. Unconscious bias of this kind needs to be acknowledged and especially as a British, middle-class, white female researcher awareness of the need to decolonize one's thinking and approach is essential. Andrée Grau points out that there is a 'danger inherent in any research dealing with identity in that it can be seen to "ethnicise" its subjects' (2001: 24) and therefore intense scrutiny is needed in the construction of this text to avoid any sense of othering.

To practise reflexivity is to question those aspects of knowing, of unconscious bias – the assumptions, cultural preferences, binaries of right and wrong, attitudes, and importance ascribed to various actions that we hold – and to discover how, in this case, the dancer Ram Gopal might classify and categorize his own culture and movement practices. To put it another way – it is to try to understand the emic perspective. Without such understanding, as researchers, 'we cannot begin to enter a dialogue with others about what *they* think it means to be an embodied person, and so what it means to do dance, or sign, or engage in ritual and ceremonial practices' (Farnell 1999: 156). My own long-term engagement with dance and with Indian classical dance spanning most of my lifetime as a practitioner, spectator, researcher and writer on Indian dance and ritual (see David 2007, 2010a, 2010b, 2010c, 2012a, 2012b) helps ease the bridge between my own relatively privileged British upbringing and the colonial and post-colonial Indian world in which Gopal grew up and from which he emerged.[13] The three years I knew and engaged with Gopal as a friend and colleague before his death adds a personal and poignant touch to the academic analysis of his story (see below).

Film and imagery as sources

Engaging in research that relies on an investigation of visual sources that include film and photography requires a scrutiny of such resources. Such visual recordings of dancers are subject to the filmmaker or photographer's selective processes and therefore have limited scope to convey a rich, thick level of a dance in performance. Film and photography capture forms but are unable to convey

[13] I studied bharatanatyam under the tutelage of Smt Rati Karthigesu at the Bhavan in London for 5 years and later 4–5 years of kathak with Smt Sushma Mehta and Damayanti (aka Anne Steenhuis-Hesterman) in Holland. I took some classes in odissi with Smt Priya Pawar and have performed in all three styles. I have been a spectator in the UK at Indian dance performances for over forty years and a researcher of this area for a similar time. My PhD (2005) examined the dance practices in UK Gujarati and Tamil Hindu communities.

implicit meanings, so only a partial reality may be communicated. Due to the ephemeral nature of performances of dance and music, film and audio recording are especially important as tools for instant recording but need to be utilized by the researcher with an awareness of these facts. Kirsten Hastrup suggests that textural and film accounts have a hierarchical relationship where the text can bring a 'thick' description, whilst film techniques may offer only a 'thin' one. She notes that 'they are not in conflict, nor are they just complementary modes of expression, because they do not operate on the same logical level' (1992: 21).

Hastrup describes how film has 'an immense power of seduction' (1992: 14), persuading the viewer that what is being watched exists as an accurate reality, rather than a selected and constructed representation and therefore the use of film can seem to be unproblematic. Film is often only recorded from one camera position at any time, creating a 'front' to the action, as in a staged performance. Yet many dance performances are not enacted in this way, so that when action turns away from the camera, it cannot be seen, thus creating a partial recording. Despite the limitations of the medium of film, the strengths of such recording lie in the fact that the footage can allow for repeated viewing of particular sequences of dance, and this in turn offers the possibility of movement analysis. Technological restrictions of the earlier period mean that little film footage remains of Gopal's actual dancing and so reduces the possibility of analysing in depth his movements and style to create a more detailed understanding of his choreography and movement vocabulary.

Historical contexts

The now much-documented histories of Indian dance were playing out in full force during Gopal's formative period in the 1930s and 1940s. It was an age of unsettling, cataclysmic, global turbulence of the world war and a period of drastic change during which time India shook off the shackles of colonialist rule, developing a new nation state supported by nationalist agendas that played out through political thought and cultural activities, and that was particularly constructed through a re-constitution of its dance styles. As Pallabi Chakravorty aptly describes, '[t]he ideas of purification, reform and national regeneration prompted the nationalist, English-educated elite to hark back to the spiritual roots of the nation's past, which, they argued, reside in traditions of arts, aesthetics and culture' (2008: 46). The use of dance as a tool to perform nationalism is not a new phenomenon. There are numerous examples worldwide of nationalist frameworks utilizing language and the arts to scaffold and to foreground their ideals: Eastern-bloc countries such as Romania and Poland where trained and sponsored state dance-ensembles were sent on tours to represent their supposedly young, outward-looking, modern and energetic countries (see Giurchescu 1994, Shay 1999); the use of folklore in Turkey for consolidating national identity (see Ozturkmen 1994); and the creation of a universal folk dance for the newly emerging nation state of Israel (Gibert 2007). Gopal's clever and strategic manipulation of the forces behind the changes in Indian dance is highlighted and discussed in the chapters that follow through an analysis of his pre-war and post-war performances. I seek, too, to indicate how his use of a modern classicism enabled him to navigate a path through the complexities and hierarchies of such Indian dance histories. Questions however remain. Why did Gopal never appear to engage in the political sphere considering the turbulence of the times? Through all his writing, interviews and recorded discussions, Gopal does not involve himself in political comments or debates. Bearing in mind the age he lived through, one of the most turbulent world periods including the withdrawal of Britain as a colonial power in India and the subsequent devastating partition of the land, this seems somewhat surprising. It raises questions about whether Gopal was apolitical in some way, or whether as a colonial subject, he did not feel free to speak out, perhaps silenced by the enforced power dynamics? I explore further these complexities in Chapter 4.

Existing literature

Recent scholarship on Indian dance, such as Sitara Thobani's (2017) meticulously researched writing on transcultural and post-colonial representations of Indian classical dance, Priya Srinivasan's (2012) candid uncovering of the transactional and transnational labour of Indian dance, Chakravorty's (2008) informative book on new directions and practice in kathak, and Purkayastha's (2014) critical writings on Indian modern dance reveal the breadth of current research work through practice-based approaches. Further, there are pertinent volumes on *odissi* as a neoclassical form by Nandini Sikand (2017), a detailed exploration of kathak's history by Walker (2014), new writing on contemporary Indian dance in an edited volume by Ketu H. Katrak (2011), and Royona Mitra's (2015) thought-provoking book on dancer Akram Khan and interculturalism. Davesh Soneji's extensive, detailed research into the *devadasi* dancers and forms of bharatanatyam is a significant addition to the work in this area (see Soneji 2008, 2010, 2012), and all these published editions contribute to the growing and significant research into Indian dance across the world.

The present book follows in the genre of published volumes/articles examining male dance performance (Burt 1995, Desmond 2001, Fisher & Shay 2009, Gard 2006, Krishnan 2009) whilst creating a specific frame relating to the politics of nationalist paradigms and the rapid changes created by the demise of colonialism and the new classicist agenda for the arts in India. New analytical work on practices of masculinity in kuchipudi dance by Harshita Mruthini Kamath (2019) opens the door to a discussion on South Asian masculinities and the male dancing body. Kamath sees 'masculinity as an inherently relational, social practice of the body' (2019: 8) and seeks to move away from Western hegemonic gender binaries that are irrelevant in global and, particularly, South Asian contexts, where gender fluidity and what I have previously called 'gendering the divine' (David 2010c: 75) are pertinent concepts.[14] It is worth noting a new growth in studies of South Asian masculinity and its disruption (see Kamath 2019: 9–10, 171 n.25 and Osella & Osella 2006). This published material adds to significant articulations on Indian male dancers by Hari Krishnan in his work on hypermasculinity in Indian dance (2009) and Anna Morcom's writings on marginalized male (and female) dancers in India (2013).

Apart from Gopal's autobiography (1957), his own book on Indian dance co-authored with Serozh Dadachanji (1951), and Ambrose's book on classical Indian dance (1950) which features his dance pieces, there exists only a small amount of any substantial writing and documented work on Gopal and his performances. These include Ambrose's self-published small, forty-page booklet *The Story of Ram Gopal* (1951) and Sunil Kothari's published interviews with Gopal (1991[1984]), his newspaper and magazine articles (2000, 2017) and his talks on Gopal's performances (2022); and Ashish Khokar's tributes on Gopal's death (Ashish Mohan Khokar 2003) amongst his other work on Gopal (1998) including a Sahapedia page (2018) and Veejay Sai's online writing on Gopal (2015).[15] The Indian publication *Nartanam* devoted a complete issue to Gopal at his death with a series of articles on him, as did *Sruti* magazine; Anne-Marie Gaston included Gopal in the dancers she interviewed and discussed in her important work on bharatanatyam (1996). A 1947 Indian publication on *Dance in India* by Govindraj Venkatachalam has a rather unflattering chapter on Gopal. More recently a chapter was written on Gopal in *Gay Icons of India* (2019) by Hoshang Merchant and Akshaya K. Rath, and Rebekah J. Kowal raises a detailed discussion of Gopal's visit to Jacob's Pillow in the 1950s and his earlier New York debut in her book on globalism in dance in

[14] This article in the *International Journal of Hindu Studies* examines the less frequently observed phenomena of female leadership of Hindu ritual in London which challenges orthodox male-dominated practice (David 2010c).

[15] See https://scroll.in/article/689145/a-visual-tribute-to-ram-gopal-indias-forgotten-dance-superstar (accessed 20 August 2020). Khokar set up the Ram Gopal Award for best male dancer after Gopal's death.

America mid-century (2020). Finally Ajay Sinha's book on Gopal's encounter with American photographer Carl Van Vechten in 1938 brings some crucial evidence to light through his close, analytical approach to the creation of such images (2022). Many newspaper reviews of his performances exist, and Gopal features in some dance encyclopaedias as well as in general books on dance. But to this date, no extensive, detailed work that focuses solely on Gopal has yet been published.

A personal narrative

My own connection with Gopal is relevant here. Many years ago, deciding on a topic for my MA dissertation in dance, I spoke with my father, John White. Knowing my avid interest and commitment to the world of Indian dance, he told me of his own witnessing of Gopal's dancing in 1951 and the powerful impression it had made on him. He went to find the original programme that he had kept. Although yellowing, the programme was in remarkably good condition. It is of the performance at the Cambridge Theatre, London, in January 1951, a thin, four-page document, costing six pence. On the cover is a small, black-and-white photo of Gopal in his Siva headdress, titled 'Ram Gopal, with his Indian dancers and musicians'. The eighteen items of the evening's concert included musical pieces by the Indian orchestra, followed by dances from Manipur, Ceylon, kathak, kathakali and bharatanatyam. Gopal's famous *Garuda*, golden eagle dance and his Siva *Dance of the Setting Sun* were central to the programme.

Inspired by my father's story, I set out to find out more about this extraordinary dancer, fuelled in part by my father's enthusiasm when he described 'the arrival of Ram Gopal with his colourful costumes, the "exotic" sounding music, and a form of artistic expression that was totally fresh and unfamiliar, made a great impact … Then we were deeply impressed by the grace and beauty of his movements, and by the realisation that his perfection of technique must have sprung from years of training' (interview with author, August 2000). I began to investigate sources and libraries, particularly the V&A Theatre Archives then based in Covent Garden, London, to find more programmes and evidence of Gopal's performance in the UK.[16] I eventually discovered that he was living in a nursing home forty minutes' drive from my house, although elderly and very frail. I made a connection and thus began a three-year friendship consisting

[16] These are part of the extensive Victoria and Albert Museum (V&A) archives, now lodged at Blythe House in West London. By 2023, they will be relocated in the new Collections and Research Centre in Stratford's Queen Elizabeth Olympic Park, London.

of regular visits to talk with him, peruse books and photos together, and meet some of his friends. I have since published work on Gopal (David 2001a, 2001b, 2001c, 2006, 2010a) and given many public and academic talks about his work.[17] Although very well known in his day, Gopal spent his last years in the south London nursing home in relatively obscure circumstances and died in hospital in October 2003. After his death, a small, moving memorial service and cremation was held during which several of us spoke about his life and work. Despite this sense of obscurity, Gopal has often been regarded as a dancing legend and as the elder statesman of Indian dance by dancers and aficionados of Indian dance performance. Bharatanatyam teacher at the Bhavan Centre in West Kensington, Prakash Yadagudde, invited Gopal as the chief guest for his first student's *arangetram* and the Academy of Indian Dance in London (Akademi) honoured him in their grand, site-specific millennium performance which I discuss below.

As I have acknowledged, Gopal did outlive his fame, surviving until his ninety-first year. In the last decade, over fifty years after he retired from the stage, there has begun to be a renewed interest in his life in India where he was largely forgotten and in other parts of the world. Some early footage of Gopal dancing has been uncovered in Bangalore by filmmaker Ayisha Abraham which is being shown at regular seminar events in India and the United States, and art historians have been looking once again at the imagery captured in stills of his dance career (Sinha 2017, 2022). *The Hindu* newspaper ran an article showing the early press interest in this book, interviewing me whilst researching in India in 2017, and a new book on gay lives in India dedicated a whole chapter to the dance work of Gopal, as noted above (Merchant & Rath 2019).[18]

Younger generations of Indian dancers all over the world are now raising questions about Gopal's dance identity and his place in Indian dance history. His famous dance of *Garuda*, the mythological golden eagle, was the subject of a project funded by the UK Lottery Heritage Fund in 2015–16, and the project's website includes educational materials for future generations to use.[19]

[17] Public talks given by the author on Gopal include the National Portrait Gallery, London (2003), at the hanging of Gopal's full-length portrait, painted by Feliks Topolski; the V&A Museum, London (2016) to launch the new lottery-funded film on Gopal's dance of *Garuda*; the British Library, London (2018) as part of their South Asia talk series, and the Museum of Croydon (2023). Additionally, I have given over ten international conference presentations on Gopal.

[18] The Hindu article is at https://www.thehindu.com/life-and-style/a-book-on-the-late-indian-modernist-dancer-ram-gopal/article22435266.ece (accessed 10 August 2020).

[19] Titled 'Garuda – Celebrating the Legacy of Dancing Legend, Ram Gopal', the project had a £85,400 grant and was run by SADAA (South Asian Diaspora Arts Archive) in conjunction with the V&A. It includes a twenty-five-minute documentary on Gopal's work and life; see https://sadaa.co.uk/projects/garuda-project. Accessed 6 November 2020. I was interviewed for the film and participated in the final public presentations at the V&A.

Additionally, Gopal featured in a photographic exhibition titled *Black Chronicles: Photographic Portraits 1862–1948* at the National Portrait Gallery, London, in December 2016. In the millennium year 2000, Akademi celebrated its twenty-first birthday in a groundbreaking spectacular event at the Southbank Centre, London (see also Chapter 6). Titled *Coming of Age,* this was a site-specific work created by Keith Khan, spanning over two days and featuring nearly 100 dancers. Akademi honoured the elderly Gopal in this tribute at the end of the event, stating:

> Another lull as Ram Gopal is brought to the stage nearest to Hungerford Bridge. He sits, regally watching the scene, while the Millennium wheel revolves slowly round in the background and another circle echoing the wheel frames him in lights. As the dancers turn to pay their respects, a tangible link is made between the very early days of South Asian dance in Britain and now – it's coming of age.
>
> (Akademi website)

The international significance of Ram Gopal's work in the early part of the twentieth century has begun to be recognized, and this book contributes to the growing understanding of his innovative role in bringing Indian dance to Western audiences. It continues the work of memorializing this extraordinary dancer, cultural icon and pioneer so that generations to come will have access to his work that wove together cultures of performance, pedagogy and histories of Indian dance. In the light of the current period of increasing nativism and populism in both India and the UK that thrives on naive and intentional stereotyping and compartmentalization, the story of how such a man surmounted differences in cultural thinking and expression, bringing a modern, international form of Indian dance to global audiences and interrupting orientalist perceptions of performance for over thirty years is of utmost significance.

The story unfolds

Using an imaginative historiography, as discussed above, I examine Gopal's life and work as a performative, creative artist through selected key pivotal moments, represented by certain selected artefacts or objets d'art related to specific times and places in his life. These quintessential moments form a powerful nucleus, a central point of significance that draws together the events, the contexts and the processes. Rather than follow a chronological order by year, this framework offers a more fluid, creative approach to the historical details of Gopal's life, whilst placing them in the context of the powerful international political turmoil in 1947 of India's independence from Britain, its subsequent partition into Pakistan, Bangladesh and India, and the processes of nationalization and new transnational migrations.

Chapter 1 begins with Gopal's passport, a copy of which is stored in the British Museum in London. The narrative develops around Gopal's 'British Indian' (colonial) identity and nationality, his home, his family – including bringing to the fore unpublished archival details of his extended family of six siblings and two step-siblings – and his early travel for performances, as well as clarifying his much-disputed date of birth. This passport allowed him to travel extensively initially with American dancer La Meri (born Russell Meriwether Hughes), a pivotal point in 1936 that begins his international career and subsequent travel to the United States, Europe and Britain, pre–Second World War.[20]

Chapter 2 focuses on an iconic photograph of Gopal's dramatic Siva headdress from his famous kathakali piece *Dance of the Setting Sun*, setting the scene to examine the deity Siva's place in the newly forming, nationalist revival/reconstruction/renaming of classical Indian dance in India.[21] The political agenda embedded in the reformulated dance styles includes a construction of hypermasculinity that looked to the great god Siva as embodying this sensibility. Hari Krishnan (2009: 384) records how 'the new male performers of the 1930s such as Ram Gopal became famous for the dances describing the hypermasculine icon of the god Siva Nataraja ("King of Dance") whom they literally "represented" onstage'. The chapter considers the historical importance of the figure of Siva, intellectually, morally and politically in India and his growing significance worldwide, using the context of Ananda Coomaraswamy's orientalist essays on Indian art and culture, *The Dance of Shiva* (2011 [1918]) and Ted Shawn's performance of the *Cosmic Dance of Siva* (1926).[22] Discussion includes Gopal's presence onstage dancing across and beyond binary cultures of race, gender, politics and the racialized body, interweaving patterns of new understanding, growth and renewed interest.

A copy of the passenger records of July 1947 aboard ship RMS *Alcantara*'s voyage from Bombay to Southampton takes the narrative forward in Chapter 3,

[20] La Meri, born Russell Meriwether Hughes in Kentucky, USA, in 1899, was a dancer, choreographer, teacher and writer, known for presenting dance performances from many cultures, especially those from India and Spain. She founded the School of Natya in 1940 in New York which changed its title to the Ethnologic Dance Center in 1942.

[21] As the 'S' in Siva is pronounced as a sibilant, it is often written in the anglicized form 'Sh'. I choose to use the single 'S' spelling as this is the usual transliteration from Sanskrit.

[22] Some brief film footage of this dance remains, where Shawn steps out of a giant sculpture featuring Siva's circle of flames.

informing the reader of Gopal's post-war departure from India. The end of the Second World War and India's independence bring Gopal back to Britain, where he famously dances at the opening of the exhibition in the Indian section at the V&A museum in London. He returns with a new company and musicians, after touring in India as part of ENSA and running a school of dance in his family home in Bangalore in addition to new training in bharatanatyam style. I examine the seven years Gopal spent in India, learning these new dance techniques. For him it is a period of consolidation and local travel, that is continued in Chapter 4 as Gopal's post-war performance tours internationally to the United States, across Britain and Europe, are scrutinized, utilizing his printed 1948 programme as a key pivotal artefact. Gopal's dance of *Garuda* is analysed as one of his key performance attractions and his innovative technique and theatricalizing agenda addressed. This chapter acknowledges Gopal's momentous decision to settle as a British citizen in Britain; it examines his connections with the British ballet world, his being feted by celebrated ballet photographers of the time and his desire to use ballet technique in his teaching and performance of Indian dance. It engages with the type of critical reviews and audience reactions Gopal received and the role that affect and rapture may play in such reception as well as examining the need for patronage and impresarios for the extending of Indian dance performance internationally.

Chapter 5 takes a 1939 watercolour sketch of Gopal by Feliks Topolski as its starting point to examine Gopal's representation by artists and photographers. The sketch is one of a series of twelve, now housed in the collections of the British Museum. These delightful, fresh and evocative watercolour paintings were created in the wings during Gopal's first performances in London. The chapter introduces the varied artists who worked with Gopal and the many society photographers who created iconic images of him onstage and offstage. I argue how such artists helped create a star image, using a potentially homo-erotic lens in their work in showing a beautiful, racialized body onstage. Gopal's own penchant for glamour is noted. The chapter discusses the importance of the moving image for a performative star and his place in popular culture by considering the few existent films of Gopal's dancing and his work as a film actor during the 1950s.

Adverts in the 1960s for Ram Gopal's School of Classical Dance reveal his attempts to start a dance school in London, providing a moment of reflection after nearly thirty years onstage. These adverts set the scene for the final chapter, *Endings*, which considers these endeavours and Gopal's role as 'elder statesman' in the British dance world, as well as the easing, during these later years, of his previously rather tense relationship with India. Echoing the great dancer Uday Shankar before him, Gopal embarks on a new, iconic duet with ballet dancer Dame Alicia Markova, as *Radha and Krishna* (1963); he works intensively in London with the Asian Music Circle and is finally feted in India and Britain through the awards of the Indian Sangeet Natak Akademi Fellowship (1990) and the OBE for services to dance in Britain (1999). The chapter leads the reader to the point of Gopal's death in 2003, and reflects on the previous discussions, drawing the many threads together to conclude the book.

1

Gopal's passport

In the vaults of the British Library, London, a duplicate copy of Ram Gopal's passport is stored. A small, stitched document, with printing on the inside cover spelling out 'PASSPORT, Empire of India', it was issued by the Viceroy and Governor-General of India and stamped by the Secretary to Resident in Mysore and Chief Commissioner of Coorg on 16 March 1937. National status is given as 'British protected person, subject of the Mysore State' and profession is recorded as 'Indian dancer'; height 5 feet 8 inches and colour of eyes brown; hair is noted as black. A small black mole in the centre of the forehead is documented as the only visible distinguishing mark. Turning over the pages, a black-and-white photo of the young holder Ram Gopal stares out with a calm, serene gaze, strikingly handsome with clear skin, bright eyes and a well-proportioned face. Gopal is wearing an open-necked white shirt and collared jacket made in a houndstooth check material. His signature underneath frames the photo. A blank space is left for a photo of a spouse, indicating a time when married women would not usually own their own passports but of necessity travel on their husband's one. The following pages are blank, ready for visas and stamps for port of entry and departure. Its original hard, navy-blue outer cover is now missing and has been replaced by plain beige card for protection, presumably by the British Library. The lost cover would have shown 'British Indian Passport' on the front and underneath the emblem of the British Empire (the Royal Arms of the United Kingdom), and the words 'Indian Empire', blatantly a colonial representation.

These documents were required from 1920 onwards until the independence of India in 1947 and marked the colonial status of the holder. As Mark B. Salter notes, passports function as legitimators for the movement of individuals but do not guarantee entry into other countries, and a 'passport not only prompts questions of immigration, nationality, globalization, travel and belonging, but also connects the individual to the realm of the international' (Salter 2003: 1). Passports offer a certain freedom (to some individuals) yet also reveal inequalities for those who do not have the fortune to own one.

(Photo)

WIFE-FEMME

3

PHOTOGRAPH OF BEARER

SIGNATURE OF WIFE ET DE SA FEMME

SIGNATURE OF BEARER SIGNATURE DU TITULAIRE

Sd/ Bassano Ram Gopal.

2

DESCRIPTION

SIGNALEMENT

Wife - Femme

Profession / Profession: Indian dancer

Place and date of birth / Lieu et date de naissance: Bangalore, India; 20th November 1912

Domicile / Domicile: Bangalore

Height / Taille: 5 ft. 8 in. ___ ft. ___ in.

Colour of eyes / Couleur des yeux: Brown

Colour of hair / Couleur des cheveux: Black

Visible distinguishing marks. / Signes particuliers: Small black mole in centre of forehead.

CHILDREN - ENFANTS

Name / Nom	Age / Age	Sex / Sexe

Figure 3a & 3b Ram Gopal passport, 1937. In collection of British Library, London.

The passport provides a pivotal key in shedding light on Gopal's life story. Disputes for many years over his birth date, understanding of his identity and nationality in relation to the changes happening in colonial and post-colonial India, and his future world travels are both clarified and complicated by this official documentation. The significance of such an identifying record changed radically over the course of Gopal's lifetime, as the British Empire collapsed. Gopal's passport in the name of Mr Bassano Ram Gopal is a British Indian one, number 5296, issued in Bangalore for five years.[1] The date of birth is unmistakably 20 November 1912 although Gopal often gave it as 1917 or even 1920, taking five or eight years off his real age, a deliberate act of concealment that persisted even into some of the obituaries written at his death. Naseem Khan's obit in *The Guardian* quoted his response when asked directly about his age: 'I always say, by God and the Bible … over 21' (13 October 2003: n.p.). The ambiguity continued throughout his life even though *The Telegraph*'s obituary confirmed that 'Ram Gopal's most prized possession was his British passport' (24 October 2003: n.p.), a document that allowed him to leave India for the first time on a tour with the American dancer La Meri in 1937 and to travel extensively on solo tours to the United States and Europe (1938–9), something quite unusual for that time. I discuss these early tours in this chapter as they form significant building blocks for his later career. This ease of travel was remarkable and presents a striking contrast to immigration restrictions young dancers from India who wish to work in Britain in contemporary times have to endure.

Although Gopal's passport allowed him relatively easy access to worldwide touring, he was later refused a visa to travel on two separate occasions. First, a planned performance in Copenhagen, Denmark, in May 1948 as part of a tour to Norway and Sweden was cancelled as Gopal was denied an entry visa (*Derby Daily Telegraph*, 8.5.48: 1). In 1953, a trip to South Africa where a six-month tour had been planned had to be called off. As reported in *The Times* on 16 April 1953:

> Mr M. C. Rouse, the manager of Mr Ram Gopal, Indian dancer, has announced that Mr Gopal's proposed tour of South Africa has had to be cancelled because the South African Government has refused the necessary visa. Application for this visa was made a month ago but was only refused on Tuesday. No explanation is said to have been offered for this refusal.
>
> (*The Times*, 1953: n.p.)

[1] Bassano as he was born on the 20 November and *bees* is Hindi for twenty. He spelt it Bissano, sometimes Bisano and his family shortened it to Sono.

The counties for which Gopal's copy passport was valid are listed as 'British Empire (see regulations 10 and 11), France, Italy, Belgium, Holland'. His father's name and address are given as Mr Ram Gopal, Benson Town, Bangalore. The document states (to the authorities of all other states) that '[t]hese are to request and require in the Name of the Viceroy and Governor-General of India all those whom it may concern to allow the bearer to pass freely and without let or hindrance, and to afford him every assistance and protection of which he may stand in need'. After 1915, all subjects born in British colonial settings were British subjects but were not officially British citizens. Citizenship, however, could be applied for after one year's residence in Britain and there is evidence in the National Archives at Kew, west London, of a duplicate Certificate of Naturalisation no. RI /19668 being awarded to Bissano Ramgopal by the Home Office on the 10 January 1958. Gopal was registered in the British Electoral system from 1950 onwards.

Gopal, as I discuss in Chapter 3, returned to the UK in 1947 to live permanently. Although the British Nationality Act of 1948 offered British nationality to all former British Indian subjects, by the mid-1950s, governmental attitudes began to change in India and in Britain. By arrangement with the British Home Office, the Indian government instigated a vetting process for all those wishing to obtain a passport to travel to the UK, requiring that they possessed enough money and a stable financial status as well as literary and spoken knowledge of English (Chatterji 2018). Given that this was the first time Gopal had left home to travel overseas with his father's name indelibly stamped in his passport, the chapter starts with a detailed account of his family home and life, commencing with his father's story. These aspects of Gopal's life have not featured in any of the existing accounts of him and importantly weave a narrative around the newly uncovered factual elements that throw light on his character and subsequent international life. The chapter continues by exploring Gopal's first experiences as a dancer, his professional work touring abroad with American dancer La Meri and his debut solo performances in Japan, the United States, Poland and France in 1938, all made possible by the possession of his new passport. These shows were followed by sell-out performances in London in 1939 with a touring group of dancers, discussed in some detail along with an exploration of Gopal's use of professional musicians. His pioneering intercultural performance work and the cultural production of modernism and explored and reviewed.

Gopal's father, Ramgopal

Gopal was born in Bangalore, south India, the fifth child of six from a mixed-race marriage. His father (1866–1945) also Ramgopal, the eldest of four sons, grew up in Kota, near Ajmer, Rajasthan (then Rajputana) and attended the local Government College before travelling to London for further education.[2] He first studied English literature at King's College, London, where he developed a life-long passion for Shakespeare and then went to Middle Temple, London, from 1888 to 1891 to train as a barrister. Members of the family recall that he was said to be an outstanding student and because of his ability and potential, his education was paid for by missionaries who sponsored his legal studies. Ramgopal's father, Gopal's grandfather, was Lalla Futteh Lal, a settlement officer in Udaipur (Odeypore), in the former Rajputana Agency.[3] He was the Amin of twelve villages in Udaipur on a salary of Rs. 80 per month, according to his son Ramgopal (Jones 1976: 100).[4] As a settlement officer, he worked to uphold the British system of land revenue collection and land administration, primarily identifying the existing land rights and their beholders. Family members believe he was the village headman and a teacher.

Prior to leaving for London, Ramgopal had an arranged marriage with a young woman from Ajmer, originally from the region of Peshawar (Punjab), and had two children with her, Rajoo (known as Mohan) and Nani (also known as Rajbhai), stepbrother and stepsister to his second family of six. Whilst studying law in London, he lived in Notting Hill Gate at 39 Colville Terrace, London, W.10, and later at 6 Station Terrace, Woodford, Essex. He was one of seventeen Indian students in a cohort of 121 admitted to Middle Temple in 1888. Archives of the Middle Temple show recorded details of his admission on 15 November 1888 and of his financial transactions there. Each term's course then cost 10 shillings.

On 13 January 1890, Ramgopal is listed as passing a satisfactory examination in Roman Law, and in March 1891 *The Times* announced his certificate awarded by the Council of Legal Education, having successfully passed a public examination.

[2] Because of the closeness of both names, I use 'Ramgopal' for the father (which he often used) and 'Ram Gopal', thenceforth Gopal, for his son the dancer. Ramgopal is thought to have died in 1945 but the exact date is not recorded.

[3] Rajputana Agency was founded in 1553 by Maharana Udai Singh of the Sisodia clan of Rajput, when he shifted his capital from the city of Chittorgarh to Udaipur. It remained as the capital city till 1818 when it became a British princely state, and thereafter the historic Mewar province (of which Udaipur was the capital) became a part of Rajasthan when India gained independence in 1947.

[4] An Amin was an assessor and collector of revenues, an office that carried 'considerable prestige and importance' (Rashid 1950: 194).

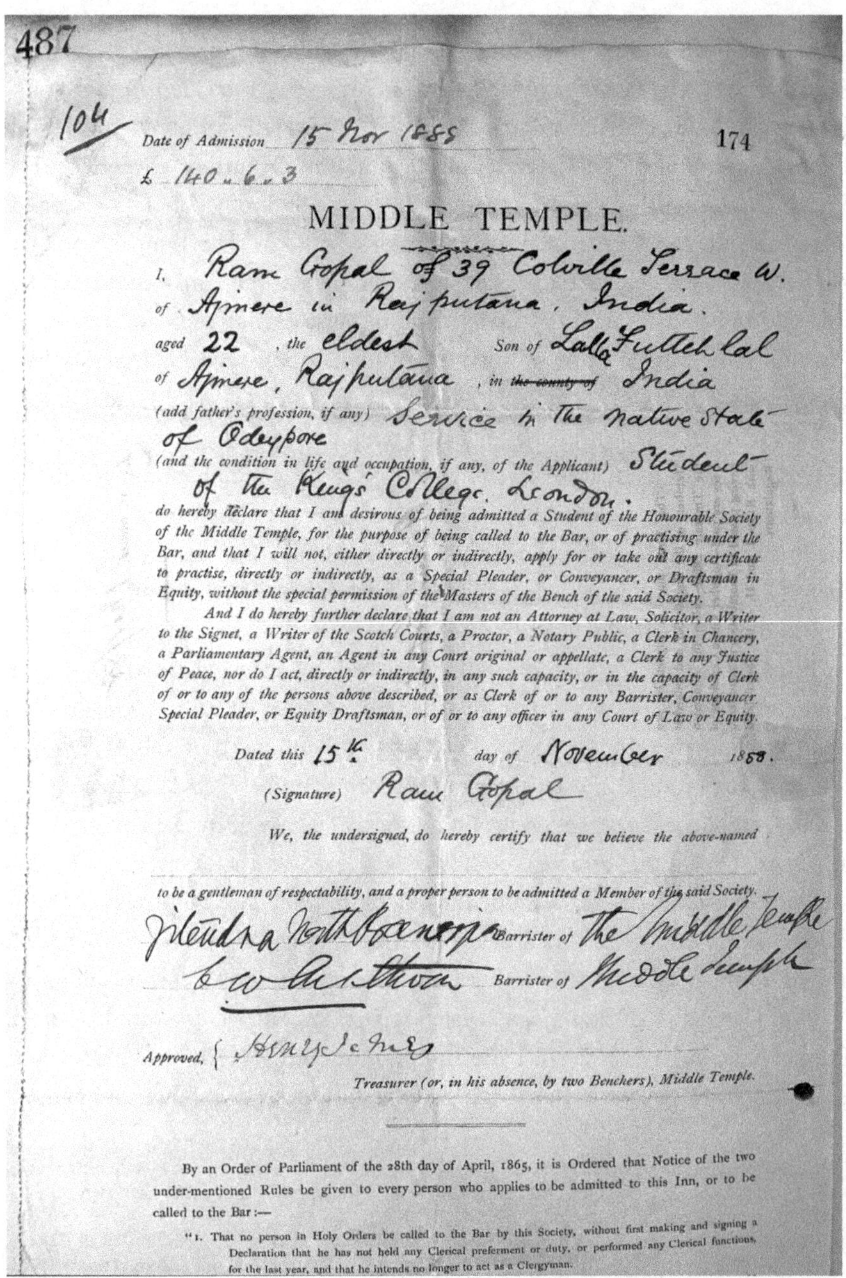

487

104

Date of Admission 15 Nov 1888 174

£ 140. 6. 3

MIDDLE TEMPLE.

I, Ram Gopal of 39 Colville Terrace W.
of Ajmere in Rajputana, India.
aged 22, the eldest Son of Lalla Futteh lal
of Ajmere, Rajputana, in ~~the county of~~ India
(add father's profession, if any) Service in the native State of Odeypore
(and the condition in life and occupation, if any, of the Applicant) Student of the Kings College London.

do hereby declare that I am desirous of being admitted a Student of the Honourable Society of the Middle Temple, for the purpose of being called to the Bar, or of practising under the Bar, and that I will not, either directly or indirectly, apply for or take out any certificate to practise, directly or indirectly, as a Special Pleader, or Conveyancer, or Draftsman in Equity, without the special permission of the Masters of the Bench of the said Society.

And I do hereby further declare that I am not an Attorney at Law, Solicitor, a Writer to the Signet, a Writer of the Scotch Courts, a Proctor, a Notary Public, a Clerk in Chancery, a Parliamentary Agent, an Agent in any Court original or appellate, a Clerk to any Justice of Peace, nor do I act, directly or indirectly, in any such capacity, or in the capacity of Clerk of or to any of the persons above described, or as Clerk of or to any Barrister, Conveyancer Special Pleader, or Equity Draftsman, or of or to any officer in any Court of Law or Equity.

Dated this 15th *day of* November 1888.

(Signature) Ram Gopal

We, the undersigned, do hereby certify that we believe the above-named to be a gentleman of respectability, and a proper person to be admitted a Member of the said Society.

Jitendra Nath Banerjea *Barrister of* the Middle Temple

[illegible] *Barrister of* Middle Temple

Approved, [illegible]

Treasurer (or, in his absence, by two Benchers), Middle Temple.

By an Order of Parliament of the 28th day of April, 1865, it is Ordered that Notice of the two under-mentioned Rules be given to every person who applies to be admitted to this Inn, or to be called to the Bar:—

"1. That no person in Holy Orders be called to the Bar by this Society, without first making and signing a Declaration that he has not held any Clerical preferment or duty, or performed any Clerical functions, for the last year, and that he intends no longer to act as a Clergyman.

Figure 4 Admission form of Ramgopal senior to Middle Temple, London, 15 November 1888. Courtesy of the Archives of the Middle Temple, London.

He was called to the Bar on 10 June 1891 and returned to Ajmer, enrolling as an advocate in the Allahabad High Court. The following year, he travelled to Rangoon (Yangon) as an advocate in the Chief Court starting his own practice in Bassein (Pathein), the largest city and capital of the Irrawaddy (Ayeyarwady) region of Burma (Myanmar), then a British Indian province.[5] Bassein was about 190 km west of Rangoon and was accessed along the Bassein river, where river steamers carried supplies and passengers between Rangoon, Bassein and Mandalay. Ramgopal took on the presidency of the local Bar association in Bassein. It was said at the time that 'he has a good deal of literary ability and is an occasional contributor to various periodicals' (Wright 1910: 387).

In the 1890s, there was scant interest in Burma by those living in Britain and the United States. It was often thought to be part of India (which it was officially until 1937).[6] Whilst living there, Ramgopal met a young woman called Mabesant (or Mabezan), of Karenese ethnicity, who had been educated in a Baptist Missionary School; the region was home to the Karen people, an ethnic minority group from the hill area.[7] It is thought she either came to him for legal advice or was working in his house as a housekeeper. Despite the difference in ages and complications of their status (Ramgopal was nearly twenty years her senior, and was already married with two children, although he may have been widowed at this stage), they began a relationship and married. Andrew Selth (2016: 174) notes that 'cohabitation with local women was … common', and about '90 per cent of the British men there had local mistresses'. Their first two daughters, Jessie and Florence (known as Flossie or Flo), and son John (Jumbo because of his prowess in boxing), and third daughter Elsie (Goodu or Gulshan) were born there. Jessie and Flossie also went to school in Burma.

The family home, Bangalore

Eventually, around 1910 Ramgopal moved back to India, having made a substantial amount of money in Burma through his legal work and other businesses. He had shares in Rowe & Co., a company with several large

5 Nick Cheesman writing on Burma's legal framework notes that '[t]he British … in 1872 had set up a judicial commissioner's court for Lower Burma, although the court did not publish official rulings. In 1892 a judicial commissioner's court installed in Mandalay became the first court in Burma to do so. In 1900 a newly-established Chief Court in Rangoon followed suit' (2014: 78).

6 There had been three Anglo-Burmese wars, in 1826, 1852 and 1885. The last completed Britain's conquest of Burma.

7 An Anglicized version of the Burmese word 'Kayin'.

department stores across Burma and he owned several properties.[8] The family settled in Bangalore, a town popular for retirement and known for its Anglo-Indian and European community. Bangalore was then a cantonment town, the largest in south India with significant areas (about 13 square miles) dedicated to the British Military Garrison, home to the British Indian Army. Spacious bungalows were built for the officers around the garrison creating suburbs such as Benson Town, Cox Town and Fraser Town.[9] Ramgopal purchased a large bungalow called Torquay Castle at 1 Miller's Road, Benson Town, Bangalore, in 1911 from an English seller, as he found the climate more suitable than in Bassein, Burma, where they had been living. With the large income from his

Figure 5 Torquay Castle, family home in Bangalore. Photographer unknown. In collection of family.

[8] Rowe & Co started in 1866 in Rangoon. Their iconic colonial building was constructed between 1908 and 1910. It had three storeys and a basement, with a tower, and featured electric lifts and ceiling fans. The huge department store, known as the 'Harrods of the East', imported European goods and stocked everything that a good-quality department store would house, including clothes, furniture, toys, kitchenware, shoes, prams, saddlery and even motor bikes. The company published a 300-page illustrated catalogue four times a year. Branches of the store were also established in Bassein, Mandalay and Moulmein.

[9] The suburb of Benson Town was named after P. H. Benson, a surgeon for the Mysore Court, and was established in 1883.

work and properties in Burma he was able to retire at a relatively young age (mid- to late forties) and in his fifties took up further studies of Sanskrit and Shakespeare, spending time reading, writing and publishing. The British Library in London has a copy of Shakespeare's *Othello* with annotated notes and an introduction written by Ramgopal with fellow scholar P. R. Singarachan and published in Bangalore in 1928. Housed in the British Library is also a copy of *Sociology or the Law and Progress of Mankind and Their Institutions*, written by Ramgopal and G. R. Josyer and published by the Bangalore Press in 1926. In 1931 Ramgopal produced two edited volumes, *Selections from Ingersoll, Vols 1 & 2* published by the same press.

Ramgopal and Mabesant had two more children in India, Ram (Bissano, often shortened to Sono) and Alice. All the children were given English names (and pet names/nicknames), and educated at Catholic schools, their father being rather keen for them to be anglicized. The two older children by Ramgopal's first wife, Rajoo and Nani, initially lived with them, but eventually the eldest son, Rajoo, returned to Ajmer where his mother had lived and where he worked as a lawyer. Nani had an arranged marriage to a teacher from Ajmer, Dr M. Karamchade Wade who had migrated to Bangalore and who received a large dowry from the marriage.[10] The children spoke Burmese (possibly the Karen dialect) with their mother as her English was not extensive, but English as a family and Hindi with the staff. Joy Jones, Gopal's niece, who lived in India till she was eighteen, remembers her grandmother being very kindly, with a passion for cooking. Mabesant certainly provided affection to the children in contrast to the strict, formal relationship they had with their father. Gopal writes 'My mother was Burmese, a Karen … I was always proud of my mother when I used to walk with her in Bassein or Rangoon when I went with my parents on those few occasions as a child when they took me for my mother's annual visit to her native land' (1957: 9–10).

There were maids, cooks, gardeners and a family retainer from Rajasthan who worked with them all their lives, known affectionately as Gulab or Gulu. Extensive grounds surrounded the substantial house and when Ramgopal added additional wings and floors to the single-storey bungalow, Torquay Castle began to resemble an English stately home. From the front, two large wings extended either side of the front portico at the end of a long drive; the first floor had wide

[10] Wade was an associate of Jawaharlal Nehru and principal of two different government arts colleges in Kumbakonam, Tami Nadu (in 1918), and Rajahmundry, Andhra Pradesh (in 1946). Both Nani's and Rajoo's birth dates are unknown.

balconies with white balustrades, and a smaller second floor jutted above the whole building with a large roof terrace. Mock Gothic arches adorned the two side wings; there were tiled roofs, wrought-iron staircases and a place for poultry at the back. Amongst the many rooms were an extensive library, a billiard room, drawing room (which was made into a bedroom when Ramgopal became ill in the early 1940s) and a substantial dining room. The house was accessed by a long drive and at the front was an ornamental fountain and a garage for the cars. Dogs were kept as family pets. Smaller cottages in the grounds were rented out to various friends and the extended family. Gopal described it as a large, somewhat rambling but beautiful colonial house that had an exotic garden. The grounds also housed two tennis courts in the front right garden (Gopal was an excellent player), a fern house and a pigeon house. It was certainly an advantaged and cultured upbringing. His autobiography conjures up a poetic vision of loveliness in the garden:

> My mother's garden looks from time to time like a still water-colour fresco suspended over the earth, unreal. What a profusion of colour, yellow and red hibiscus, honeysuckle, flame of the forest *Gold Mohur*, that wonderful tree of fire-red blossoms and grey bark, like smoke. The lawns lie like jade, and lizards run from corner to corner; the four wonderful silver oaks seem to sigh, their trunks strongly rooted, their tops swaying from side to side and I catch a glimpse of the silver leaves.
>
> (Gopal 1957: 1–2)

Despite the idyllic setting and the privileged lifestyle, home was not always an oasis of calm. Ramgopal was known for his outbursts of anger and his Victorian strictness, and the children lived in fear of crossing him. On his return to India, he became quite political, joining firstly the Arya Samaj and later the Brahmo Samaj supporting nationalist Indian home rule and Hindu reform.[11] But he fell out with these organizations and left. He certainly did not approve of his son Bissano dancing and wanted him to train in law. Gopal writes in his autobiography how unthinkable it was for his father to accept his dancing. Gopal's mother however supported him in his artistic pursuits, and in fact Gopal recalled his maternal grandmother in Burma being a talented singer and actress (Viswanathan 1996: n.p.). He was the only one of the siblings to pursue an artistic career.

[11] Both are Hindu reform movements: the Arya Samaj began in 1875 and campaigned against caste discrimination amongst other issues. The Brahmo Samaj evolved in Calcutta in 1828 and particularly flourished in Bengal.

Gopal's relatives

The detailed family section that follows is especially significant as Ram Gopal (dancer) did not talk about his family, and it was widely assumed that he was an only child. Nothing to this date has been written about his siblings and their children, nor the detail of his parents' lives and backgrounds. Interviews were carried out by the author with Joy, daughter of Flossie, and Susan, Jessie's granddaughter as well as Peter, eldest son of Jumbo.

Ramgopal was keen for his children to have arranged marriages and to live at home in the extended house. Jessie, the first-born, had an arranged wedding to Gobind Ram Sahgal, a professor in engineering who had studied at the University of California, Berkeley. They later separated and she returned to live at home with her two sons, Ian Inderjit (Gunju) and Narsingh. Both boys trained at the military academy in Dehradun and became commissioned officers in the British Indian Army: Ian a Brigadier and Narsingh a Major. Jessie lived in a ground floor apartment at the back of the house and often wore Burmese clothing, following her mother's example. Second daughter Flossie was more rebellious and managed to marry Tamil-speaking Welshman Tom Mellor, a man whom

Figure 6 Ramgopal family portrait outside Torquay Castle. Photographer unknown. In collection of family.

she had met at the tennis courts and with whom she had fallen in love. Tom was working in Bangalore as a British missionary, so they lived in Bangalore and, in the hot summer months, in Ooty. Their daughter Joy attended a local Catholic convent school and came to London at eighteen to attend art school (interviews with author, 2016–19). She remains living in London at the time of writing.

The first son (and third child) of Ramgopal and Mabesant was John Alpha Ramgopal (Jumbo, 1903–71), who married Hyacinth, an Anglo-Indian Catholic. They lived with their five children, Peter, Ronnie, Christine, Christopher and Paul, in a spacious family flat on the first floor of the house.[12] Elsie, fourth child and the next daughter, had an arranged marriage to the first director of All India Radio in Madras, Dr Victor Paranjoti, from a Tamil-speaking Christian family. Later they separated and Elsie returned to live downstairs at Torquay Castle in the east wing with her two daughters, Santosh and Susheila. The fifth child of Ramgopal and Mabesant was Bassano Ram Gopal (Sono), born 1912, whose life this book discusses, and finally came Alice, who died aged eighteen, probably from diphtheria or pneumonia.

Peter, Jumbo's eldest son, now living in the Midlands in Britain, remembers playing with Narsingh, his cousin at Torquay Castle. He loved to build model aeroplanes and they would fly them together. They used catapults to knock down fruit from neighbour's trees for fun and would also pick mangos, guavas and huge jackfruit from their own large garden. He recalled too the neem and tamarind trees in that garden. Peter recalled how his father Jumbo became the head of the household after the deaths of Ramgopal (believed to be in 1945) and Mabesant (possibly 1944) and how Jumbo looked after his sisters, Peter's aunts, who both had returned home to live. Later, as Jumbo's family grew and included his mother-in-law and some of his wife's siblings, the whole family used Gopal's apartment as well as their own, spreading across the complete space of the first floor whilst Gopal was away on dance tours in India and when he left for Britain in 1947. The two large balconies of the first floor were home to Hyacinth's many pot plants, and where the children would fly their kites.

Gopal had his own apartment on the first floor of the rambling building, accessed by a spiral staircase and with its own entrance. He filled it with paintings, many by the Russian painter Nicholas Roerich who was living in Bangalore at the time, and with Rajput miniature paintings and Russian icons, sculpture, antiques, books, sumptuous carpets and cushions collected on his

[12] Hyacinth, or Cynthia, was from Calcutta and worked in Bangalore for the British Army as a stenographer. She died in Bombay in 2018.

travels in India and around the world. Kathak dancer Kumudini Lakhia who joined Gopal's troupe after the Second World War described how Gopal 'was a voracious reader and had a wonderful library' (interview with author, December 2017). By all accounts, it was an exquisitely beautiful place. Later, he was to build his own dance space in the front part of the garden where he taught classes and rehearsed for performances. 'I had constructed a garden studio. The stage was covered with a tiled roof. The floor was slightly raised. The "auditorium" was large enough to accommodate about a hundred people. And it was in that studio that all my pupils came and worked from morning to night,' he recalls (Gopal 1957: 140).

During rehearsals, the dancers would retire to Gopal's apartment in the lunch break and discuss the next day's work, looking at imagery from books to enhance their understanding of the characters being played and the iconography reflected in their costumes and jewellery. In the dance company at that time was a young Polish woman, Hanka Dytrych (see Chapter 3), who remembers being chaperoned by Jessie and Elsie and being inseparable from Elsie's daughters Santosh and Susheila. She recalls a separate house in the grounds where some of the dancers, musicians and teachers were accommodated, although she and another Indian female dancer, Sohan, lived next to Jessie in two rooms on the ground floor (Dytrych 2009: 447). The family left the house finally in 1969.

Ram Gopal, the dancer

From a very early age, Gopal had loved to dance. He recounts dancing freely and ecstatically in the garden during a monsoon downpour, aged about seven. Later, as a teenager, he was asked to perform by the Yuvaraja of Mysore, Kanteerava Narasimharaja Wodeyar, at a special Durbar.[13] The Yuvaraja was to become his first royal patron. By 1932, Gopal was accompanied by his young Bangalore friend, Krishna Rao, who played drums for the performances. Krishna Rao later trained in dance and performed extensively with his wife, Chandrabhaga Devi, both joining Gopal's troupe in the 1940s in India. Inspired by a performance of kathakali at Bangalore Town Hall, Gopal decided to train at the Kerala Kalamandalam school (KK) where he could study kathakali intensely under the great guru Kunju Kurup.

[13] A public reception held by an Indian prince or a British governor or viceroy in India.

Gopal records that he went there 'intermittently from 1933–34' and then adds, 'I think I went there right up to 1938' (cited in Kothari 1991 [1984]: 12). He continued to visit and train there when back in India during the war years.

The Kerala Kalamandalam (KK) school was started by poet and social reformer Vallathol Narayana Menon in 1930 to revive the flagging interest in the dance form of kathakali that had once been highly valued and patronized by the local Maharajas. 'Involving the unfolding of stories in dance or dance-drama, Kathakali originated from Krishnanattam (Sanskrit plays in praise of Lord Krishna) and Ramanattam or Attakatha (Malayalam plays in praise of Lord Rama) in the coastal state of Kerala during the seventeenth century,' note Amit Sarwal and David Walker (2015: 306). Diane Daugherty writing specifically on arts funding in Kerala notes that the 'first playwrights were members of regional ruling families' (2000: 239). This institutionalization of kathakali at KK was mirrored in Rukmini Devi's setting up of the Kalakshetra Foundation near Chennai in 1936, first named the International Academy of Arts, Madame Menaka's institution Nrityalayam in Khandala, Maharashtra, in 1941 for the teaching of kathak, and Rabindranath Tagore's school in the early 1920s at Santiniketan, West Bengal.

I interviewed founder Vallathol Menon's daughter, Vasanthi, in December 2017 during a visit to KK. Then aged eighty-nine, she remembered seeing Gopal dance there when she was a young girl about nine years old, probably in 1936 but was away at college when he returned for further training in the mid-1940s. Unfortunately, no archives or records exist of this period of the school, but Gopal would have been attending at the old Cheruthuruthy site, set up in 1935 a couple of miles away from the current university college. He may have also attended the original school at Ambalapuram village, in the Thrissur district of Kerala which was there between 1930 and 1935. In 2017, I was fortunate to visit the Cheruthuruthy setting, close to the Nila River with quiet and beautiful open grounds and large trees providing shade. It has been restored and is still utilized by senior post-graduate students and professional dancers. Several whitewashed buildings sit amongst the old trees, with wide spaces between. Sounds of music waft up from the open doors and windows, and peering in, rehearsals are under way for the next production. There I talked to senior teachers and watched some of the classes in this peaceful, dedicated site of practice.

The Maharajas of Cochin (Malakulam Palace) and Travancore supported the setting up of the school here in the 1930s with the Maharaja of Travancore buying the land. They were keen supporters of the arts, and the Malakulam Palace at Thrippunithura 'was popularly known as "Kathakali Palace" due to the royal family's patronage of artists and performances there' (Daugherty

2000: 240). Gopal writes of KK: 'The "school" I must hastily add was a pale blue-coated "choonam" paint-washed building of some dozen or more rooms that housed kitchen, costumes, offices and some living rooms, all very ascetic and simple' (1957: 30). Describing his journey to study kathakali there, Gopal notes: 'A third-class ticket, scant information, notebooks and pencil in hand, with a pathetic roll of bedding and a pillow, and off I went to the Kerala Kalamandalam School of the eminent, kind, laughing, humorous and very lovable poet genius of Malabar, Vallathol' (1957: 29). Gopal was taught intensively by senior guru Kunju Kurup, enduring an exacting routine of very early morning starts, gruelling eye exercises where ghee (clarified butter) is poured into the eyes to lubricate them, full-body massages followed by the learning of rhythms and postures. Evenings were set aside for training in gesture and facial expression. 'Then and now, Kathakali remains for me the greatest, most exciting of dances,' he later remarked (Kothari 1991 [1984): 12). The large, extensive university college at KK is now state-run. Nearly forty years later in 1969/70, Gopal was to visit his guru, now almost ninety, and Kurup recognized and blessed him. This moving moment was recorded by Claude Lamorisse for her film *Aum Shiva* (1970).

Touring with La Meri

Returning to Bangalore from KK, Gopal continued to give dance performances and in January 1937 appeared at the Globe Theatre, Bangalore, at a charity event. The Parsee manager, Mr Cooper, introduced him to the famous American dancer, La Meri.[14] Her tour had already visited Ceylon, in Columbo and Kandy, and Madras in India between December 1936 and January 1937. According to Gopal, she asked him to teach her kathakali and then invited him to join the rest of her Indian tour, followed by performances in Singapore and Japan. La Meri had studied bharatanatyam for a short time in Madras with Papanasam Vadivelu Pillai and M. D. Gauri. Gopal recalled that '[s]he had a remarkable ability to concentrate and to study our dances which I have rarely seen either among Indian or Western dancers. She studied *alarippu*, *swarajathi*, the *navarasa shloka* and *tillana*' (in Kothari 1991[1984): 14). La Meri pens a different narrative regarding their meeting, as her biographer Nancy Lee Chalfa Ruyter notes: '"a handsome young boy" named Bissano Ramgopal (1912–2003) came to her hotel to audition

[14] An American 'ethnic' dancer, La Meri was born Russell Meriwether Hughes in 1899. She died in 1988.

for her company … Impressed with both his knowledge about Indian dance and his performance, La Meri and Carreras arranged with his family that he could become a part of their small company' (Ruyter 2019: 104–5). Gopal joined her group in Bombay for performances at the Capitol Theatre in February 1937, before moving onto Nagpur and Calcutta, where Rabindranath Tagore watched them perform, and Delhi. Then in April 1937 with his new passport, Gopal left with the company for performances in Burma, Malaysia, Java, Singapore, the Philippines, Hong Kong, China and Japan. Gopal's precious document, his passport, came into its own at this point.

The financial agreement for joining the tour relied heavily on contributions from Gopal's family, which Kay Ambrose, close friend and some-time manager for Gopal, described:

> Backed up by the business-manager [Italian Guido Carreras, also husband of La Meri], the leader of the troupe [La Meri] announced they could not engage a new member unless he could pay certain expenses himself. Ram was thus faced with a final show-down with his father who, understanding at last that his son would become unmanageable unless he had his own way, agreed to pay a fixed amount to the leader of the troupe to cover a given period, for which she was to teach Ram stagecraft – and he was to teach her some *Kathakali* dancing.
>
> (Ambrose 1951: 27–8)

Ruyter comments on their Indian tour, describing how Gopal

> joined them in Bombay on February 25, went with them to Nagpur (February 28 to March 2) and then on to Calcutta and beyond. La Meri writes about their long hours of working together to develop dances for him to perform. For example, after their all-night train ride and morning arrival in Nagpur, they worked seven hours setting two pieces to add to the concert programs: an Indian duet, 'Krishna and Radha', and 'Jarabe Tapatío', the Mexican dance that La Meri had often done with Lilian as partner (1977a, 100–101; 3/9 letter to Lilian). His first appearance on stage with La Meri was at her Globe Theatre concert in Calcutta on March 10 when he performed his own solo, 'Siva,' and 'Krishna and Radha' with La Meri (*Star of India*, Calcutta, March 9, 1937). He also danced with her in Delhi and in performances scheduled in other countries after India.
>
> (Ruyter 2019: 105)

In April 1937, the group performed twice in Rangoon, Burma, and gave several concerts in Malaysia in Penang, Ipoh and Kuala Lumpur and in Singapore's Capitol Theatre (Ruyter 2019). They moved from there to Java in May for five weeks followed by a return trip to Singapore and then travelled for four

Figure 7 Ram Gopal and La Meri, Java, May 1937. Photographer unknown. Author's own collection.

scheduled performances (they only in fact did two) in the Philippines (Manila), and three performances in Hong Kong in July. Their final destination was Japan, where they arrived on 15 July in Yokohama and settled in Tokyo for the next five weeks (Ruyter 2019).

Gopal choreographed the *Krishna-Radha* piece for La Meri and himself and danced three solos in the programme of *World Dance – Shiva, Indra,* and the *Peacock,* performed in kathakali style as well as the two duets he created for himself and La Meri.[15] The cover of a programme of their April 1937 Singapore performances has a full figure photo of La Meri, and printed on the front, 'LA MERI Assisted by RAMGOPAL', Gopal clearly still an apprentice in the eyes of La Meri. Inside he was named Bissano Ramgopal. In the first half of this programme, La Meri's four Spanish dances were followed by a bharatanatyam *tillana* and a kathak *nautch*. In between her two Indian items, Gopal performed his *Siva* dance, ending with their *Krishna-Radha* duet. The second part of the programme consists of *Interpretative Dances* by La Meri, and the programme

[15] They performed the *Krishna-Radha* duet again together in 1958, when Gopal invited her to tour with him to Trinidad (Ruyter, personal communication with author, 2019). La Meri included a bharatanatyam *tillana* and *alarippu* in her 1945 performances and in 1946 danced a *Krishna-Radha* duet with Ted Shawn at Jacob's Pillow.

featured only her photos. In other venues on the tour, they danced a Mexican and an Indonesian duet to recorded music. Not only was Gopal an unpaid dancer with the company he also had to work backstage which he did not enjoy, but which provided good training in stagecraft for his own future performances in Europe and the UK. Whilst touring he took lessons in the Burmese *Pyu* dance and Javanese dance in Batavia and Solokarta, 'with Suharsono, a former court dancer turned medical student' (Cohen 2011: 153). He also bought local costumes, which he later used in his own concerts.

Their relationship, however, was not an easy one and La Meri and Gopal were to part ways at the end of the tour in Japan in September 1937. Their narratives of this period differed.[16] According to Gopal, his reviews during their tours were excellent, whilst those for La Meri were rather lukewarm. He notes rather dramatically that La Meri finally told him to leave the company, abandoning him penniless and with no contacts in Tokyo. La Meri's account (1977: 96, 126) states that as war closed in, their Japanese tour was cancelled and the company had to return to the United States, so a passage was booked for Gopal to travel to India. He however had made good friends in Tokyo and wished to remain there.

Joan Erdman (1996: 290) describes this kind of relationship between dancers as a transnational 'dialogue … [which] was a complex interchange of expectations and discovery'. Classical Indian dance affected and influenced the performance of the oriental interpretive dancers, and the American and European dancers had something to offer dancers from India. In this case, touring with La Meri had an influence on the stage technique and presentation that Gopal developed to bring Indian dance to Europe. Gopal's trained classical technique was passed onto her. Anna Pavlova's influence on both Uday Shankar and Rukmini Devi has been noted by many scholars (Erdman 1996, Venkataraman 2005) and is indicative of the powerful stimulus artists of different traditions, of varied backgrounds and differing time periods have on each other.

Debuts in the United States, Poland and France, 1938

After leaving La Meri's tour, Gopal remained in Tokyo for four months, where he became close friends (probably lovers) with Aleksanda Janta-Polczynski. Janta was from a wealthy land-owning family in Poznan, Poland, and employed

[16] See Kowal (2020) for a further discussion on their relationship and alternative narratives.

as an international journalist and foreign correspondent for *Gazeta Polska* in Asia, living in Japan for two years. He was well-connected and an excellent organizer, later becoming an extensively published author and cultural activist. Janta writes about his fascination for India, 'I was attracted to that country since the time when in 1935 I crossed the continent, with memories of my stay at the school of Rabindranath Tagore in Santiniketan and a meeting with the poet in Calcutta remaining one of most important and cherished' (Janta 1970: 6 [transl. Garapich]).

Janta organized sell-out solo performances for Gopal in Tokyo, followed by further concerts in Yokahoma, Osaka and Kobe.[17] One of the revue theatres in Tokyo commissioned two new dance pieces and costumes, rather than a cash payment to the artist (Janta 1970). Janta remarks that Gopal's 'first performance was met with brilliant press and public reviews' (1970: 7). During this time, Gopal received invitations to perform for Emperor Showa's brother, Yasuhito, and twice at the Polish embassy in Tokyo. Then, on 29 December 1937 with Janta as his manager, Gopal sailed on the NYK (Nippon Yusen Kabushiki Kaisha) Line, the MS *Chichibu Maru* from Yokohama to Hawaii for his first US tour organized by Janta, arriving on 5 January 1938. They remained in Hawaii for almost three weeks.

On 19 January and 2 February, Gopal gave two performances at the Dillingham Hall, Honolulu, and one concert on 25 January at the Academy of Arts, having been invited by the cultural director of the Academy, Edgar C. Schenck. In the programmes, Janta was named as Gopal's manager and was clearly very active regarding publicity. The main Hawaiian newspapers, the *Honolulu Star-Bulletin* and the *Honolulu Advertiser* both carried nine mentions each of Gopal; these included pre-announcements of his concerts, short interviews, his attendance at social events and two reviews of his performances. Some of the publicity material included drawings of Gopal created by American artist John Handforth in Tokyo. Gopal dined with the Hawaiian Governor and was a house guest of wealthy locals Mr and Mrs Ray M. Allen in Kauai. California-born Allen worked as manager of the Koloa Sugar Cane company and the Allens were renowned for their generous parties. Gopal and Janta attended a special party given in their honour by Claude Albon Stiehl, distinguished architect and President of the American Institute of Architects in 1937. Already Gopal was mixing with the wealthy elite, a pattern that continued during tours to Europe and Britain after the United States.

[17] Gopal had already performed in Tokyo with La Meri and had given lecture-demonstrations with her there 'in the auditorium of the historically significant Meiji Seimei Kan building' (Ruyter 2019: 112).

At this stage, Gopal did not have musicians with him and this necessitated dancing to recorded music. Nevertheless, his performances were sold out and the Honolulu Advertiser claimed that 'more than 1,100 persons attended the public recital given on Tuesday night at the Honolulu Academy of Arts. Approximately 2,000 persons did not get in to see the dancer and police officers were called to deal with the heavy traffic. The Indian dances fascinated an enthusiastic audience' (27 January 1938: 5). Gopal's programme included items titled *Krishna & Radha, Mayura Nrittya (Peacock dance), Indra, Bhakti Bhava, Kathak dance* and *Siva, a South Indian temple dance.* By popular request, Gopal was invited to give a final extra performance, delaying his departure to Los Angeles by a few more days. For this concert, he performed some new items including the *Cobra Devil Dance, Devali Puja, Arati, Bhayananka, Kite Dance,* Boddhisatva and *Mogul Serenade.* Critical reviews printed in the local *Honolulu Star-Bulletin* of his final performance remarked that 'subtlety, fine distinction and precision of detail characterises every movement. Facial expression, the flicker of an eyebrow, twitching of lips, movements of sensitive toes all contribute as much to the illusion as movement of graceful limbs' (Oakley 1938: 11).

Gopal and Janta left Hawaii on 5 February 1938 in spectacular fashion to the sounds of a Hawaiian orchestra playing for their departure and garlanded with celebratory leis.[18] Sailing for five days on the ship SS *Matsonia*, they docked at Los Angeles Harbour on 10 February. Shipping documents showing the passenger lists for this journey record Gopal's nationality as British (from India), with a visa for the United States that was issued in Tokyo on 17 December 1937. Gopal's passport, the pivotal document at the heart of this chapter, once again allowed him to travel safely and securely on his first visit to the United States, giving him the freedom for such international and intercultural movement. On arrival, customs officers carefully examined Gopal's trunks of costumes and accessories, exclaiming, 'Say, is this the wardrobe of a man or a woman?' (Gopal 1957: 58). Shipping records reveal that Janta travelled on a Polish diplomatic passport and had already visited the United States in 1934. Passenger lists record Gopal's real age of twenty-five, but he tells journalists in interviews that he is twenty, sometimes amending it to twenty-one. Press announcements heralding Gopal's arrival on the West Coast and his very successful performances in Hawaii are made in the press: the *San Pedro News Pilot* headlines, 'Indian Dancer Arrives at Port' (10 February 1938: 1) and the *Los Angeles Times* remarks, 'Hindu Dancer Will Appear at Ebell' (25 February 1938: 34). The news reports state that

[18] Garlands of flowers customarily given on arrival or departure from Hawaii as a symbol of affection.

Gopal and Janta will be staying at the Hotel Roosevelt, Hollywood, for several weeks before debut performances in New York.

Gopal's first performance in Los Angeles was on 11 March at the Wilshire Ebell Theater, 4401 West 8th Street, with two further shows on 4 and 11 April.[19] The first was sponsored by film director Cecil B. DeMille, fashion designer Adrian, actor Melvyn Douglas and theatre producer Max Reinhardt. Gopal met his benefactors at dinners in the homes of DeMille and Adrian, along with other Hollywood stars and socialites. Letters of introduction to DeMille and to impresario Sol Hurok had been sent by Janta when in Tokyo which greatly facilitated his stay in Hollywood. Gopal described DeMille's house: 'He took me around his house, filled with so many relics and antiques of rare beauty and value … He was handsome, with the distant, detached, cool look of a sage, a seer, a sort of *rishi* of the cinema world … And he was kindly' (Gopal 1957: 59).

Janta rang impresario Sol Hurok from Los Angeles, after sending him reviews of Gopal's Japanese and Hawaiian shows to see if he would help them get a booking in New York. Hurok agreed on the conditions that it would be at their cost, warning Janta that charges for the rental of a theatre, accessories and advertising could cost up to $1,000 per day. After ten weeks in Los Angeles, it is probable that Gopal and Janta travelled New York via Chicago by sleeper train or by car with a driver, although no details are recorded, taking three to four days to get there. They were certainly in New York by April 1938. Gopal's New York debut was on Sunday 1 May at the 46th Street Theatre, close to Times Square and promoted by Hurok.[20] Critic John Martin noted in the *New York Times* that

> Ram Gopal, a youthful Hindu dancer, made his New York debut last night at the Forty-sixth Street Theatre, and came through the ordeal with flying colours … Here are … the makings of a fine dancer. Gopal has a beautiful carriage and handles his body well … He is certainly not without technical knowledge and skill … the high point of the evening was the Cobra dance.
>
> (Martin 1938: 15)

Music recordings were used for the performances in Hawaii and LA but Gopal this time was able to employ a drummer (unnamed) to accompany him. Gopal is billed as a 'Hindu Temple Dancer' and the programme 'a recital of the dances of North and South India and authentic Hindu temple dances'. Gopal performed

[19] Built in 1927 and seating nearly 1,300 the theatre was named after Adrian Ebell, a pioneer in women's education and organizer of societies for women in the 1890s (see https://ebellofla.com/theatre/history/ accessed 20 August 2021).

[20] This theatre was built in 1925 and is now called the Richard Rogers Theatre.

ten items (with two intervals), this time including his famous *Garuda* dance, as well as the *Dance of Siva*, *Mayura Nrittya* (Peacock dance), *Indra*, *The Cobra* and the poem *The Glory of Spring*. The one-night concert was a great triumph, and Hurok returned $200 to Janta from the sales of tickets.

Renowned photographer Carl Van Vechten was in the audience for the 1 May concert and wrote a pleasing review, noting:

> The dancing of Ram Gopal begins by being technically proficient and when I say technically proficient I mean it in the sense that I would mean were I speaking of Heifetz and his mastery of the technic [*sic*] of the violin. Indeed, in the matters of muscular control and rhythmic continuity, in his ability to communicate his intentions simultaneously to each forefinger, toe and eyelash, I can only compare Ram Gopal with Nijinsky. The dancing of Ram Gopal goes beyond technical proficiency. He is young and extremely beautiful; his costumes are as perfect for his purpose as art can make them; but it is the spirit of the dancer which demands and receives the spectator's concentrated attention. So, when he dances as Siva or Indra, the god himself seems to be setting foot on the stage, or rather the stage becomes a bank of clouds, a dewy mountain top, or any suitably elevated location for a god to dance.
>
> (Van Vechten, New York, 8 May 1938)[21]

Van Vechten invited Gopal and Janta to his apartment where he also had his photographic studio and, over two days, took many evocative images of Gopal (see Chapter 5 for discussion).[22] Hollywood society photographer George Hurrell's photos of Gopal were used for publicity in the *New York Times* and one of Handforth's drawings was printed on the front of the printed programme.

On 16 May 1938, two weeks after this very successful New York debut, Gopal boarded the ship MS *Batory* of the Gdynia-America Line, sailing for Poland with Janta and Janta's mother, who had joined them in New York. Onboard the ship, he romantically mused how he 'loved every single instant of my first visit to America. On the night I sailed away, a crescent moon hung low in the sky and the stars were bright. Of course it was Siva, winking at me sleepily from the heavens, telling me that this city was something dreamed up out of his imaginations' (1957: 63). After a relaxing break at the stately home of Janta's family in the village of Mala Komorza, playing tennis, enjoying dinners with

[21] This is taken from a typed copy in the archives of the Library of the Museum of the Opera, Paris. There is no information as to whether it was published, but it is signed and dated by Carl Van Vechten.

[22] See art historian Ajay Sinha's book that focuses on these photos of Gopal by Van Vechten (2022).

the family and their friends, and giving impromptu dance performances to locals, Gopal travelled to Warsaw with Janta in June and performed to great acclaim at the Grand Theatre. This theatre suffered extensive bomb damage and was almost destroyed the following year in the siege of 1939. The success of this performance brought invitations to perform in other cities – Lviv, Krakow, Katowice, Poznan and Tonin in that June/July period of 1938.

From Poland, the pair travelled by train to Paris; Gopal spent time visiting the city and meeting with celebrity friends, such as Mercedes de Acosta (whom he had been introduced to in New York), Gertrude Stein, dancer Serge Lifar, Princess Krasinsky Kshesinskaya (a Russian ballet dancer) and Alice Toklas, whilst Janta prepared the ground for Gopal to dance there in the late autumn of that year. In November, Gopal gave a performance at the Musée Guimet, with invitations sent out to the Association Français titled 'Dances de l'Inde, par Ram Gopal', and which drew an ecstatic write-up in *The Figaro* by Serge Lifar (13 December 1938). He also took part in a gala performance at the Théâtre de la Gaité-Lyrique on 26 November organized by impresario Eugene Grunberg, billed as 'Concert de Gala avec RAM GOPAL, danseur de Temple Indou'. Contracts were signed for a return visit the following year with a full company of dancers and musicians.[23]

First performances in London, 1939

The scene is London, July 1939. A pivotal moment in Gopal's career. His passport, the document that allowed his departure from India to tour the Far East, and that has travelled with him to the United States, now provides him with legitimate access to Europe and finally Britain. At the Aldwych, one of London's main West End theatres, there are queues outside the door with a sign stating 'House Full'. Gopal, the young, classically trained modernist Indian dancer is making his debut in the capital and the planned two-week season has been extended to four to accommodate the audiences flocking to see him dance. Despite the tensions in Europe of the impending Second World War, the twenty-six-year-old Gopal had already won over audiences in Warsaw and Paris as well as the United States. Prior to these London performances, he had successful appearances in Paris for the second time in June and July of 1938 with his company of dancers and musicians. In his London audiences were dancers, balletomanes, wealthy arts patrons and art connoisseurs in addition to the

[23] See Appendix 1 for details of these performances.

general public. Ballerina Alicia Markova and her dance partner, Anton Dolin, visited on two consecutive nights and effused to Gopal afterwards in his dressing room, 'We had to come, we love your dancing, [we] admire it so much … What rave notices!' (quoted in Gopal 1957: 110). Such panegyrics were repeated everywhere. Barbara Gregory, a dancer with London Ballet, remembered going backstage with Australian artist Eilean Pearcey to meet Gopal after the show. Whilst talking, he demonstrated some movements and Gregory remarked that his second position plié was far superior to hers. She recalled his *Dance of the Setting Sun* as having 'a marvellous costume and glorious backcloth. It was just so glamorous and he was so charismatic, and with such beautiful features and body' (personal communication with author, August 2000). Cyril Beaumont, the renowned dance historian and publisher, attended Gopal's 1939 performances and wrote later in a programme note to Gopal's 1956 season at the Royal Festival Hall, London:

> Ram Gopal was not the first Indian dancer I ever saw, for in the twenties I witnessed young Uday Shankar dance with the famous ballerina Anna Pavlova … None the less, it was Ram Gopal, through his initial London recitals in 1939 who first opened our eyes to the various styles and rich vocabulary of Indian dance, a revelation and education which were to grow in force over successive years as the young artist developed, and constantly enlarged his repertory.
>
> (Beaumont, programme note 1956: n.p.)

The daily newspapers and monthly magazines were replete with tributes to Gopal and his company of musicians and dancers, many supporting their articles with photos. Comments were made on his fine technique, his physical presence and his powerful ability to evoke mythological characters on stage. An anonymous reviewer in *Cavalcade* stated, '[T]o see him is to realise the essence of dancing. His technique is magnificent. The perfect eloquence of his body is the final expression of the exquisite control of each individual muscle' (August 1939: n.p.). The *New Statesman*'s journalist praised 'his unearthly physical control', stating 'Mr Gopal's art is so inspired and so finished that it is as if one were observing the dances of Siva and Krishna themselves' (cited in Gopal 1957: 108). Gopal's fame attracted artists such as Kay Ambrose known for her books on dance; Feliks Topolski, celebrated pen and wash artist; and artist Pearcey (mentioned above) who sat in the wings drawing him at his performances. He was even invited to take tea with Queen Mary at Marlborough House by Lord Lloyd, an ex-Governor of Bengal (Gopal 1957).

Post-modern theories of affect and reception, developed in film studies and sociology and extended to other disciplines, shed light on the way viewers' bodies, as well as their cognitive and emotional faculties, are affected by performance. Susan L. Foster points out that even in the 1930s, critics such as John Martin were using the word 'contagion' in relation to the effect of dance and movement on the viewer. He argued, as Foster summarizes, that 'viewers' bodies, even in their seated stillness, nonetheless feel what the dancing body is feeling – the tensions or expansiveness, the floating or driving momentums that compose the dancer's motion. Then, because such muscular sensations are inextricably linked to emotions, the viewer also feels the choreographer's desires and intentions' (Foster 2008: 49). This is understood today as kinaesthetic empathy or muscular sympathy. I have written elsewhere (David 2021) about recent developments in film theory that investigates haptic affect through the sense of seeing, but it is well worth revisiting here. Laura Marks coins the term 'haptic visuality', where she implies that there is a kind of touch through seeing (2000: 162). As Marks puts it, 'in haptic visuality, the eyes themselves function like organs of touch'. She observes that 'haptic looking tends to move over the surface of its object … more inclined to move than to focus, more inclined to graze than to gaze' (2000: 162). This, she argues, engenders a relationship of 'mutuality' (2000: 184). Haptic visuality brings a closeness of touch and produces an affective intensity, a sensuous engagement of bodies (see David 2021). This helps in understanding audiences' and critics' responses, even of the early period, whilst remaining aware that perception and reception were additionally affected by a colonialist gaze that othered and exoticized bodies unfamiliar to their own. Stuart Hall's contribution in the 1970s to reception theory emphasized that in watching, an audience is not just passive but is creating meaning. The meaning is constructed through the relationship between audience and performer (Hall 1973).

Gopal's dance programmes

After such acclaimed performances at the Aldwych, Gopal was booked to appear at London's Vaudeville Theatre in November and December 1939 for three weeks, extended into a four-week stay. His programme of dances at the Vaudeville Theatre, running eight performances a week (Monday to Saturday evenings plus matinees on Tuesdays and Fridays), consisted of twenty-one items described in the printed programme as 'genuine Kathak and Kathakali and of the classical school of India'.[24] The eleven short presentations of the first half were two instrumental pieces, and nine dances with Gopal dancing four of those as solos. Retna Mohini, his Javanese leading female dancer, married to the French photographer Henri Cartier-Bresson, danced two solo items. Two other main dancers Chandra Vali and Sohan Lal presented one duet and two solos. After the interval the remaining ten dances were a similar assortment of styles, performers and length, apart from the last, the *Ras Leela*, an Indian ballet of the story of Krisna and the Gopi girls (cowherds) of longer length and employing the whole cast. The timings of the pieces, the mixed programming of different styles and the inclusion of an interval indicate that Gopal had clearly conceived and directed his performances to a Western audience. In this he brought a modernist aesthetic sensitivity, as Shankar had done before him. Gopal's training in kathakali with Kunju Kurup laid the ground for genuine innovation in his kathakali pieces. The adaptation of kathakali, for example (traditionally performed through the night with no break), to retain a certain authenticity as well as creating accessibility for Western audiences is described by Erdman (1987), writing about Uday Shankar's work, as a technique of 'translation'. Gopal's performance structure crossed the barriers between classical and interpretative, being neither strictly classical in its presentation nor presenting an imagined, fantasized, colonial view of India. Rather than simply translating one form to be more accessible to different audiences, I argue that Gopal evolved a new cultural production of modernism, changing structures, weaving culturally different forms and historically sourced dance and music that disrupted identities, origins, styles and geographies.

Gopal realized that he would have to 'prune the traditional dances of all repetitive movement, light the stage adequately and costume my dances and ballets with the best available copies of the frescoes and sculptures and bronzes that my tailors could duplicate' (1957: 55). He tells how, from watching Shankar's performances and later from his experience touring with La Meri, he discovered more about the intricacies of stage presentation, lighting and the rigours of touring. Gopal spoke of being inspired by Shankar's performances and of the desire to dance like him (interview with author, August 2000) and Kumudini Lakhia, who later performed with him, admitted that she thought that he secretly idolized Shankar. In an interview in 1976, Gopal talked of the 'perfection of his productions – lighting, costuming, music and dance' and how he created a sort of magic (Gopal 1976: n.p.).

[24] Gopal also added an extra Friday matinee performance on 1 December for a charity performance to raise funds for Indian seamen affected badly by the war, with the proceeds distributed by the Hindustani Social Club.

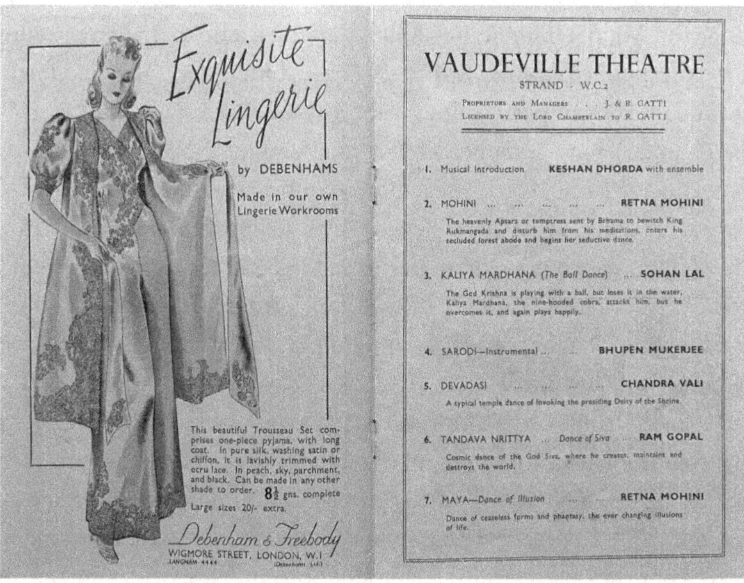

VAUDEVILLE THEATRE

STRAND · W.C.2

Proprietors and Managers . . . J. & R. GATTI
Licensed by the Lord Chamberlain to R. GATTI

1. Musical Introduction **KESHAN DHORDA** with ensemble

2. MOHINI ... ... **RETNA MOHINI**

The heavenly Apsara or temptress sent by Brhama to bewitch King Rukmangada and disturb him from his meditations, enters his secluded forest abode and begins her seductive dance.

3. KALIYA MARDHANA (*The Ball Dance*) ... **SOHAN LAL**

The God Krishna is playing with a ball, but loses it in the water, Kaliya Mardhana, the nine-hooded cobra, attacks him, but he overcomes it, and again plays happily.

4. SARODI—Instrumental ... ... **BHUPEN MUKERJEE**

5. DEVADASI ... ... **CHANDRA VALI**

A typical temple dance of Invoking the presiding Deity of the Shrine.

6. TANDAVA NRITTYA ... *Dance of Siva* ... **RAM GOPAL**

Cosmic dance of the God Siva, where he creates, maintains and destroys the world.

7. MAYA—*Dance of Illusion* ... ... **RETNA MOHINI**

Dance of ceaseless forms and phantasy, the ever changing illusions of life.

Figure 8a & 8b Vaudeville Theatre programme, November 1939. Author's own collection.

In fact, Gopal spoke and wrote quite frequently about Shankar who he had seen dance in Bangalore at the Excelsior Theatre and later in Delhi. 'And I must say it was enchanting, bewitching. Considering the fact that it was not genuine Kathakali, nor pure Bharatanatyam, the impression his dancing created was amazing. I thought I was in the Elephanta Caves, or Ellora, or at the temples at Halebid and Belur – looking at the friezes actually coming to life,' said Gopal (cited in Sunil Kothari, 1991 [1984]). He acknowledged Shankar's use of creative staging and adaptation of dance to suit Western audiences: 'Uday Shankar was not far wrong when he said that his success was due to a carefully planned, timed and executed modern programme, incorporating the old gestures and steps with new variation and his own personal style which is lyrical and fluid, added to a superb modern Indian orchestra' (Gopal 1957: 45). Erdman, writing further about Shankar's translation technique, stated that he 'produced programs which mediated between what westerners had come to expect as oriental dance and the ways in which it was presented in indigenous contexts' (1996: 293). Gopal also remarked on Shankar's prowess as a pioneer, stating that '[i]n my opinion it was Shankar and Shankar alone who surpassed them all, as he still does in his wonderfully creative ballets' (Gopal: 118). Shankar choreographed ballets for his troupe in the early 1930s and Gopal followed suit with his own *Ras Leela* in 1939, as described above.

Although their upbringing differed radically, both fathers had trained in law at the Middle Temple in London. Shankar and Gopal were mutually feted by the public, especially in their early tours, and Gopal followed in Shankar's footsteps in performing in the United States and in Paris. He also invited Shankar's long-term French partner, Simkie, to perform in his troupe in Turkey in the early 1950s. Hurok looked after Shankar and Gopal as their impresario in different periods. Both trained in the dance style of kathakali and used that training in their performances (although for Shankar this was for his later concerts). Live, trained musicians were a key to both men's strategic staging: Shankar famously utilizing the talents of his brothers, uncles and younger brother Ravi, and Gopal selecting some of the best musicians available for touring. Gopal, however, used aspects of a traditional *margam* in his programmes and often choreographed duets or trios which Shankar did not do. Bisakha Sarker, speaking about her training with Shankar's wife, Amala, told how Shankar's dance style did not develop from a *margam* but emerged from very successful stage productions into a style. As students they not only learnt creative, modern dance but also were trained in strict classical Indian dance styles and group choreographies.[25]

Musical arrangements

A distinctive element of Gopal's concerts from 1939 was his use of live music, as, unlike many other artists, he had the means to travel with groups of musicians. He mainly followed the staging often credited to dancer and innovator Rukmini Devi, placing the musicians stage right, when conventionally in the past they were situated behind the dancers. This was noted, for example, by the *Journal des Débats Politiques et Littéraires* on 13 August 1838 after the performance of the *Bayadères* in Paris, and Shankar followed this with his musicians in the late 1920s and 1930s. The positioning of the musicians on stage right continues to this day for classical Indian dance performances, although Gopal confided to me that he would vary the staging in early programmes. For some items the musicians would be at the back of the stage; for others, on stage right. Dance aficionado Lionel Bradley (discussed below) noted that in the 1939 performances at the Aldwych, the musicians moved from stage right to the back especially for Gopal's *Dance of the Setting Sun.*

Gopal helped change the perception of Indian dance and music for his Western audiences, who at that time were more familiar with 'exotic' or 'interpretive oriental' artists performing to recorded pieces from varied Indian or Western repertoires, as noted above. An *India News* journalist commented in 1949 that companies 'have specially prepared gramophone records for their background music' (1949: 4); many of the exotic/oriental dancers during 1900s to 1930s performed to Western classical music or exotic music played on Western instruments (David 2001). Examples include Ruth St Denis's famous portrayal of *Radha* (1906) danced to excerpts from Delibes's orientalist opera *Lakmé* and interpretive dancer Nyota Inyoka's performances at the Arts Theatre Club, London, in 1930 where her Western musicians played clarinet, bassoon, piano and drums. She was billed as 'a Hindu dancer' and the programme titled 'Brahmin India'. Even La Meri utilized records for her early solo shows.

[25] Sarker spoke in a live Facebook discussion that I also participated in for South Asian Heritage month in August 2020, run by Sampad.

A review of her 1936 London debut rather candidly noted that 'she was greatly handicapped by the accompaniment of badly-worn gramophone records; these must have been uninspiring to La Meri and were most depressing to the audience' (*Dancing Times* 1936: 753).

Gopal's sell-out performances in London in July and August at the Aldwych and November 1939 at the Vaudeville theatre were accompanied by a group of classical Indian musicians and vocalists, led by Keshan Dhorda and named as Gopal's 'Hindu orchestra' or 'ensemble', in the programmes. The group played *sarod*, *veena*, flute, *tabla* and *mridangam* amongst other instruments. The musicians also performed instrumental-only pieces in addition to playing for the dance items, revealing Gopal's innovative staging for Western audiences. In this way the live musicians were foregrounded as artistes in their own right, as well as being accompanists. It also gave audiences a chance to gain some familiarity with instruments they were unaccustomed to hearing or seeing, whilst retaining the historical practice of maintaining dance and music as an integral whole, something that Shankar had also introduced in his Western concerts. The new modernist aesthetic that Gopal developed included shortening longer items for acceptability and accessibility, programming two halves and an interval, and presenting spoken introductions to the dances with explanations of the mime content – the latter being an element that exists in classical Indian dance performances to this day. The idea of interweaving cultures emerged as artists and their troupes able to travel (using privileges such as passports and having the means to pay shipping fares) were demonstrating by bringing largely unknown cultural performances to audiences in Britain and in Europe, a practice of weaving of intercultural artistic values, aesthetics and knowledge. Thus, Gopal and his performers in this period and after the war introduced the concept of diversity, which, as Jonathan Bollen explains, 'was emergent as a cultural value in this period' (2020: 11).

Reviews of the time, of course, tended to focus on the dance. Any discourse on the music veered rather to confessions of ignorance, along with the use of certain pejorative language as would be understood now, such as 'native' musicians and 'repetitive' melodies. *The Sunday Times* critic noted on 30 July 1939 that 'the music, mainly of a repetitive melodic order, was supplied by native tambourines and flute, on which Keshan Dhorda is an expert performer'. Dhorda was singled out again by the *Daily Telegraph*'s critic as a 'good flautist'; other critics spoke of the 'haunting strangeness' of the music. One of the 1939 programmes (in author's collection) notes the evening beginning with an introduction played by the musical ensemble. The all-male musicians were not named in this programme; there was simply a note that 'Authentic music' would be played 'comprising the

Veena, Tambour, Flute, Medallam (Keralan drum), Chendai (Keralan drum), Tablas, Symbols and Temple Drums of South India'. After two dance items came a sarod instrumental piece by Bhupen Mukerjee, who was later to become music director of Indian dancer Rafiq Anwar's performances during the war. In the second half, Dhorda played a musical interlude on the flute.

Lionel Bradley, an enthusiastic music and dance lover, wrote in the mid-1930s and 1940s what would be known today as a 'dance blog' – a series of unpublished, handwritten accounts of varied London dance performances, called 'Ballet Bulletin', which are now stored in the V&A archives.[26] Having seen various performances, Bradley, who was a professional librarian, would pen his account and then send to friends and other dance aficionados. They would pass it on to other acquaintances to read, and in this way, he gained a significant readership. After his visits to two of Gopal's shows at the Aldwych on 1 and 3 August 1939 he penned the following description of the music, also singling out Dhorda for his beautiful playing:

> This was a fascinating show and well worth a second visit, even without a change of programme. One should begin, perhaps, first with the white clad and mostly imperturbable musicians – but their eyes were bright and alive – since the programme began with a musical introduction. There were six or seven of them and (apart from one or two instances in which a gramophone record was used) the music was composed or arranged by Keshan Dhorda, who led them himself and is an inspired flute player. The other instruments were mostly various drums or tom-toms which marked the rhythm with varying intensity, and two little things like shells which made an attractive sharp *plok plok* distinct from the duller heavier drum notes and a big stringed instrument like a double bass which was I think, always played pizzicato. Often there were only three – a cylindrical drum (resting on its side on the knee of the cross-legged player), the plok-plok, and the lovely flute, like the music of some heavenly singing bird. Often the music reminded me of water splashing through a garden or dropping a deep note from a conduit into a pool, several distinct but congruous sounds not really monotonous and with the flute song rising and falling.
>
> (Bradley 1939: n.p.)

The rather naive but delightful account provides further information that there were six to seven players and that some dances were accompanied by

[26] Extended thanks are due to Jane Pritchard, curator of Dance, Theatre and Performance at the V&A, for not only drawing my attention to the existence of Bradley's 'Ballet Bulletin' but allowing me access to read them in the archive.

a recording – possibly these were Retna Mohini's Javanese ones. Thanks to Bradley, much more is known about these performances than from the scant reviews published in the daily press.

At these same performances, Bradley made a point of writing about Gopal's solos. Here he reflects on Gopal's physical magnificence in his famous Siva item, the *Dance of the Setting Sun* (or *Dance of Siva*), 'Ram Gopal's arms are very beautiful and he has the most perfect muscular control so that he is able to produce a lovely rippling motion which starts with his fingers and passes upwards like a wave along the whole length of his arm to the shoulder' (Bradley 1939). Chapter 2 takes up the theme of Siva as dancing deity – Siva Nataraj – exploring the significance of Siva's emerging role in the reformulation of the classical dance of that period.

The innovative performances Gopal and his newly formed troupe offered in pre-war London were possible in part due to the ease of travel for privileged dancers such as Gopal, sporting a British Indian passport with its own political and cultural capital, and in part because he had money to pay for dancers and musicians. By contrast, in recent years after the millennium, dancers coming to Britain have spoken about their difficulties in obtaining visas to work and perform. Anusha Kedhar, travelling from her home in the United States to take up a contract of dance work with the contemporary South Asian Dance company *Angika*, writes of her detainment for several hours at the UK border in 2004. She writes (2011: 3),

> When I arrived at London's Heathrow Airport, I was locked up in a room and my possessions were confiscated after my 'intentions' for coming to the UK were deemed suspicious by one of the UK Border Agency's Entry Clearance Officers (ECOs). The officer's concern, he informed me, was that I was going to overstay my six-month work visa, try to illegally settle in the UK, and, eventually, be a drain on public resources.

Kedhar was granted a work visa under the Tier 2 category for the hiring of foreign 'Creative Artists and Entertainers', a category which no longer exists within the British immigration system. After finally being released, Kedhar wryly commented that 'while my brown body initially posed a barrier to my transnational movements, the political and economic capital of my American passport eventually granted me access, albeit limited, to enter the UK' (2011: 4). Other Indian dancers experiencing visa problems include Mavin Khoo, who was forced to return to Malaysia in 2006. He recalled, 'I had to leave London and go back to Malaysia … I remember going back to Malaysia and really being in deep depression' (Manch UK talk, 22 January 2021).[27] Bharatanatyam teacher Prakash Yadagudde spoke of his travels to Britain, 'The Bhavan … asked me to come quickly to do a performance for the ministry of Education here. However, my immigration was not cleared and I was pushed back and forth between the Emigration offices in Bangalore and Bombay, with no idea what to do.' Yadagudde stressed how much a significant barrier immigration clearance could be for an artist, underlining the lack of freedom he felt at the time (Manch UK talk, 3 July 2020). Negotiating the complexities and anomalies of the UK's immigration and visa systems remains a tedious and often tortuous process as these examples indicate. These more recent illustrations can be directly contrasted with the experience of Kumudini Lakhia, who came to join Gopal's troupe from India in 1948. She later commented, 'In those days, you could get a visa in four hours!' (interview with author, December 2017).

[27] These regular talks were set up online at the start of the Covid-19 epidemic in March 2020 when all theatres, galleries and events in the UK were closed. Started by Mira Kaushik with a team of five other women, the initiative created a new digital platform bringing inspirational talks and discussions with South Asian dance, film, music and drama artists to a large online audience.

2

Siva Nataraja

Sumptuous jewels – pearls, turquoise stones, green sapphires and pink corals – adorn the spectacular headdress of Gopal's Siva costume. Now in the archives of London's V&A Museum, the headdress tells magnificent tales of the onstage iconic figure of the dancing god Siva, realistically created with accuracy and acute detail by Indian jewellery makers. A tight-fitting magenta silk headcap, worn just above the eyebrows and curving down over the ears rises up to a serpent-shaped piece above the head, encrusted with pearls, with curved strands of turquoise stones shaped to create height. It is lined with brown velvet. From each side of the head, two 'wings' with tassels stand out and from them hang down to the shoulders four tiers of circular rose-shaped jewels. Costume experts at the museum add a further description:

> The front band is decorated with a zig-zag of gold sequins, within each of which is a 'flower' or large gold sequins centred with a coloured 'jewel' and surrounded by 'foliage' in gold metal braids and cords; above this to either side is a similarly decorated band topped by a high fan-shape, each 'leaf' outlined in blue jewels and gold metal cord and filled in with gold metal braids and cords.[1]

The whole costume piece is ablaze with colour, intricate design and opulence, even in its now damaged form (See headdress in Plate 1 of colour insert).

Gopal's recreation of the *Dance of Siva*, taken from a kathakali dance drama was one of his signature danced pieces.[2] For this item, titled *The Dance of the Setting Sun* or *Dance of Siva* in his programmes, Gopal wore the beautiful headdress described above. Excerpted film footage and photographs fortunately do exist, and therefore it is possible to reconstruct a sense of the impact of the dance. The photos and film are all black and white, so it is only seeing this costume now preserved in a museum, that the full colour of the headdress makes

1 https://collections.vam.ac.uk/item/O106799/theatre-costume-unknown/ (accessed 5 August 2021).
2 The dance evolved from its kathakali base with Gopal adding movements from bharatanatyam and kathak.

Figure 9 Ram Gopal as Siva. © Hulton Deutsch, Getty Collection.

an impact on the viewer. It is breathtakingly beautiful. The dance was one of two items Gopal performed as Siva. The second piece was taken from bharatanatyam repertoire, titled *Siva's Dance of Creation*, or *Natinam Adinar*, a dance which became part of his repertory after the Second World War, when he trained in bharatanatyam. This item became a regular piece in many dancers' repertory as I discuss later. Taking Gopal's stunning Siva headdress as an evocative starting point, the chapter examines Siva's emerging role in the dance of this period, that is, from the early twentieth century to the time of India's independence when the reconfiguration of classical dance became part of the nationalist agenda. It focuses on Gopal's specific Siva roles as well as other dancers of the time who danced as Siva Nataraja (Siva as lord or king of the dance).[3] The place of the Indian male dancer during this time of change and rupture is addressed,

[3] In his role as Lord of the Dance, Siva is depicted in Indian iconography standing on his right leg, with left leg held up in front of him. His right foot tramples a small demon, *apasmara*, or representation of forgetfulness. Both right and left hands are extended out to the right side, joined, the right in position of *pataka* in blessing, *or abhaya hasta* (fear not), and the left with dropped wrist facing down in *dola*, showing compassion and pointing to the free raised foot, representing liberation. Two other arms are outstretched each side, the right in *katakamukha*, holding the drum or *damaru* that beats the rhythm of creation. The right is in *ardha-chandra*, holding a flame, symbolic of the destruction of the universe. Siva's body is centred in a large circle of flames.

interrogating new notions of hypermasculinity as a political tool as well as the provocative usage of nomenclature of the dance terms.

In addition to this extraordinary headdress, Gopal wore a layered neckpiece at least 15 centimetres deep, again laden with colourful jewels (this necklace varied at different performances) and jewelled armbands on his upper arms that were made to match the headdress. These were designed in a 'horned' motif, with metal settings coloured blue, silver and magenta to look like jewels, with a fabric strap and magenta 'pompoms' dangling at the back. Gopal wore a tightly fitted, short, gold-coloured silk or possibly lamé garment, round his loins, leaving his chest and legs uncovered. Naked chests for male dancers were in homage to Siva, still seen in Hindu temples today where priests are required to remain bare-chested during worship as a mark of respect. The costume material was gathered at the front and fell as a longer, narrow piece just above the knee, although there are some later photos of Gopal wearing a tied silk *dhoti* for this dance that hung longer to the ankles.[4] Round the waist he wore a substantial, gold metal, intricately designed belt, and his straps of large pear-shaped ankle bells were tied in two rows around each ankle. The fingers on his right hand were extended with long metallic coverings, often used in kathakali technique to emphasize important hand gestures.[5]

Gopal (1957: 55) discusses how he created his costumes, seeking to 'capture the fine and brilliantly coloured robes, ornaments and jewellery' that he observed in the Indian bronzes, sculptures and paintings in temples and museums. 'That was how I designed and created my Setting Sun head-dress of the God Siva; also for the Cosmic dance of Creation, Preservation and Destruction, for which I duplicated the famous headdress, since so widely copied by other dancers in India, in heavy gilded bronze and gold, down to the exact detail' (1957). Before the creation of this spectacular headdress, Gopal used other prototypes in the earlier period – smaller and simpler headdresses that followed the style of Siva depicted, for example, in the Chola bronzes.[6] A number of his costumes and some of his dance jewellery pieces are in the archive collection of London's V&A museum, although not on show, gifted from his estate after his death. Some are the same pieces he wore at the

4 See, for example, John Lindquist's photos of Gopal as *Siva* in 1954 at Jacob's Pillow Dance Festival, where Gopal wears a full-length yellow silk pleated *dhoti*.

5 Not all images of this piece show Gopal with extended finger coverings. In the 1948 film *Lord Siva Danced* by Sarah Erulkar, where this dance is captured on film, he does not wear them.

6 Made during the Chola dynasty from the ninth to the thirteenth centuries in Southern India, these famous bronzes combined qualities of the sacred and the sensuous in the beautiful, stunning imagery of the deities.

V&A museum in 1947 when he famously danced in the Indian galleries (see Chapter 3).

Gopal had been performing this excerpted Siva piece since his first public concerts in 1937 which he learned from his kathakali guru Kunju Kurup at KK in the early 1930s. He describes,

> In my dance of Siva's Sandhya-nritta-murti, the dance Siva performs at the setting of the sun, 'He, Lord of the evening dance' I could not help feeling in this purely personal dance creation of mine, that I was on Mount Kailasa … I had to convey the gentle rhythmic movements of the oceans, the winds and the twinkling stars of the evening.
>
> (Gopal 1957: 35)

One final chapter in his autobiography is devoted to the Dance of Siva, where Gopal again identifies with the power of the symbolic dancing god, speaking once more of his total absorption into the potency of this mythological form. He quotes from Henrich Zimmer's 1946 writing on 'Siva's sacred dances' (1957: 207), as well as using theosophist Ananda Coomaraswamy's well-cited work on Siva (2011 [1918]) in his programme notes for this dance at his debut performance in New York in 1938. In aligning himself with scholars interpreting Hindu mythology for the West, Gopal stakes a position that speaks of his own Western education and his idea of cosmopolitanism that spanned East and West, stating how he loved the West, 'of course I am Westernised, bridging the gap between the East and the West. I am gloriously Westernised' (1957: x). He recounts that even as a small child, dancing as if possessed at various occasions, in the garden at home in a thunderstorm and again when older dancing for the Yuvaraja of Mysore, his identification was with Siva as the deity of dance. Gopal's empathy with Siva as 'Divine Dancer' (1957: 47) is foregrounded again when he narrates how all Indian dance arises from Siva's cosmic dance (1957: 47), a trope used extensively in the recodification and realignment of classical Indian dance to a nationalist agenda after 1947. His autobiography invokes the dancer's prayer to Siva, written both in Sanskrit and in English on the frontispiece – 'To Whom the Whole World is the movement of His body, All Music is his speech, Adorned with the Jewels of the Moon and the Stars in His hair, deep in stilled meditation, To this Almighty Being Siva, I make my Obeisance' (1957: v). This prayer is taught by most bharatanatyam teachers to their students and is often performed at the start of a class.

Associating his identity with the powerful, potent form of Siva, Gopal's dance consciously creates a persona of masculine virility – a hypermasculinity – perhaps all the more important at this turbulent time of transition in Indian dance and significantly so for a gay man. Perhaps Gopal may also have been playing with the concept of Siva as *ardhanarshwara*, the more fluid mythological representation of Siva as female as well as male energy and power. In this way Gopal could portray both aspects on stage. Ashish Khokar, writing about Gopal in 1998 emphasizes this, stating, 'Ram Gopal considered himself to be *ardhanarshwara*: the concept of half man, half woman. "My left side is Bharata Natyam; the right, Kathakali"' (1998: 69). Rather than adhering to colonial and Western constructs that emphasize gender binaries, this more changeable perception of differing attributes as part of one whole suited the young Gopal. Like the great ballet dancer Vaslav Nijinsky before him, with whom he was likened (he was called 'the Indian Nijinsky' by critics in the United States in the 1930s), and to a certain extent ballet dancer Rudolf Nureyev who followed him, Gopal's ability to depict a tender, lyrical side in addition to the powerful, vigorous aspect discussed above, was a compelling factor for his audiences.[7] In his dance items, he could express qualities, such as 'sensuality and sensitivity (conventionally feminine) with extraordinary strength and dynamism (conventionally masculine)' (Burt 1995: 84). Peter Stoneley (2006: 74) suggests the term 'omnisexual' to describe the mix of strength and sensitivity shown by Nijinsky, a term that also works for Gopal.

The kathakali-based *Dance of the Setting Sun* appeared as part of the programme in Gopal's debut performance in New York on 1 May 1938 at the 46 Street Theatre (close to Times Square), remaining in his repertoire for over thirty years. He had also included it in his tour with La Meri in 1937 under the simple heading 'Shiva'. The headdress discussed had not been crafted at this point, so Gopal wore an earlier prototype. Fortunately, footage of the dance is featured in British film director Sarah Erulkar's 1948 film, *Lord Siva Danced*. This is a twenty-three-minute filmed portrait of Gopal that includes parts of repertory by Gopal and his company. Predominantly shot in Bombay by the Shell Film Unit, the film 'had significant cultural impact not only in India –

[7] This accolade introduces several layers of meaning: Nijinsky transformed dance for men at the turn of the twentieth century, challenging gender stereotypes (Burt 1995); he was arguably one of the first male star dancers; and he was powerful and agile on stage as well showing an 'extraordinary expressiveness' (1995: 66).

where it came to be treasured as a documentary classic – but also in Britain, where it won huge accolades and triggered enthusiasm for Indian dance in the west', notes Katy McGahan in Erulkar's obituary (2015: n.p.). The film's commentary, written by Erulkar, underscores the mythological trope of Siva as a cosmic being dancing at the beginning of all time. It opens on the bronze sculpture of Siva Nataraja, with focused close-ups of the head and hands before showing Gopal dancing. As the film closes, Gopal is performing his *Dance of the Setting Sun,* and an actor's voiceover poetically and dramatically enunciates, 'Lord Siva on Mount Kailash. From the darkness of his meditations, he is roused by the glory of the sun before it sets and dances to its beauty … And Lord Siva danced.'

Gopal as Siva

As noted above, Gopal had two particular Siva dances in his repertoire, the adapted kathakali *Dance of the Setting Sun* for which the spectacular headdress was created, and the bharatanatyam-styled *Natanam Adinar* (discussed below). The *Dance of the Setting Sun* is a short item, running four and a half minutes in length, commanding in its presence and grandeur. There are extensive arm movement and poses but the foot and leg work is minimal and relatively simple. Accompanied by a haunting flute melody and rhythmic drum, Gopal takes a standing pose on his left leg, with the right heel up, his body angled in a soft *atibhanga* and creating liquid, rippling movements with both arms.[8] Movements flow from the shoulders down to the fingertips and back again. Grand, slow steps coming forward are accompanied by majestic gestures; the arms starting in front of the body, ending with a flourish with one arm up and the other out to the side and fluid, serpentine hand movements. Gopal utilizes both bharatanatyam and kathakali hand gestures, showing both hands to the front of the body, fingers outstretched and fluttering, whilst making a turning motion in each hand. His hands change from *alapadma* (open lotus) to *katakamukha* (opening in a bracelet), alternatively as he moves backwards on stage. Dramatically he takes the classic Siva Nataraja pose with left leg up raised in front of his body and both hands to the right side, whilst performing small jumps up and down on his right heel. He lunges to each side and then again

[8] Sanskrit term for position with slight bend in body with the opposing knee bent, often used in Siva iconography.

makes discrete leaps to the left and the right as his arms make wide sweeping gestures. In the final part Gopal kneels on his left knee, with the right leg and foot stretched out at an angle behind. His arms are slowly and very deliberately brought up in front of his body and then majestically over the head to the sides. In a close-up shot, Gopal gently turns his face to the side, eyes cast down, as if in an act of meditation, and invoking the *santa rasa* (peaceful or meditative emotion). A powerful yet sublime moment, caught on camera as it lingers in a detailed close-up on his face.

Writing of Gopal's performance of this dance in December 1947 at the Princes Theatre, London, critic Bernard Peacock said, 'The *Dance of the Setting Sun,* in Kathakali technique, danced by Ram Gopal, was as perfect an exhibition of grace, rhythm and control as one could ever wish to see; the rippling arm movements were so fascinating that I became more and more hypnotised at each performance. To me it is the outstanding item of his repertoire this season' (1947: 5). This dance always impacted strongly on audiences. Dancer Barbara Gregory recalled its 'marvellous costume and backcloth. It was just so glamorous, and he was so charismatic and with such beautiful features and body' (personal communication with author, August 2000). After a performance at the Cambridge Theatre, London, in 1951, critic and writer Richard Buckle wrote that 'I still prefer *The Dance of the Setting Sun,* which he renders as ever with a grand serenity. This dance conveys well the idea of Shiva, alone on topmost Himalaya. Extending to the world his sunset benediction, then with a gesture of infinite pity, putting it to sleep' (*The Observer* 21 January 1951: 6). The notion of affect, discussed in Chapter 1, is of course pertinent regarding understanding audience and critical reception in these instances. Results of the project 'Watching Dance: Kinesthetic Empathy' (2008–11) run by Matthew Reason and Dee Reynolds concluded that the question of pleasure was key to their findings that were both rich and complex.[9] As they recount, '[t]he consideration of pleasure alongside that of kinesthesia allows us to recognize that for one spectator the empathetic response might be to allow themselves to be bodily carried away by an escapist flow of movement, while for another, it is to feel viscerally involved in an awareness of effort, muscle and sinew' (2010: 72).

Gopal was proud of his masculine-type dances, particularly the second Siva dance *Natanam Adinar*, the god Siva's energetic, cosmic dance of creation and

[9] This AHRC-funded project 'used audience research and neuroscience to investigate arguments that kinesthetic empathy is central to consciousness and to spectator response to dance' (http://www.watchingdance.org/) (accessed 10 October 2020).

destruction (a hypermasculine ideal itself), created by his bharatanatyam guru Meenakshisundaram and which lasted a full six minutes. The dance tells the story of Siva descending from the Himalayan mountains and dancing for devotees in the famous temple hall at Chidambaram. Gopal stated (incorrectly) that 'I was the first to perform it ... It should be danced by a man' (quoted in Gaston 1996: 103), although it was becoming at that time part of female repertory. Anne-Marie Gaston learnt the piece from her guru K. Ellappa Mudaliar in the late 1960s and performed it as a regular item in her bharatanatyam performances (Gaston 2011). Matthew Harp Allen traces the *Natanam Adinar* piece back to 1939, danced then by Lakshmi Sastri. He acknowledges dancer Sarada Hoffman's account of Rukmini Devi's performances that told how Devi would end her recitals with this piece (Allen 2010 [1997]: 227). Allen notes also that this popular song of *Natanam Adinar* was already sung in vocal concerts and was amongst others 'imported into dance in the 1930s and 40s as an explicitly articulated strategy of revival' (2010 [1997). The appearance of *Natanam Adinar* in the 1930s, not part of the *devadasi* repertoire prior to this period, clearly celebrated Siva as the icon of the dance.

Gopal discussed his training with hereditary bharatanatyam teacher Meenakshisundaram Pillai, describing in an interview with Sunil Kothari how Pillai created specific movements for him.

> For instance in the dance of Shiva – in the number *Natanam adinar* – he made me jump higher than was usual in a normal recital ... He made me do a lot of exercises and taught me very powerful footwork. He made my movements extra-broad, extra-sweeping, with big bends, and advised me to match my expression to the theme of the dance.
>
> (in Kothari 1991 [1984]: 16)

No doubt it was inspiring for the hereditary teachers to have a male pupil. It was choreographed for Gopal as a *varnam*, 'with a beautiful *trikala tirmanam* and a *chittaiswaram* at the end' (personal communication between author and Rajyashree Ramesh, August 2017) and not as a *kirtana* as it popularly became.[10]

[10] *Trikala tirmanam:* This is typically a *jathi*, which usually contains syllables like *tha*, *dith*, *thaka*, *jham*, etc. Usually in a *Varnam* the *trikāla jathi* is rendered after singing the *Pallavi*, the first section once. The *trikāla jathi* uses all three speeds and ends with a *tirmāna-adavu* which is usually *kita thaka thari kita thom* or *tha thin kina thom*; *chittaiswaram* comes in the *second* part of the *varnam*, sung with both lyrics and rhythmic beats.

The piece is set to a famous hymn to Siva composed by Gopalakrishna Bharati and set in *Adi Tala*;[11] it glorifies the dance of Siva and praises Siva as he steps down from Mount Kailash as lord of the dance. Mrinalini Sarabhai, who danced with Gopal in the 1940s and 1950s, noted that 'his "Natanam Adinar" danced in the real Pandanallur style was one of the finest I have ever seen' (2003: 52). Gopal's close friend and renowned dancer U. S. Krishna Rao supported this view, stating 'his interpretation of *Natanamadinar* was considered to be unparalleled' (2003: 27). Rao added that 'Thatha [Meenakshisundaram] had a great sense of what is proper in his teaching of dance. He would fashion his instruction according to the personality of the student, his background and culture' (2004: 25). Gopal considered this as part of his suite of Tanjore dances, where he removed what he called the monotonous parts of the piece and used 'three passages of rhythmic dance in that classic style' (1957: 56). There is no film footage of Gopal dancing the *Natanam Adinar* although photographs remain. More significantly, some of Gopal's handwritten notes on the dance survive in notebooks, and in her book, Ambrose includes sketches of selected movements of the dance's first sequence, accompanied by the hand gestures and the floor pattern of the piece. Seventeen drawings show both static and moving poses and are accompanied by the lyrics of the dance: 'Thus danced Lord Siva. So he dances in the golden hall of Thillai … with celestial exquisiteness' (Ambrose 1950: 56–7). Gopal noted in an interview with Gaston in 1984 that '[a]t the beginning of the dance I often preferred to do a few Siva poses and get into a sort of trance' (Gaston 1996: 275), once again, underlining his wish to be identified as the deity, almost as a form of possession when he danced.

Recordings made of the music for Gopal's performances in 1958 that include *Natanam Adinar* by the Asian Music Circle (see Chapter 6) as well as other items in his dance programmes featured Ravi Bellari as singer and general music director, Anura drumming for the Kandyan pieces and other musicians named as Raman Lal, R. Shinde, Namboodri and Satyavan. The *Natanam Adinar* runs for four minutes in this recorded version. Raman Lal played *tabla* and accompanied Gopal at his Jacob's Pillow, USA, performances in 1958. Namboodri also featured as a dancer in the 1956 performances and of course, Anura had been with Gopal as a loyal dancer and drummer since 1947.

[11] One of the most frequently used rhythm cycles in Karnatic music, *Adi Tala* is a repeating eight-beat cycle.

During the earlier period in Bangalore, Gopal's *nattuvangar* and singer for this piece was Vidwan Lokkiah, who accompanied many well-known dancers such as Indrani[12] and who was also known as a *kuchipudi* teacher. Dancer Rajyashree Ramesh, now in Berlin, informed me that she learnt the same composition of *Natanam Adinar* from Vidwan Lokkiah in the 1970s in Bangalore. Lokkiah used to play for Gopal in Bangalore. 'I have not seen any other school or dancer performing this version,' she said, confirming that it was an unusual composition created for 'blossoming male dancer Ram Gopal'. When Ramesh learnt it from Lokkiah, it was longer, about 12–15 minutes in length (personal communication with author, 2017).

Siva's onstage appearance

The allure and power of the iconic mythological figure of Siva believed to be dancing at the onset of creation touched many writers, poets, artists and dancers during India's colonial period and subsequent independence. This included thinkers who formed part of the

> new Orientalist (as they came to be known) under the leadership of Havell and reformer Tagore, [who] reclaimed 'Indian arts and antiquities' as 'Indian art and aesthetic'. The significance of this reformulation lay in the fact that Indian art was no longer in the realm of mere technical expertise but elevated to the realm of 'aesthetic and spiritual empathy'.
>
> (Chakravorty 2008: 47)[13]

Indeed, Siva as a figure was deeply implicated and foregrounded as Lord of the Dance in the reconfiguration of the dance forms as a nationalist trope, as I discuss below. Famously, Ted Shawn created his own *Cosmic Dance of Siva* as early as 1926, described by Paul Scolieri as 'a theatrical rendition of the sacred postures, gestures, and rhythms associated with the Hindu "Lord of the Dance"'.[14] Shawn appears at the start of the dance inside a giant set of the sculpture of Siva's

[12] A *nattuvangar* is the vocal percussionist for a bharatanatyam item, leading the dance and in conversation musically with the dancer. He/she keeps the rhythm using small cymbals.

[13] Theosophist Ernest Binfield Havell had been superintendent of the Madras School of Arts and the Government Art School in Calcutta in the late 1800s.

[14] See Scolieri's essay (2020a) on the Jacob's Pillow webpage at https://danceinteractive.jacobspillow.org/themes-essays/men-in-dance/ted-shawn-defense-male-dancer/ (accessed 10 February 2021).

circle of fire, in the position of Siva Nataraj. He is the cosmic dancer, left foot up in front of him, hands in *pataka* and *dola* positions on the right side, taking the iconic position where Siva is described as stamping out the existential ignorance that exists in the world. Shawn emerges from the sculpture and performs a short, one-and-half-minute interpretive solo dance, accompanied by a dramatic musical piano piece (composed in three sections by Lily Strickland). Smoke representing incense emerges from the pedestal (Scolieri 2020b). The choreography includes stamping on the ground, body twists, rippling arms, lunges, turns and head movements from side to side. Shawn commissioned the dramatic set from an Indian foundry 'that agreed to create a life-size *prabhamandala*, the symbolic ring of flames that surround Siva in the bronze statues that depict him in the form of Nataraja' (Scolieri 2020b: 211–12). It was made in pieces so it could be shipped and re-formed on stages for performance. The founders created his special headdress, representing Siva's symbols of coiled serpent, 'flowing hair … crescent moon' and the head of *Ganga* (2020b).

The costume was similar to Gopal's, a short, tight pair of trunks with a decorative front piece hanging slightly lower, as depicted in the iconography of Siva Nataraj and accompanied by ankle bells and jewellery – necklace, bracelets and armbands – that Shawn had bought on his travels in India. Like Gopal, Shawn wrote of his seeming sense of total absorption whilst dancing this role, stating, 'I never gave a performance of that dance without consciously asking Siva to take possession of my body to use as an expression of the power and the rhythm of his being' (Shawn 1979 [1960]: 198). Shawn was clearly influenced by Coomaraswamy's 1918 writings that he read at the time, as well as many of the other orientalist writers of the period (Shawn: 1979 [1960]). He was also famously setting an agenda in the United States for the male dancer as a virile, athletic, hypermasculine, performative agent, stating, 'Dancing is for men, American men' (Terry 1976: 30) and promoting the strength and beauty of a toned male physique. Coming out as gay was not an option for Shawn and his male dancer colleagues at that time, so it was necessary to adopt this performative, stereotypical and normative male identity.

Other dancers focused on Siva as part of their repertoire in the early period when interest in the classical forms was growing. Kathak pioneer Madame Menaka (born Leila Roy) choreographed a *Dance of Siva* in the early 1930s for her dance partner Ramanarayan Mishra that was included in their European tour of 1936–7. Footage of the piece can be seen in the 1938 film *Temples of India*, directed by Hans Neiter, where it is called *Shiva's Dance of Destruction*. The dance runs for three and half minutes and is accompanied by music of drums and *jaltarang*, and the style is interpretive, rather than the kathak style known today.[15,16] Mishra is dressed in a silk dhoti, with one leg exposed and with bare chest. He wears (like Gopal and Shawn) a necklace, decorative arm bands and a Siva headdress in the form of a helmet, copied from Hindu iconographic portrayals.

Prior to this, the infamous dancer Mata Hari (born Margaretha Geertruida Zelle) performed in Paris in 1905, dancing in the library of the house of art collector and industrialist Emile Guimet, in front of his large bronze dancing Siva Nataraj sculpture.[17] She 'performed her sensational choreographies on the theme of creation, fertility, and destruction, ending with her removing almost all of her clothes in front of the figure. Her scandalous performances contributed significantly to popularizing the Nataraja' (Beltz 2011: 211). Gopal also danced in front of this same bronze Nataraj at the Musée Guimet in November 1938 during his first trip to Paris (see Chapter 1). Gopal writes:

> Later, I went straight to the Musée Guimet ... I had to see the Gods and Goddesses of India, Tibet and China, and besides, I was told in Warsaw that this museum had lectures and even a performance of my dances was possible. I remember reading, in connection with Garbo's picture *Mata Hari* that this remarkable spy had danced there her version of Hindu Temple Dances ... would I dance there too? Possibly.
>
> (Gopal 1957: 80)

Shankar also created a *Dance of Siva* for a performance in Britain at the British Empire Exhibition at Wembley in 1924, no doubt as part of the cultural programme put on in the Indian Pavilion and probably invited by his mentor, William Rothenstein (Bhattacharjya 2011: 488).[18] Shankar later admitted to

[15] Walker's excellent analysis of kathak performance history suggests that Menaka's work was more akin to the oriental dance still seen in the 1930s – a period 'of flux during which the canon was gradually established' (2014: 111) when Indian audiences were more suspicious of the early dancers, perhaps seeing them as having too much European influence.

[16] The *jaltarang is a* melodic percussion instrument originating from the Indian subcontinent that consists of a set of ceramic or metal bowls filled with water.

[17] The house and collection later became the Musée Guimet.

[18] 'Built by architects Charles Allem and Sons, the India Pavilion was modelled on the Jama Masjid in Delhi and the Taj Mahal in Agra. The white building was divided into 27 courts, each dedicated to the exhibition of products from one of the twenty-seven Indian provinces. It was one of the few pavilions where food was served. It also hosted an exhibition on Indian art curated by the India Society with the involvement of William Rothenstein, who made available over twenty-three paintings' (see http://www.open.ac.uk/researchprojects/makingbritain/content/1924-british-empire-exhibition). The overall Indian site covered five acres, with the Palace covering three acres and costing £180,000 to build. Paul Greenhalgh (1988: 61) comments that 'one of the main functions of the building was to show all that Britain had done for India since her arrival there'.

not knowing very much about Siva and just made up the steps to the music. In fact, he had been given a copy of Coomaraswamy's book of *The Mirror of Gesture* in 1923 that contained photos of Siva Nataraj (Bhattacharjya: 2011), but he recalls that he did not really look at this in any detail till his time in Paris in late 1924.

The enduring worldwide popularity of the iconic bronze figure of Siva dancing is exemplified by the modern installation of a 2-metre-high bronze Siva outside of the headquarters of CERN in Geneva (Conseil Européen pour la Recherche Nucléaire). Donated by the Indian government in 2004, the statue not only commemorates Indian's long association with CERN since the 1960s but is there in recognition of 'the metaphor between the cosmic dance of the Nataraj and the modern study of the "cosmic dance" of subatomic particles' (CERN website: n.p.). For over 150 years, art collectors have treasured this representation of Siva; sales at Christie's auction house in New York in 2019 realized $1,035,000 for a 22-centimetre-high Chola bronze of Siva Nataraj, and over £20,000 was paid at Bonhams, London, auction house for a much larger bronze Siva piece 103 centimetres high in 2005. The famous Siva Nataraj at the V&A Museum, London (that Gopal was photographed in front of in 1947), was bequeathed to the museum in 1935 by Lord Ampthill, Governor of Madras from 1900 to 1906, a relic of colonial India.

Siva and emerging masculinity

Siva's significant role as an iconic figure, as Lord of the Dance, aka Siva Nataraj, the strong, potent masculine presence in the reconfiguration of the dance forms during the 1930s–50s in India, has been well documented (Allen 1997, Gaston 1996, Krishnan 2009, Meduri 2008b). Not only was the repertoire changed and reinvented as is now well understood, but as Hari Krishnan writes, 'gender was reimagined under colonial and upper-caste nationalist frameworks that invented the male dancer as a hypermasculine, spiritual and patriotic icon for the emergent nation' (2009: 378). These examples indicate how colonialism becomes a highly gendered process. Anthony Shay emphasizes that the creation of hypermasculine dance styles, seen in many middle eastern states as well as in India, was a direct response to the civilizing missions of the colonial period. He sees it as an invented tradition (Fisher & Shay 2009). Shay reminds the reader that in dance in areas such as Egypt, Iran and Uzbekistan in relation to the legacies of colonialism, not only did there need to be '"proper" images for male dancing bodies' but also both male and female dance forms were 'frequently sanitized'

(2009: 287–8). Describing the changes in Indian dance during this period, Davesh Soneji similarly acknowledges 'the moralizing projects of colonial and postcolonial modernity' (2012: 3). Gopal underlines these points in his own discussion of Rukmini Devi's role in the dance revival in India. He accused her of sanitizing the new bharatanatyam choreographies in her decision to eradicate the more erotic elements of the *devadasi* repertoire expressing *sringara* (erotic and sexual love).

Interviewed by Gaston in the 1980s, Gopal rather caustically commented, 'Rukmini … has bleached Bharata Natyam … we worship the *linga* (male sex organ) and the *yoni* (female sex organ). That is sex. How can we deny sex between a man and a woman. It is a charge between human beings' (Gaston 1996: 94). There is no doubt that Devi reformulated the dance to reflect the spiritual and the devotional elements, the *bhakti,* in contrast to the human and the passionate. She described how she retained some elements and discarded other aspects that she felt were seen as improper. In his comment above Gopal rehearses one of the two alternative accounts of Devi – firstly that she rescued the dance from a practice that was dying, debased and that had become devalued; secondly, that she had changed the form out of all recognition, appropriating it and transforming it into a 'purer, spiritual', middle-class, respectable dance style (O'Shea 2005).

Despite these narrow binary views, Devi was without doubt a visionary nationalist, as well as dancer, choreographer and revivalist, 'a towering, multi-faceted personality who left her impress in the multiple domains of Indian culture and the arts' (Meduri 2005: 3). Interestingly, Canadian Teresa Hubel, writing of her time spent training at Devi's dance institution Kalakshetra in the mid-1980s, notes that 'Kalakshetra, though it was many wonderful things, was one of the least erotic places I have ever been. The rules there were strict, especially concerning the behaviour of its young female students … in the realm of dance, sringara was not permitted, and young dancers who demonstrated this expression were thought to be vulgar' (2010: 175–6).

Gopal's dances of the deity Siva and his virtuosic leaps as the giant mythological eagle *Garuda* (see Chapter 4) represented a strength and virility that created a public display of masculinity – more important at that time when high-caste Indian males were not encouraged to dance and when homosexuality remained a criminal act in India and Britain. He took care to dance only masculine roles, stating, 'You can look like an emasculated eunuch if you are a male dancer' (quoted in Gaston 1996: 101). This was a necessary and strategic move for Gopal, as his beauty and femininity were also highly renowned. Kumudini Lakhia was later to say of him that felt himself 'too beautiful to be a man' (quoted in Shah 2005: 47). Whilst dancing in his troupe in the late 50s and 60s, she remembered how well dressed he was in gorgeous silks and wearing perfume (2020).

During this period in India, the classical dance form of bharatanatyam that was part of Gopal's post-war concerts was in the process of being revived and reconfigured. To avoid being reductive and to illustrate the complexity of this process, Allen describes it as

> re-vivification or bringing back to life, ... a re-population (one social community appropriating a practice from another, a re-construction (altering and replacing elements of repertoire and choreography), a re-naming (from *nautch* and other term to *bharata natyam*), a re-situation (from temple, court and salon to public stage), and a re-storation (as used in Schechner 1985: 69), a splicing together of selected 'strips' of performative behaviour in a manner that simultaneously creates a new practice and invents an historical one.
>
> (Allen 2010 [1997]: 63)

In concert halls and on proscenium stages, Siva's sculptural form began to preside at the side of the dancer, in full view of the audience, as homage to his role as patron of the newly formed bharatanatyam classical dance style, and to be worshipped at the beginning of the evening's performance. As Allen notes, the 1930s saw the advent 'of Nataraja as both a patron deity *for* dance and a subject for portrayal *in* dance' (2010 [1997]: 798). Most writers (see Allen 1997, Gaston 1996, Meduri 2008b, O'Shea 2007) credit Rukmini Devi as being one of the first to place the image of the dancing Siva on stage, and indeed she claimed to have started the practice. The earlier hereditary dancers, however, did not agree with bringing temple worship to the stage as they saw it. Balasaraswati favoured, for example, songs devoted to Krishna and Murugan (O'Shea 2007) rather than Siva, and her daughter, Lakshmi Shanmugam-Knight, said, 'It is not in our tradition to have Nataraja. I am carrying on my mother's tradition' (quoted in Gaston, 1996: 316). But by the 1940s Siva was now not only appearing as a significant element in the dance items but also being worshipped as a deity of the dance on stage. He became the new hero of the dance (Allen [2010] 1997). Gopal did not use a Siva icon onstage in his concerts, perhaps as part of his spirit of resistance.

Dances as described above were performed by women, as noted, but more significantly formed part of the new nationalistic masculine identity for male performers, an identity strongly promoted by Devi at her famous dance school, Kalakshetra. Devi's male dancers, trained in the strong, dramatic style of kathakali as well as bharatanatyam, took on the masculine roles in her dance dramas. Krishnan argues, '[F]rom the period between 1940 and 1955, this new hybrid dance technique came to be seen as the normative movement vocabulary for the male performer of bharata natyam' (2009: 385). The masculinization of this aspect of dance by Devi not only reflected the new nationalist agenda but was in opposition to cultural and homophobic discourse that, as Jonathan Bollen notes, 'attributes feminising and homosexualising connotations to male participation in dance' (2002: n.p.). It was also effective in partially eradicating the important female role of the *devadasi* dancers of the earlier period along with the more sexually explicit aspects of their *abhinaya* repertoire (as indicated above; see also Gaston 1996, Soneji 2012).

Mahesh Dattani's renowned play 'Dance like a Man' (2013 [1989]) engages with the issues of supposed masculinities in the dance environment.[19] Set in the patriarchal attitudes of post-independence India, the play shows the lives of three generations of an Indian family, where the son and daughter (Jairaj and Ratna) and their daughter Lata are bharatanatyam dancers. Jairaj's position as a professional dancer is vehemently opposed by his autocratic father, Amritlal. The play questions strongly held views on the place of dance in society, challenging who should or should not be allowed to dance and the effects of those choices on the family dynamics. Dattani, who studied bharatanatyam in his twenties, cleverly subverts and redefines masculinity as the story unfolds. In its first showing in Bangalore in September 1989, Dattani played the character of Jairaj and the choreography was created by U. S. Krishna Rao and his wife and dancing partner Chandrabhaga Devi (Gopal's long-term dance colleagues).

Terminologies of bharatanatyam

Selected from the group of dances listed at that time as classical, bharatanatyam became the form most associated with the new nation state of India. As discussed earlier, it was mainly removed from the domain of the *devadasi*,

19 I watched Lillete Dubey's 2011 staging of the play at the Waterman's Arts Centre, west London. The original production was mounted there in 2003.

restructured, re-presented and recalled by the middle- and upper-class milieu. Terminology used by the *devadasi* had been varied but included the names *dasi attam, sadir attam, sadir kacheri* and *sadir nautch,* as well as *bharata natya.* Krishnan makes the important point that, contrary to many accounts, the 'new' term of 'bharata natyam' (often written bharatanatyam or sometimes bharatha natyam) was not invented at the time but rather foregrounded at that point for the nationalist agenda (Krishnan 2009). Indeed, the Music Academy in Madras was using the term 'Bharata Natyam'/'Bharata Natya' in its conferences and dance programmes from 1931. One of their programmes states, '[T]he Conference of 1931 is again memorable for the great lift it has given to the declining art of Bharata Natya by including it, as an important item, in its daily evening concerts' (1931 Conference brochure: n.p.). From that time, the name 'bharata natya(m)' became the preferred nomenclature for the revised dance style.

Gopal's 1947 article in *Ballet* magazine includes a discussion of the style of 'Bharata Natya' (1947: 43), explaining the different items that make up the *margam*, but in his autobiography in 1957, he uses only the term *dasi attam,* not 'bharatanatyam'. He continues by describing what he considers the four main Indian styles of dance, emphasizing the male presence in these forms. 'The Kathakali dance drama of Malabar performed by an entire troupe of dancers and musicians are all male; the Kathak dancing of Delhi and Jaipur which is mainly a solo dance; the Manipur dancing of Assam, lyrical and graceful in character; and the Bhagavata Mela Nataka, all-male temple dance drama,' Gopal writes (1957: 49).[20] This was also the case for his pre-war programmes, which named dances in kathakali, kathak and 'South Indian Temple Dances', as this was before the time that Gopal had undertaken any instruction in bharatanatyam. Back in India from 1940, he took up training in bharatanatyam with renowned teacher Meenakshisundaram Pillai in the Pandanallur tradition and Muthukumaran Pillai, the later coming to teach at Gopal's school of dance at his home in Bangalore from 1940 to 1942. In Gopal's international concerts after the war, and during the war in India, 'Bharata Natya' (as his programmes called the dance) items taken from the *margam* repertoire such as *alarippu, tillana, natanam adinar, jatiswaram* and *padams* appeared in his performances. He continued to use, however, the terms 'Dance of the Tanjore Temples,

[20] Although Gopal does record that there were women at KK learning and performing mohiniattam (1957).

South India' and 'Bhagavata Mela Nataka' as well as 'Bharata Natya'/'Bharata Natyam'/'Bharatanatyam' in his printed programmes up to the mid-1960s. In most of his concerts he would name the style of the dance after the title, for example, 'Garuda, the Golden Eagle' (*Kathakali*), 'Moghul Miniatures' (*Kathak*) and 'Natanam Adinar' (*Bharata Natya*) in his 1951 Cambridge Theatre, London programme.

Gopal's references to the *Bhagavata Mela Nataka* tradition from Tanjore (more closely linked to the kuchipudi dance style) were probably influenced by his teacher Meenakshisundaram Pillai who was trained in both styles. Gopal states in his book that 'the "Dasi Attam" of Tanjore derives from the Bhagavata Mela Nataka, the male dance drama *par excellence* of the village of Soolamangalam in Tanjore district itself' (1957: 143). Reginald Massey (2004) confirms that this tradition of dance-dramas continues to this day at an annual festival in the village of Saliyamangalam (Thanjavur district, Tamil Nadu), where a cycle of four plays in *Bhagavata Mela Nataka* style are performed in the temple. Some shorter elements of the long dance-dramas have now been absorbed into female bharatanatyam performance.

Construction of a (dancing) male Indian identity

In his book on male dancers, Ramsey Burt notes how 'masculinity as a socially constructed identity is not a stable entity, but one made up of conflictual and contradictory aspects' (1995: 7). He reminds us how in different forms of cultural expressions, gender representations 'do not merely reflect changing social definitions of femininity and masculinity but are actively involved in the processes through which gender is constructed and norms reinforced' (1995: 11–12). Much has been written about the construction of the Hindu male identity during the colonial period (Alter 1994, Banerjee 2005, Chattopadhyay 2011, Gupta 2011, Kamath 2019). This is a complex area but there is no doubt that British colonizers identified with a highly masculine ideal – assertive, aggressive, strong, violent and virile – and in direct opposition to, as they depicted it, the effeminate, vanquished and weak Indian. Sikita Banerjee in her writings on nationalism and masculinity in India traces this creation of a certain type of masculinity in empire back to Protestant belief that 'emerged in the mid-nineteenth century, when British imperial power was at its zenith and drew upon various traits: self-control, discipline, confidence, martial prowess, military heroism, heterosexuality, and rationality' (2012: 26).

The particular colonial image held of the Bengali male, appallingly and contemptuously described in 1841 by Thomas Babington Macauley was of a man 'feeble even to effeminacy. He lives in a constant vapour bath. His pursuits are sedentary, his limbs delicate, his movements languid … Courage, independence, veracity are qualities to which his constitution and his situation are equally unfavourable' (Macauley 1967 [1843]: 386).[21] Banerjee argues how this pejorative view revealed the British administrators' penchant for use of 'a gendered and racialised lens to classify Indians into various groups, one of the most important being "martial" and "nonmartial" races' (2012: 15). A study published in 1908 by Herbert Risley scientifically measured bodies of Indians and separated those who were 'tall and fair-skinned, with light-coloured eyes (e.g. the Pathans or Sikhs)', from those who were 'short and dark-skinned with dark eyes (e.g. Bengalis)' (quoted in Benerjee: 32). Skin colour and gender were two powerful tropes of colonial power. At these times of colonial rule, as Joseph Alter argues, 'virility was a metaphor for political power and sociomoral strength' (Alter 1994: 55). The imposed construct of the Hindu male, othered in relation to both British and Muslim men, gave rise to a determined necessity to deal with such humiliation by a counter construction of masculinity. This re-masculinization, or notion of a hypermasculinity, commonly forms part of nationalist agendas and of colonial critiques, discussed earlier and explained by Alter (1994: 61), 'the ideology of nationalism is arguably one of the most masculine expressions of patriarchal politics'. Murali Balaji and Khadeem Hughson underscore this view confirming how the 'cultural production of masculinity has long been tied to nationalistic subtexts' (2014: 207). As is now well understood masculinities (and femininities) as identities are always socially, culturally and historically constituted.

Indian nationalism gave birth to several different types of new masculinities: Swami Vivekananda, famously speaking at the 1893 Congress of the World Parliament of Religions in Chicago, redefined Indian manhood with an emphasis on a type of spiritual masculinity in which religious discipline offered moral superiority, courage and strength. His daily prayer to the goddess Kali finished with the line 'Take way my unmanliness and make me a man!' He exalted his followers to stand up, be energized and be 'manly' to better understand the

[21] Cheesman identifies two other derogatory, stereotypical attitudes of the British colonizers towards their male subjects alongside that of the Bengali, that they were 'The Sinhalese was a drunkard and gambler (Rogers 1987: 210–11). The Burmese man was indolent except when provoked' (2014: 81).

spiritual discourses of the Upanishads. Vivekananda along with the Tagore family was part of a Bengali elite that created a counter and resistant model, establishing their own articulation of a muscular nationalism. John J. MacAloon (2006: 296) calls Vivekananda's idea of a spiritual masculinity a 'muscular Hinduism', likening it to the Victorian idea of 'muscular Christianity' that was in vogue and underpinned colonial thinking. 'During the late 1850s, the tenets of Muscular Christianity became an integral part of the public school educational system. The primary reason was to encourage Christian morality and help develop the character of the future captains of industry and political leaders, and in turn strengthen the British Empire,' note Nick J. Watson, et al. (2005: 7). Dancer Navtej Johar, discussing the disenfranchised body in yoga and dance, adds that this notion of muscular Christianity influenced 'Veer Savarkar, the father of the extreme right-wing Hindu movement of Hindutva, who dreamt of an India that would be energized by a Masculine Hinduism' (2017: 154).[22]

Gandhi, in a similar fashion, created an ascetic masculine ideal to counteract Western aggression and violence, where self-control, discipline and sexual abstinence created a 'celibate body [that was] regarded as being supremely fit' (Alter 1994: 46; see also Krishnan 2009). This emphasized spiritual superiority and domination as an alternate performance of masculinity. Banerjee in an earlier work argues that the two main constructs of masculinity of 'the Hindu soldier and the warrior-monk' (2005: 2) came out of the British colonial period in direct response to the classification of Indian men as the effeminate other. The warrior-monk has both physical prowess and spiritual superiority. Banerjee coins the term a 'muscular nationalism' that she describes as 'the intersection of a specific vison of masculinity with the political doctrine of nationalism' (2005: 2). Sanatan Dharmists and Arya Samajists were also implicated in the rise of new masculinities as movements that embraced Hindu reform and Brahminical patriarchy.

The nationalist ideal in terms of cultural and artistic expressions led, as discussed above, to a middle-class construction of dance and music that fitted into Brahminical (and binary) notions of men identified with strength and vigour and women who depicted chastity and femininity. Lata Singh emphasizes the point that 'the whole issue of masculinity and effeminacy also came into the nationalist discourse' (2009: 275). The spaces for men were the public arenas and therefore, in contrast to this, the home was designated as the woman's place.

[22] Paul Scolieri acknowledges how Ted Shawn was also influenced by ideas of muscular Christianity 'which brought muscularity and the male physique in line and harmony with Christian ideals' and into his choreography. (https://www.berkshireeagle.com/archives/a-closer-look-at-the-life-legacy-of-ted-shawn/article_5757f2b4-8134-5f59-8c00-b822720d2c00.html). (accessed 28 July 2021).

Krishnan too argues how the fixing of 'identities, categories and roles related to gender and sexuality during this period was predicated on Brahmanic and colonial perceptions of propriety and obscenity' (2009: 384).

These binary constructions of gender emerged out of European philosophical thought and were deeply reinforced through colonialism. In this particular and biased cultural model, masculinity is associated with the white male body, that creates an Other of the colonial subject. These rigid conceptualizations are at odds with new thinking and theorizations on the complex ways of being a man or a woman that differs widely across cultures, contexts and communities; theorizations such as Judith Butler's (1993) that fracture and trouble notions of fixed sexualities. Butler's new understanding proposed that gender is socially constructed and that sexuality needs to be uncoupled from biological sex. In terms of masculinities, this means 'uncoupling *what men do* from *what men are*' (Haywood & an Ghaill 2003: 15). This reconceptualization of gender shows that there are complex ways of being a man or a woman that vary widely 'across culture, context and community' (Jackson II & Balaji 2014: 25).

In the millennium period, commentators are writing on the creation of the 'lean and muscular ... new Indian male' (Baas 2015: 445), much influenced by the chiselled, gym-toned bodies of male Bollywood stars and by the affluent middle class who wish to signify 'socio-economic success, cosmopolitanism and even professionalism' (2015: 445) through such fitness and bodily developed strength. I have written elsewhere about the impact of the gym bodies of the Hollywood stars such as Shah Rukh Khan that privilege fitness and workouts – a trend that began in the mid- to late 1990s led by Salman Khan who was a keen body builder and was often depicted semi-clad or in transparent, revealing shirts in his films (David 2015). In the film *Om Shanti Om* (2001), half-way through the song 'Dard-e-Disco', Shah Rukh Khan emerges from water, showing a naked upper body, oiled, and with a muscled physique, that flaunts six-pack abs and rippling arm muscles, and which the camera lingers over in full close-up. Depicted here is a marked change in the focus of desire. Instead of the attention being specifically on the bodies of the female stars, the male leads (and their bodies) now attract as much attention. As Chara Gupta underlines, Shah Rukh Khan's body

> can be a delight for the women's gaze. The object of desire is not so much the female, but the male. Gender roles are ... reversed here ... The embodied performances ... to a degree subvert notions of a dominant male gaze, mutate hegemonic masculinity, questions neat heteronormative categories, and undermine prescribed gender spaces and fixed gendered representations.
>
> (Gupta 2007: n.p.)

Gopal's extraordinary impact on audiences, especially through the portrayal of the Hindu god *Siva* with his androgynous yet stunningly beautiful presence on stage, conveyed, to some, an exotic and desirable representation of the East. I argue that Gopal played with such exoticism knowingly, aware of his attractiveness to men and to women, both on and off stage. Like all dancers, he had a heightened sensitivity to his own bodily presence as it was the tool of his trade. His attention to the detail of costuming, lighting, jewellery and make-up was renowned. Offstage, he was flamboyantly well dressed with a penchant for long dramatic caftans, colourful silk turbans and expensive gold rings. He always had an eye for the camera, even in his older years. In the audience's affective reception can be found aspects of gendered and embodied moralities through the scopophiliac and sometimes homoerotic gaze placed on the Indian male dancer, perpetuated not only in performance but also in the imagery produced for publicity purposes. At the time of Gopal's early performances, this gaze was filtered through orientalist and colonial constructs that viewed him as highly exotic and somewhat erotic.

Dance critics of this prior period (1930s–1950s) were predominately white men who knew little of the world of Indian dance and reinforced this gaze through their discourse of the seductive power of such representation of the East. *The Sunday Times* critic in July of 1930 wrote, 'Ram Gopal and his company of Hindu dancers and musicians … are artists of uncommon ability. Even to the unversed European it is obvious that they hold high ideals of physique and ritual … One could detect no single flaw throughout the evening' (30 July 1939). In the same season of performances, an unnamed reviewer extolled Gopal stating, 'There is no doubt that America's praise [the Indian Nijinsky] is justified – to see him is to realise the essence of dancing. His technique is magnificent. The perfect eloquence of his body is the final expression of the exquisite control of each individual muscle' (*Cavalcade*, 5 August 1939). Such pleasured, potentially homoerotic, viewing of the idealized male dancing body, and particularly in pre-war Britain, of an Indian body, conveyed both an exotic controlling gaze, as well as a relationship of power, despite Gopal's own manipulation of such dynamics. As Jane Desmond writes, '[d]ance lets us look at bodies for pleasure, indeed demands that this is what we do. This has the potential to link bodies with desire and dancing with the visible manifestation, or elicitation of, desire' (2001: 5).

Gopal mainly had relationships with men, but for a short time in the 1960s, when he lived in London, he was married to a much older woman, wealthy heiress Edith Alexander.[23] Gopal identified as homosexual and probably as bisexual although due to the constraints of the time – this was an unspoken fact. As noted earlier, Gopal presented solo dances that tended towards a hyper-masculine register, in the same way that Ted Shawn and his group of male dancers tried to show that they were not effeminate by using a display of athleticism and physical strength, as coming out was not allowable in that historical period. Burt underlines this point, arguing how 'the spectacular aspects of men's dancing generally reinforce conservative norms of masculine behaviour' (1995: 54).

In the discussion of the extraordinary role that Siva played within the dance milieu, as an icon of national power and status, as a symbol of display of masculinity and as a figure that ushered in the newly reconfigured national dances of India, Gopal's Siva dances were central to his success in his production and weaving together of dance histories and styles. The iconic headdress, emblematic and illustrative of Gopal and his powerful presence on stage, dances out of the archives with great potency as a signifier of Gopal's innovative aesthetic.

[23] Edith Julia Alexander (1887–1969) was twenty-five years older than Gopal. Gopal's obituary in *The Times*, London (2003: n.p.) notes that Alexander was a 'rich widow, many years his senior, who promised him the benefits of considerable trusts in Switzerland'. There were family difficulties regarding the money after she died, and it remains unclear as to whether Gopal received any financial benefits. Gopal laid her ashes in tomb of her late husband.

3

The war years and beyond

Gopal's return to Britain

On 2 July 1947 Gopal set sail from Bombay to England on board the *RMS Alcantara*, a Royal Mail Line ship, arriving at Southampton docks three weeks later on 23 July.[1] Named on the list of British passengers, aged 29 [*sic*], as a dancer, travelling courtesy of Thomas Cook & Son, London, in Class A (first class), the manifest notes that Gopal's 'Country of Intended Future Permanent Residence' is England, revealing his intention to take up British citizenship and settle in the UK. Passenger shipping lists have become increasingly important sources of data for historians wishing to investigate travel, immigration and genealogies, although as Robert P. Swierenga warns, many earlier lists were handwritten and therefore 'problems of illegibility plague every project' (1991: 48). Fortuitously, all the passenger shipping lists tracking Gopal's international travels that can be found, including the one cited above, are typed, although several are written over by hand. The yellowing, lined pages, alphabetically ordered, where Gopal is numbered no. 137 of approximately 970 passengers, reveal an assembly of passengers including students, housewives, accountants, tea planters, missionaries, engineers and a range of ages from children to retirees. Other shipping documents from his overseas travels reveal his travel companions: Gopal's first journey to the United States on the ship *SS Matsonia* was with manager and lover Aleksanda Janta (see Chapter 1); his second to New York in 1948 for the New York Jubilee Gala was with promoter Julian Braunsweg, and his return travel to New York in 1954 for Jacob's Pillow performances was

1 The ship was built in 1926 in Belfast as a Royal Mail Ocean liner. During the war she served as an armed merchant cruiser and as a troop ship but returned to passenger service in 1947. The *Alcantara* was scrapped in 1958.

with his later life partner Serafin Kycia, who was recorded as 'Stateless' in the travel documentation.[2]

As set out in Chapter 1, by the 1950s Gopal was on the British Electoral Register and in 1958 received a Certificate of Naturalisation from the Home Office, under the 1948 British Naturalisation Act which conferred British Citizenship. Gopal returned and settled in Britain before the flurry of legislation in the 1960s (Commonwealth Immigration Acts 1962 and 1968) which made the transition to citizenship an altogether different proposition. His ability to glide smoothly to British nationality after a year's residence is a substantive marker between his status and that of dancers today.

Gopal loved London, seeing it at that time as 'the world's most international city' (1962: 16). His concerts pre-war had been an outstanding success so this was not surprising. Leela Venkataraman's obituary for Gopal states that 'even with his love for the classical vocabulary, he chose to make his home in the West and not in India – which he visited regularly. Perhaps the different Western context gave his creative imagination freedom without tying him down to the orthodox

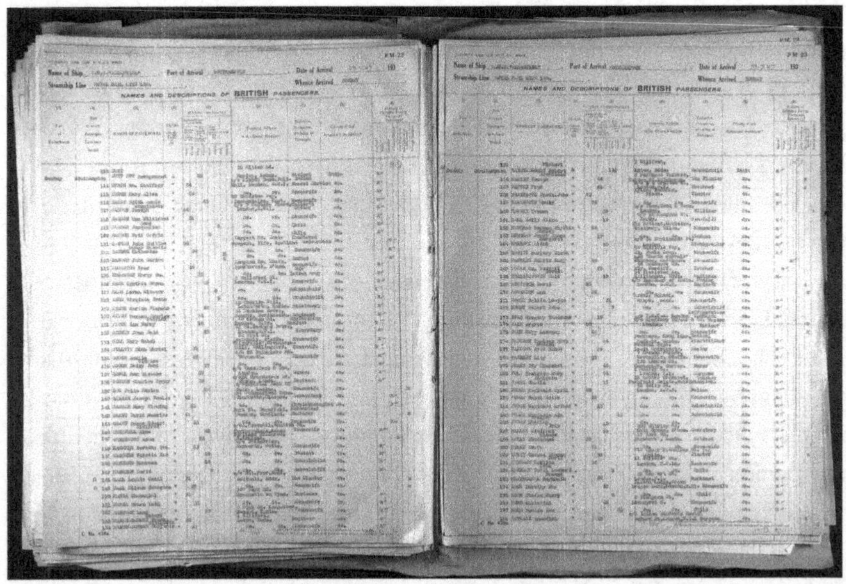

Figure 10 Passenger list, *RMS Alcantara*, 2 July 1947. Author's own collection. © Ancestry.com.

[2] Rebekah J. Kowel records the correspondence between Ted Shawn and Gopal over Kycia's presence for the trip. Gopal insisted that Kycia accompanied him as he needed an 'assistant', which Shawn challenges. Gopal eventually got his way and Kycia was allowed to travel and Gopal also insisted on a raise in his fees (2020: 183–6). Kycia had left Poland to settle in the UK after fighting on the Polish army but may not have received British naturalization. He sadly died by suicide in 1989.

presentation conventions associated with each traditional form' (2003: n.p.). I contend that this was one of the ways he challenged the status quo through acts of resistance, perhaps also because his insider/outsider status (identified in the introduction) pushed him to explore dance more broadly and to incorporate innovative ideas into his work.

The year 1947 was a significant pivotal point in Gopal's career, settling in London at various addresses for the next period of his life until his death over fifty years later. The mobility represented by the 1947 shipping document which serves as the key pivotal image of this chapter symbolizes his frequent travel in the years that followed. He returned by ship to the United States at least four more times for performances and toured productions in Europe (especially Scandinavia), Turkey, Ceylon, Trinidad as well as return trips to India documented in Chapter 4. Gopal's trans-Atlantic journeys as well as Indian trips were all by ship, except for one flight in October 1953 to New York on a BOAC (British Overseas Airways Corporation) plane. The 1950s saw the new 'jet-age' of commercial aviation and this 'expansion of international aviation enabled new patterns of touring' giving an increased mobility for artists, notes Jonathan Bollen (2020: 2). Routes between Australia, the Far East and India opened up and ships began to be seen as more old-fashioned as opposed to the notion of modernity and sophistication offered by aircraft travel. Such increased mobility for performers allowed for richer cross-cultural and intercultural exchanges between artists themselves and their audiences, bringing extended understandings of diversity – perhaps emergent as a new cultural value – and the interweaving of different cultures (Bollen 2020).

Gopal recalls this period, stating that after both his parents had died in the mid-1940s in Bangalore,

> the old house had lost its spirit and become rather like a tomb. Yes, I would follow my intuition. I must go on now, move away. Where? London of course. Where else? All my background had been with English friends, teachers and memories, those wonderful pre-war 1939 memories of the Aldwych where I danced for the first time.
>
> (1957: 171–2)

Gopal really effected a 'double presence', laying down roots and remaining in England whilst retaining unbroken connections with India. His Anglicized upbringing included a Catholic education, English as the lingua franca at home, his interest in and connections with the (then) European world of ballet, his early world travel, his father's own education in London – all these circumstances contributed to his sense of being somewhat of a cosmopolitan figure. He took pride in being a world player and retained a certain idealism for East-West connections. Judith Mackrell, interviewing him in 1989, writes that '[i]t is clear, as he studs his conversation with references to Western artists, that he views his art as part of a larger culture' (1989: 17). In obituaries written at his death, Gopal's sense of worldly engagement was remarked on by many writers, with *The Telegraph* noting, 'Although steeped in the culture of India, he was cosmopolitan' (24 October 2003).

The modern conception of cosmopolitanism, understood as that which is of the world – in other words that which is free from national, regional or local limitations and prejudices – is a complex intellectual *projet*, which started with the Enlightenment's vision of a shared human morality that would act as a guiding principle and lead to perpetual peace.[3] This belief in a universalist morality is what led to the creation of the *United Nations* in 1945 and in 2002 the *International Criminal Court*.[4] According to Helen Gilbert and Jacqueline Lo, '[f]or some theorists, cosmopolitanism operates as a prescriptive vision of global democracy and world citizenship while, for others, it offers a theoretical space for articulating hybrid cultural identities' (Gilbert & Lo 2007: 5). Cosmopolitanism is a vast field, with many idiosyncrasies, specificities and contentions. It has been labelled 'critical' (Rabinow 1986: 258), 'discrepant' (Clifford 1992), 'rooted' (Cohen 1992: 478), 'patriotic' (Appiah 1997: 633) and the apparently contradictory 'working class' (Werbner 2008: 12) to cite a few. Today's attitudes to the concept of cosmopolitanism acknowledge its colonial roots and note its loaded nature, with a sense of reviling the 'new cosmopolitan' (Pollock et al. 2000) as simply being part of the new global elite (Matthews 2007).[5] Gopal's own, perhaps ingenuous sense of identity is encapsulated at the end of his autobiography, where he wrote: 'After all I may have been born in India, but … I felt I was a living human being first, and as a citizen and lover of all mankind I felt neither Eastern nor Western' (1957: 199). Similar notions are reflected in studies carried out by Sayaka Osanami Törngren and Yuna Sato

[3] This was problematized in the writing of German philosopher Immanuel Kant, especially in his *Ideas Towards a Universal History from a Cosmopolitan Point of View* of 1784, *Perpetual Peace* of 1795, and in his last work *Anthropology from a Pragmatic Point of View* of 1798 which recognized that individuals, whilst belonging to specific political states, are also citizens of a single word community in that they share a common heritage of humanity. I thank the late Andrée Grau for her important input into this note and the section on cosmopolitanism.

[4] The ICC's founding treaty was adopted by the UN General Assembly at a conference in Rome in July 1998. After being ratified by more than sixty countries, the Rome Statute entered into force on 1 July 2002 (see https://www.cfr.org/backgrounder/role-international-criminal-court).

[5] Brett Neilson notes how Arjun Appadurai (1991) 'calls for a cosmopolitan anthropology that does not presuppose the primacy of the West' (1999: 111).

(2019) in Japan where they found that at least five of the small sample (twenty-nine multiracial and multi-ethnic individuals) self-identified neither as Japanese nor as mixed heritage but as human beings first 'without any reference to their racial and ethnic background' (2019: 815). This was an act of resistance against existing identity categories, like the defiance shown by Gopal to be categorized in any way. In the same manner, Kwame Anthony Appiah cites his own father's letter, written at his death to Appiah and his siblings '"Remember that you are citizens of the world." And he went on to tell us that this meant that – wherever we chose to live, and, as citizens of the world, we could surely choose to live anywhere – we should make sure we left that place "better than you found it"' (1997: 618).

Arriving in London in September 1947, Gopal brought a new company of dancers and musicians and, that same month, performed some of his prepared programme of dances at the opening ceremony of a new exhibition, *The Human Form in Indian Sculpture* in London's Victoria and Albert Museum's Indian sculpture section. Opened by William Hare, the fifth Earl of Listowel, who had been the last Secretary of State for India, the exhibition event was covered as a news item in the main London newspapers along with photos of Gopal posing beside the magnificent temple carvings and bronze deities in the museum's collection. An article in the *Evening Standard* (11 November 1947) captioned its coverage of the exhibition with 'Nautch in SW7'; the *Illustrated London News*, an influential weekly publication, carried a double page spread with photos (20 September 1947). According to the report, the dancers were there 'to illustrate and interpret the significance of various poses which are to be found in the statuary exhibited'. One photo shows Gopal reclining in a Vishnu pose. Arnold L. Haskell (cited in Gopal 1957: 173) gave the introductory address at the opening and spoke of Gopal as 'an exceptional artist'; Gopal commented that it was such a privilege to be asked to perform there and it was an auspicious start to his return to England. Short excerpts of film of the event exist in the Pathé News archive, in black and white and unfortunately without sound. I discuss this film in Chapter 5.

The war years in India

Commencing with the documentation of Gopal's return to the UK after the Second World War in 1947, this chapter turns back to the war years when Gopal returned from Europe to India by ship, remaining there for seven years, undertaking new training in the classical styles of bharatanatyam and kathak (discussed below), teaching in his home studio in Bangalore, and preparing programmes to tour for the Entertainments National Service Association (ENSA) in India during the same period. His significant work with dancers Mrinalini Sarabhai and later Kumudini Lakhia, who both went on to forge creative and groundbreaking paths in the field of Indian classical and contemporary dance, are discussed. I engage with the wider field of dance in Europe at that time, indicating the links with Indian and eastern performers that influenced the developing modern dance in Germany and elsewhere, as well as investigating the need for patrons and managers for Indian dancers at that time.

In London, during the war period, there were few performances of Indian dance. Some scant references can be found in theatre archives of dance reviews of Punjabi male dancer, Rafiq Anwar.[6] 'Rafiq Anwar and His Company of Indian Dancers and Musicians' performed as part of a British ENSA tour, appearing in London in June 1942 at the Rudolf Steiner Hall and again in May 1943 at the Ambassadors Theatre. The reviews were mixed, praising the presentation of the programme, but observing that Anwar 'lacks that subtlety of arm movement and unearthly quality which made Ram Gopal's *Siva* such a memorable performance' and commenting on 'his continual downward glance and heavy tread' (*Dancing Times* July 1943: 450–1). Remarks were also made about his supporting cast, mainly European dancers who did not 'seem able to interpret or sink themselves into the subtle movements of all parts of the body' (*Dancing Times* November 1942: 52). Anwar's printed programme at the Ambassadors Theatre lists several dances that are recognizable from Gopal's pre-war programmes (*Cobra Devil dance*, *Kite Dance*, *Siva*, *Ras Leela* amongst others) but there is no choreographic acknowledgement of Gopal's work, instead naming Anwar and Robin Sarkar as choreographers. One of Gopal's musicians, Bhupen Mukerjee, played in Anwar's orchestra. The order of the programmes that interspersed short, varied dances with musical items followed Gopal's programming. When I questioned Gopal about these performances he commented that Anwar had been an extra in his company before the war and had probably tried to imitate him with these dances but lacked the finesse in his gestures (interviews with author, August 2000).

After Gopal's sell-out performances in London in 1939, members of his company began to put pressure on him to return home to India as the war in Europe grew closer. He spent seven years back in India from the beginning of

[6] Anwar was studying engineering at London University. He later became a film actor, playing the lead in a Hindi classic, *Neecha Nagar (The Lower City)*, which won the Grand Prix, the top award at the first ever Cannes Film Festival in 1946.

1940 to mid-1947 based at the family house in Bangalore. Whilst there, Navy, Army and Air Force Institutes (NAAFI) and ENSA India commissioned Gopal and his dance company to tour India's major cities to entertain the Indian and British troops as well as performing in hospitals for the convalescent soldiers.[7] Gopal's troupe, touring under the name of the 'Ram Gopal Ensemble', included U. S. Krishna Rao (dancing as Krishna Ubhayakar), his wife Chandrabhaga Devi, Mrinalini Sarabhai, Janaki, Dayal Saran, Radhika, Karpaga Devi, Devakar, Vithal Dass, Retna Mohini and the very well-known Saraswati Orchestra, directed by B. N. K. Rao and led by M. S. Natarajan. This large orchestra normally consisted of twenty-five players but performed with just eleven members for Gopal's tours. As in previous years, the dance programme was interspersed with musical items. Dance pieces included Gopal's stunning *Garuda* dance, his Javanese duet with

Figure 11 Programme of Ram Gopal's performances in India (wartime). Author's own collection.

7 The first official war entertainment organization in India was the Bengal Entertainment Services Association (BESA) and lasted till 1944. ENSA took over in 1943 (Merriman 2013).

Mohini named *King Klana & Devi Srinkandi,* his other solo items *Cobra Devil Dance* and *Rajput Serenade of Love* and a *Tillana* duet with Krishna Rao amongst other pieces (see *Nartanam* 2003: 3 & 4).[8] During this period, in 1944 Gopal and his company danced in Bombay at the All-India Dance Festival, coming first in the competition. Leading local critic D. C. Shah wrote, 'Ram Gopal stood head and shoulders above the rest. Ram Gopal's was the smallest troupe at the festival and yet his two performances are amongst the season's greatest highlights' (quoted in Gopal 1957: 147). These performances included several of the dancers named above as well as Nina Thimayya and Polish-born Hanka Dytrych (discussed later).[9] The company additionally performed at the same festival the following year in Delhi.

The house and studio in Bangalore were a magnet for those in the performing arts. ENSA dancer Catherine Wells recalls in her wartime memoirs being taken to meet 'the renowned Ram Gopal' in Bombay, whom she had first seen dancing in London. She described how

> I had admired Ram Gopal's dancing immensely when I had seen him with his troupe in London, and so was delighted at the thought of meeting him in person, and on my first day in India too. We went to his studio where – in a brown and gold dressing gown – he received us very simply and unpretentiously … and his conversation was quiet and intelligent.
>
> (2001: 90)

The London Ballet Company, touring with ENSA in India, also visited Gopal's studio, and Nand Kumar (2003) writes how John Gielgud, performing for ENSA in *Blythe Spirit* and *Hamlet,* was invited to dinner along with other friends to Gopal's Bangalore house. Art and film critic, Serozh Dadachanji, visited the house with a commission from *The Bombay Chronicle* to write on Gopal's school and his dance performances. They became good friends, and later, he and Gopal jointly wrote a book titled *Indian Dancing* (1951). Gopal says of him, 'He was the friend who rushed to my side, from Bombay to Bangalore, when I lost my beloved mother' (1957: 154). Janta, Gopal's former manager, visited the family house during the war, and Michael Rouse, an Army officer who had worked in Burma, Java and India, also came to stay, becoming the new manager for the company after the war. Gopal's niece, Joy, remembers Rouse as a 'very elegant and very nice, gentle man' (personal communication with author, August 2019).

[8] A special edition of the journal dedicated to Ram Gopal on his death.

[9] Thimayya was an excellent dancer and performed solos and duets with Gopal. She was married to Major General K. S. Thimayya, one of India's most eminent generals who later became a diplomat.

The tours for Gopal and company travelled across the whole country from Lahore (now in Pakistan) to Calcutta, Madras and Bangalore. They performed in theatres and military centres for the troops, with one of the dancers T. K. Narayan stating that Gopal 'used to perform almost every day at different military centres. We were all performing with him on many occasions and Selvamani used to provide nattuvangam support' (2004: 45).[10] Narayan's daughter Gayathri Keshavan noted that her father, aged seventeen, saw Gopal dance at the Town Hall in Bangalore in 1940 and was inspired to learn. Despite his parents' opposition, he started to combine his dance training alongside his engineering studies and was allowed to stay at Gopal's family house rather than to make the 5 to 6 mile walk there and back each day. This he did for nearly four years. Narayan joined the company for some performances and went with Gopal for extra classes from Meenakshisundaram Pillai. He set up his own school of dance, the Academy of Bharatanatyam in 1948 which his daughter still runs in Bangalore (personal communication with Gayathri Keshavan, July 2019). Gopal's stint with ENSA during the Second World War forms an important bridge between the cultural work performers had taken up in the UK, the United States and South Asia. The United Service Organization (USO) in America and the Indian People's Theatre Association (IPTA) in India had convergent yet different aims in relation to ENSA and Gopal remains one of the few Indian performers involved in the cultural dimension of the war effort. Although this war period back in India was a time of growth and artistic achievement for Gopal, it was also tinged with sadness. Whilst there, around 1943–4, Gopal's mother contracted tuberculosis and died, followed shortly by his father who was already eighty.[11]

Gopal's school of dance, Bangalore

Encouraged by his mother on his return home, Gopal took the opportunity to start his own school of dance in Bangalore, building a garden studio (described in Chapter 1) for classes and company rehearsals, working with renowned dancers Mrinalini Sarabhai and Tara Chaudhri amongst others. Classes started at 8.00 a.m. and continued till sunset, with a break for lunch and afternoon rest from the hot sun. Students occasionally joined the family for breakfast in the large dining room of the family house. Gopal notes,

[10] Very little information is available for these tours, despite searching in archives in Delhi (Sangeet Natak and the Indira Gandhi National Centre for the Arts) and Chennai (Madras Music Academy).

[11] The exact dates of their deaths are unknown, but this has been suggested by family members and Gopal speaks of his mother's death being in the early part of the war period.

> I engaged the services of several dancers, Ellappa Mudaliar and Gowrie Ammal among them, who worked closely with Bala Saraswati, greatest living woman dancer of 'Dasi Attam' and Muthukumaran Pillai from Mayavaram in the Tanjore district ... Also Kunju Nair and Kunchunni, two students of the Kerala school of the Poet Vallathol in Shoranur, and a Kathak master.
>
> (Gopal 1957: 139)

K. Ellappa Mudaliar and Mylapore Gauri Ammal were both hereditary practitioners teaching bharatanatyam, and Kunju Nair and Kunchunni (from Kerala Kalamandalam) taught kathakali. The fact that Gopal and his company and students were taught by invited hereditary *devadasi* practitioners and *nattuvanars* indicates how Gopal continued to challenge boundaries and to distance himself from the nationalist agenda of the dance reformers. His own training with Tanjore hereditary teachers Meenakshisundaram Pillai and Muthukumaran Pillai in the Pandanallur style created an exciting new identity for Gopal, where the inherited tradition was being placed on a cosmopolitan, biracial (gay) body, eliciting a hyper-masculine movement style laced with virility and encompassing broad, sweeping movements, powerful footwork and incredible leaps.

Sarabhai had been excited when Gopal had persuaded her mother to allow her to move to Bangalore to study with him, and she was one of the first students to enrol in his dance school. Her family moved to a house not far away at the other end of Bangalore. Gopal wrote that Sarabhai's dancing was full of delicacy and gracefulness and he was inspired to invite her as his partner when they toured to Madras and Calcutta during the war (1957). Their collaboration was highly successful, described by a Calcutta critic as when they danced together 'the atmosphere was electrified with a subtle sense of the sublime' (quoted in Sarabhai 2004: 78). In her autobiography Sarabhai recalls of Gopal that he 'had a fine presence on and off the stage' (2004: 76) and in a tribute to him after his death, she wrote, 'Ram Gopal was a superb dancer and I enjoyed my work with him' (2003: 52).

Sarabhai's professional relationship with Gopal was not only as dancers performing together but of an understanding of shared aesthetics. They offered the audience a unique sensory encounter which was achieved in part through the Indian intertwining of music and dance with the classical traditions of sculpture, painting, music and literature. This experience somehow transcended cultural boundaries. Both had trained with hereditary dance gurus Muthukumaran Pillai and Meenakshisundaram Pillai and engaged with what they felt was a 'pure' classical tradition. They did not always see eye to eye, however, and they also diverged at time in their opinion of other artists. Sarabhai, for instance, admired greatly the dance reformer Rukmini Devi, with whom she had studied briefly. What especially appealed to her in Devi's work was 'the aesthetic values of her productions' (2004: 49). In contrast, Gopal was occasionally quite scathing about Devi as discussed in Chapter 2. Conversely, he was full of praise for Balasaraswati, the renowned Indian dance reformer of the period, calling her a 'superb artist' (cited in Ambrose 1950: 95). Sarabhai argued that whereas she could admire Balasaraswati's skills as a dancer, she thought her rather coarse and slightly vulgar, not having the grace, beauty and taste she saw in Devi. Sarabhai and Gopal later worked together on tours in London and other parts of the UK in 1950 and 1951, and they retained a friendship that lasted over many years. They both, of course, came from highly educated, multilingual, well-travelled and wealthy backgrounds.

Two sisters, Nina Thimayya (previously mentioned) and Boli Cariappa, from outside Bangalore attended Gopal's school, and Thimayya became one of the main dancers in Gopal's troupe. Shevanti, Janaki(e) and Rajeshwar joined as pupils and later performed at the above-mentioned All India Dance Festival

Figure 12 Ram Gopal's dance school at his family home, Bangalore. Author's own collection.

as well as in Gopal's ENSA tours. Gopal describes them all: 'Shevanti from Bombay, whose every line and movement were filled with grace and beauty; Janaki, a young Brahmin girl from Madras, who moved like Parvati, Goddess of the Dance herself; Tara, the dancer from the Punjab, who had grace and vitality; Rajeshwar, whose slim waist was the envy of every girl in the company and who danced like a gazelle' (1957: 146–7). Other dancers attending classes in Gopal's home studio over the years and performing with him were Gopal's childhood friend Krishna Rao and his wife and dance partner Chandrabhaga Devi, Australian dancer Louise Lightfoot, Retna Mohini and Lilavati Devi. The hereditary teacher K. Ellappa Mudaliar, mentioned above, whilst working in Bangalore with Gopal brought along one of his young students considered a child prodigy. Baby Saroja – Madras Kadiravelu Saroja or M. K. Saroja – began to train in dance aged five and had her debut performance aged nine. Saroja danced with Gopal and Sarabhai from 1940 to 1943, joining his classes and performances. At the age of eighty-six, M. K. Saroja recalled her memories of Gopal, stating, 'He was a very great person, a good heart, and had an understanding how to use the art' (interview with author, December 2017). She also remembered travelling with his company to London to perform after the war.[12] Gopal said fondly of her, 'She had acting genius and a great spiritual quality' (1976 audio interview).

During the war period, Gopal met Tagore and Gandhi, who advised him to preface his dances with verbal explanations, even for Indian audiences. This Gopal did and it proved to be successful and became part of his modernist strategy, tailor-making the programmes to suit audiences unfamiliar with Indian classical and folk dance genres. His troupe's final tour in India was in 1946–7, finishing in Delhi where Nehru came backstage to meet Gopal and his dancers and spoke effusively to Gopal about his performances, stating he enjoyed in particular the dances of Siva, the *tillana* and the *Rajput Serenade of Love* above the rest (Gopal 1957).

The war period in India was marked by thousands of displaced people from all parts of the world arriving there as part of the British Empire, a mass migration that is rarely written about. These included refugees displaced by the war raging in Europe and elsewhere (Burma, Poland, Greece, Malta and the Middle East, for example), new recruits to work in the British system and those displaced from elsewhere in the then British Empire (Yasmin Khan 2016). I go on to discuss

[12] Saroja and family (husband Mohan Khokar and son Ashish Mohan Khokar) retained a strong connection with Gopal and he stayed with them in their house near Chennai many times. Mohan collected artefacts relating to Gopal's career (programmes, articles and photos) that remain in his extensive archive and Ashish has written several articles on him (see Beginnings chapter).

below one Polish refugee who joined Gopal's company in India but consider first some of the intercultural connections and inspirations in the dance world during the war and pre-war period.

Connections across Europe

Evidence reveals a dancing dialogue between Europe and the East/Far East, with networks that traversed styles, performances, teachers, students and continents. Additionally, Gopal always maintained a special love for Poland and the Poles. As set out in Chapter 1, after leaving an international tour with La Meri in 1937 in Japan, Gopal met Aleksander Janta Polczynski, wealthy journalist, cultural activist and playwright, who befriended him and became his tour manager in the United States and in London. In 1939, Gopal made friends with the Polish war artist Feliks Topolski whose delightful sketches of Gopal in the wings of London's Aldwych Theatre are held in the British Museum (see Chapter 5). Topolski's later full-length portrait of Gopal is currently on semi-permanent loan to the National Portrait Gallery, London. Sources suggest that Gopal probably had relationships with these two Polish men. He certainly spoke some Polish. Gopal's long-term life partner in Britain was Polish architect Serafin Kycia and they shared a house at 15, Draycott Avenue, Chelsea, in London and later in Craignish Avenue, Norbury (a south London suburb). Sadly, Kycia suffered from serious depression and later took his own life. One of Gopal's family members suggested he had been a boy soldier and had been forced to fight for the Nazis, which had badly affected him. Kycia had completed some training in architecture when he arrived in the UK and found some employment undertaking architectural drawings and structural engineering work. He travelled to the United States with Gopal on tour in 1954 on the S. S. United States liner from Southampton (see further discussion in Chapter 4).

Gopal loved dining at the Polish Club in Kensington. He had a close friendship with Polish actor Vladek Sheybal, who wrote in his memoirs, 'Ram Gopal, a great Indian dancer and one of my greatest friends for years would always say, "You have those Garbo eyes". He would come and see me on stage in every single part I played – just to see my eyes in the spotlight.'[13] Sheybal accompanied him

[13] www.vladeksheybal.com (accessed 10 June 2020).

to India House, London, in 1990 when Gopal was awarded Elected Fellow status of the Sangeet Natak Akademi.[14]

During the war, when Gopal was touring India under the auspices of ENSA, a young refugee Polish dancer, Hanka Dytrych, joined his ensemble and danced some kathak pieces.[15] She remembers, 'We … carried a great theatrical wardrobe – trunks of costumes, among which were the famous "crowns" set with semi-precious stones designed by Ram. The work was very exhausting … We often travelled by night and had to practise in the morning for several hours under the watchful eye of our Guru' (2009: 447). This work enabled her to leave the Polish refugee camp she was living in at Valivade near Kolhapur, Maharashtra. Interestingly, she knew of Gopal from her parents who had enthused about his performances in Poland in 1938. She first met Gopal after dancing Polish national dances in a festival in Bombay with a group of girls from the camp. Dytrych recalls, 'Wanda Dynowska, a friend of Ram Gopal's, brought him to us. Wanda asked me to dance in front of him. Later he said, "If you should ever wish to learn the classical Indian dances, I shall teach you"' (2009). After touring India with his group, Dytrych returned to Bangalore with the company in 1947 for rehearsals and preparations for an English tour. She writes of that time:

> Ram's family home was old and very spacious with a front porch, just like our Polish country residences, and in a garden setting. There was also a tennis court and a separate villa, where some members of our ensemble, the orchestra and the teachers were accommodated. Sohan and I lived in two-room quarters on the ground floor of the main building. I lived next to and under the care of Ram's sister Jessie, a charming elderly lady, who dressed in Burmese clothes.
>
> (Dytrych 2009: 447)

Dytrych recalls very early morning lessons with the kathak teacher and then having breakfast with the whole family after showering. After, they would go to the garden studio to rehearse, where Gopal was a strict taskmaster. Afternoons

[14] This prestigious award was restricted to only thirty fellows at any one time. It is recognized in India as the highest national honour conferred on practising artists, gurus and scholars.

[15] Hanka is a Polish shortened form of Hannah or Anna. The 10,000 or so Poles who took refuge in India during the war were predominately Jewish and were settled in refugee camps across the country. Dytrych (born 1924 in Poznan, western Poland) lived in the Valivade refugee camp for five years, along with her mother, part of the large number of Polish nationals deported to India during the war (Yasmin Khan 2016). Dytrych took part in many cultural activities in the camp, including dance performances. I am grateful for correspondence on this with Danuta Pniewska, one of the editors of *Poles in India 1942–1948* (2009), which includes a section written by Hanka Dytrych titled 'In the Ram Gopal School'. Here she signs herself as Hanka Dytrych-Sahanek (Sahanek was her maiden name).

were free, so were spent playing tennis, reading or going on excursions. Sometimes Gopal would take them to the cinema. Dytrych became very close to Gopal's sister Elsie's two daughters, Santosh and Susheila, and kept up a long correspondence with them after the war. Sadly, her request for a visa to travel with the company to Britain in 1947 was delayed because of the complications of her refugee status and she missed the tour. Such pioneering intercultural work that Gopal effected, the weaving together of tradition and creative practices as well as different cultural expressions and heritages are, I argue, part of the new modernist framework seen in Europe and beyond.

Gopal and European modernist dance

The movements of dancers and performers across world routes in the period that Gopal was working gave rise to a confident and productive interweaving of different performance cultures and histories that, rather than erasing differences, created new concepts, innovative ways of moving and thinking about the body, and different modes of perception. As Fischer-Lichte argues, the interweaving of performance culture was 'to be regarded as an aesthetic, artistic process but also as a social, indeed, political one' (2009: 400). Processes of the interweaving of histories and cultures affected the rise of modernism in dance, creating multiple modalities of understanding the body and its movement. Although the term 'global' was not in common parlance at that time, there was certainly 'a global dimension of modernism' (Burt & Huxley 2019: 3) in the dance being practised, as dance more easily transcended national boundaries, being a mainly non-verbal form. In the pre-war 1930s, especially in the modernist dance developing in Germany, there were strong transnational networks of teachers, students, students of students, performers and critics (Manning 2018). In his own work, Gopal espoused the ideals of modernist dance through his artistic experimentation, his privileging of cross-cultural bodily movement and a certain idealism for East-West connections. Between the wars, it was certainly a privileged time and space of intercultural and transcultural migrations and artistic exchange.

The performance work of Indian classical dance that Gopal brought to packed houses in London, New York and Europe shows evidence of the influence of European modernist dance practices. Several of his dancers had received training in techniques from Emile Jacques-Dalcroze and Mary Wigman, and in his concerts that encompassed a range of Indian, Javanese and Balinese dance items, audiences could observe traces of Delsartian training, a performative element displayed in certain rippling arm techniques. Dancers such as Indonesian Retna Mohini (see Chapter 1) who joined Gopal's touring group in 1939, bringing Javanese and Balinese dances to his concerts, had additionally trained in Dalcroze and Wigman-style movement.[16] This intercultural and interdisciplinary exchange of East-West dance vocabularies was effected through a dual dialectical relationship that reveals how Gopal and Uday Shankar before him, were influenced by the work of early modernists such as Wigman and Hilde Holger, as I set out below. Shankar too had worked with Rudolf Laban at Dartington Hall in Devon in the 1930s.

Although fragmented sources can be misleading, there were many intercultural connections between European modernist dancers and Gopal's creative work. The history of European modernist dance, already well documented (see Hodgson & Preston-Dunlop 1990, Manning 1993, and Karina & Kant 2003), reveals how the German idea of *Korperkultur* (physical training and education) embraced the importance of bodily movement, of artistic experimentation, and of natural living with a 'return to nature' idealism. Dance was a key component of such thinking. Laban and his student Wigman along with Dalcroze and François Delsarte, a music and drama teacher who developed a system of expressive gesture, were central to this new dance development (Nicholas 2007). Some of the key European-trained dancers that had direct links to Gopal were Mohini, Hilde Holger and Zohra Segal.

Holger was known as a central European modernist dancer.[17] She trained with leading Austrian dancer Gertrud Bodenwieser in the tradition of Delsarte, Dalcroze and Laban in Vienna in the 1920s.[18] At a young age, she was touring with Bodenwieser's company, afterwards starting her own group and school, the Hilde Holger Tanzgruppe and The New School for Movement Arts. Holger came from a progressive Jewish family; by 1939 she was forced to leave Austria and set off for Bombay having not been allowed to enter Britain. During her ten years in Bombay, she married into a wealthy Parsee family and performed for local Nawabs and at various society events. She opened her own conservatoire, the School of Art for Modern Movement, and photos taken on Juhu Beach, Bombay, show dramatic shots of her female dancers in modernist poses.

[16] Sometimes known as Ratna, her birth name was Carolina Jeanne de Souza. She was born in 1901 in Batavia, on the island of Java.

[17] Born Hilde Sofer (1905–2001).

[18] Born Gertrud Bondi (1890–1959). Bodenwieser was one of the judges at the First International Competition of Artistic Dance in Warsaw in June 1933 and the Head of the Department of Modern Dance in the State Academy in Vienna.

Dancers Shankar and Gopal became friends, the latter coming to dance at her studio. She wrote in her unpublished biography, 'My studio was large enough to hold private shows for invited audiences. The great Indian dancer Ram Gopal gave a solo performance there too' (Holger: n.p.). One of her students, Wolfgang Stange, now running the inclusive Amici Dance Company in London, told me, 'I remember a photograph of Ram Gopal in Hilde's office. She told us about her beginning in Bombay with Gopal. Hilde was very much influenced by Indian art and had the most beautiful finger and hand movements in her movement vocabulary which she passed on to us' (personal communication with author, 2018). Whilst living in Bombay, Hilda trained 'in different dance styles at the Uday Shankar centre' (Kampe 2013: 198) and additionally with kathak dancer Menaka, who knew Gopal well. Menaka had schooled in Europe, and she and her troupe danced at the 1936 Olympic Games in Berlin along with Wigman and Laban (see Hanley 2006).[19]

Mohini met Gopal in Paris in the spring of 1939 through an acquaintance at the Musée Guimet, where Gopal had given a solo performance (see Chapter 2). At the time, she was married to renowned French photographer Henri Cartier-Bresson. The friendship between modernist dance-trained Mohini and Gopal was a fruitful one, as Gopal noted:

> Retna Mohini, with whom I had become friendly, and who desired very much to join me in India, decided she would follow later. She would be my partner. She showed me some of her Javanese and Balinese dances. She was like an ivory figure moving with exquisite grace.
>
> (Gopal 1957: 87)

Mohini had learnt Dalcroze and Wigman-style dance in Batavia, Indonesia, in the early 1930s as a pupil of Indonesian dancer Retnowati Latip. Latip had studied under Rosalia Chladek, a Dalcroze dancer trained at the Dalcroze Institute at Hellerau, Dresden, in Germany.[20] After Mohini's arrival in India in 1939 at the invitation of Gopal, Mohini and Cartier-Bresson joined at his home in Bangalore, before setting off for training with him at the famous KK where Gopal had already learned kathakali. Gopal created duets and solos for her and later they toured India dancing in Bangalore (Town Hall), Delhi (Regal Theatre, All India Dance Festival), Bombay and elsewhere (as discussed above).

[19] Martha Graham had refused to perform at these games.

[20] Chladek developed her own system of training called the 'Chladek Dance System' and became Head of Dance in the State Academy of Austria.

Dancer Zohra Segal who worked with Gopal in London in the 1960s left India in 1931 to train in modern dance, gaining a pedagogic diploma in Dresden at Wigman's school. Segal remarked how the school had strong discipline and good management.[21,22] Wigman was particularly kind to Segal, telling her explicitly 'never to imitate the German girls in my work, but to try and evoke an inner flow, fused with my inherent rhythm. Perhaps this advice was the source of my ability to pick up Indian dancing with comparative ease in later years' (Segal 2015 [2010]: 45–6). As Susan Manning notes (2018), Segal met Shankar when he visited the Dresden School and he invited her to perform with his company after she had completed her training. She became his main partner from 1935 to 1938, and through such training, Segal bridged the realms of modernist and classical dance. In the 1940s, Segal instructed students in modern dance at Shankar's centre in Almora, India, and then moved to London in the 1960s, where she taught for Gopal at his classes in Chelsea. She wrote, 'I had heard that Ram Gopal, the renowned Indian dancer, was living in London, and one day on impulse I telephoned him. One thing led to another, and soon I was installed as the principal of his newly opened school, at a salary of £20 per week for working only from ten to twelve in the morning!' (2015 [2010]: 187).

The rippling arm movements that Gopal used in his famous *Dance of Siva* (or *Dance of the Setting Sun*) emerged directly from his kathakali training. Shankar also used this in his choreographies and Diana Brenscheidt notes how German reviewers in 1932 remarked on Shankar's 'sinuous, serpentine-like arm movements in the Indian performance' (2011: 168). Dancers would depict this movement in detail if showing, for example, Siva wearing the snake around his shoulders, by utilizing the *sarpashirsa* (snake hand) mudra in one hand and then allowing the movement to gently ripple through towards the other hand using the hand, wrist, lower arm, upper arm and shoulder on one side. It is followed by the reverse movement from shoulder, upper arm, lower arm to wrist and hand on the other. Padma Subrahmanyam has spoken about such serpentine arms being portrayed in the ancient text on dance, mime and acting technique, the *Natyasastra*, a *nrttahasta* movement termed *aviddhavakraka.*[23] She relates

[21] Born Sahibzadi Zohra Begum Mumtaz-ullah Khan in 1912 in what is now known as Uttar Pradesh, Segal was the daughter of a Muslim aristocrat. She died in 2014 in India, aged 102.

[22] Wigman had photos of Shankar and Segal in her scrapbook (Manning 2018).

[23] Described in one translation of *Natyasastra*: 'The two hands are to have Kutila (oblique) movement after touching the opposite shoulder elbow and hands. Then the palms are moved and turned towards the back. This is known as Aviddhavakraka' (Bharatamuni 1986: 148). Subrahmanyam also notes two *karanas* (element of dance phrase) called *sarpitam* and *nagapasarptuam* (both relating to snakes/serpentine).

how when meeting Shankar she told him, 'You are doing something from Natya Shasta. He cried and said he had never seen the book' (Subrahmanyam 2021: n.p.). Kumudini Lakhia, Gopal's dance partner for several years and close friend described how Gopal's 'arms were like water when he used to do his *Dance of the Setting Sun*, just like water' (interview with author, December 2012).

One key factor in the training that Holger and Mohini would have received through the Delsarte system is the isolation of parts of the body. Not only are there rotations of the arms and hands, but Delsarte adds an arm movement that he terms 'Serpentine' and that illustrates the same rippling effect. Delsarte's *System of Dramatic Expression*, compiled in 1886 by dancer Genevieve Stebbins, describes these movements in detail as follows:

> Sink wrist as previously explained; arm in breadths. Rotate wrist until fingers point to ground, palm out. Raise hand on wrist, palm in. Elbow has been stiff. Now, bend elbow until finger-tips touch shoulder, simultaneously sinking upper arm to side of torso. Without unbending, raise elbow up and out; wrist remains level with armpit, hand falls decomposed. Now, sink elbow again to side; combine last with a rotary inward movement of upper arm, which throws decomposed hand palm out and down. Straighten elbow; this will throw the hand out and up. Recompose hand.
>
> (Delsarte, in Stebbins 1886: 96)

Delsarte suggests in a note how difficult it is to write out movements and that a 'living teacher' (Delsarte, in Stebbins 1886) is really required to gain accuracy in such technique.

Lynn Wenzel and Carol J. Binkowski (2016) argue that the movement of Ruth St. Denis's undulating serpentine arms in her dance *Radha* was based on Stebbins's Delsarte performances in the late 1890s in the United States, in which she showed her Serpentine Arm Drill and Eastern Temple Drill. Denis claimed that she was 'the first dancer in the Western world to use my arms in such a fashion' and that 'it is hard to realize now, when most dancers use an arm ripple, that at this period it did not exist as a part of the dance' (1939: 97). Denis continues:

> I knew that my arm ripple was the subject of much interest and speculation on the part of the public. In the *Incense* my arms were held out from the shoulder and were raised and lowered with a subtle rippling movement which began between the shoulder blades and seemed to extend through and beyond the fingers. In the *Cobra* the arms took on the undulating ripple of the snake's body.
>
> (Denis 1939: 96)

Ann Cooper Albright's work on Loie Fuller adds a further dimension on the historical use of the serpentine arm movement. Albright, in a dedicated attempt to understand Fuller's 1891 dance 'The Serpentine', analysed and performed the dance, revealing Fuller's use of the yards of silk material manipulated through undulating movements of the arms and upper torso, in a serpentine manner. This appeared to show the Delsartian influence of a rippling arm and body technique. Conversely, as discussed above in Gopal's performances, there are traditions emerging from the Keralan dance/drama style of kathakali of comparable arm and upper body articulations utilized by Indian dancers such as Gopal and Shankar. Such expressive use of hand and arms can be found as well in kathak and bharatanatyam dances, in Egyptian belly dance (where it tends to be termed 'snake arms'), in Bollywood film dance and in contemporary breakdance and popping styles, where it is called 'the wave'.

Returning to the war period, this powerful time of seismic change worldwide caused Gopal to seriously consider how his productions were to be managed and produced as he contemplated a new vision of extensive touring as war came to an end. The poor experiences that he endured whilst back in India during the war (discussed below) convinced him that the work of patrons (both private and state), impresarios and managers was essential for an artist to survive and gain success in reaching audiences. Indeed, his 1951 book, co-written with critic Serozh Dadachanji, devotes the last section to the need for state support for artists, especially in India. They write (somewhat prophetically considering the Akademis that the Indian government were to set up in the early to mid-1950s) that

> [w]hile the dancer and his fellow artists must work to free art of the fetters that bind it, the State should also play its part in helping art to find its proper place in life … The State should grant the dancer certain facilities. It should build national theatres … At present, every dancer with a troupe has to act as his own talent-scout, producer, director, business manager and virtuoso! There should be state centres where all four arts are encouraged.[24] For the advancement of Indian dancing one of the most necessary measures is the opening of a department within a Central Dance Academy that would train promising choreographers.
>
> (Gopal & Dadachanji 1951: 111–12)

[24] Here they refer to dance, music, poetry/song and painting.

Patrons, impresarios, managers

The view of Indian dance as a highly stylized, beautiful and somewhat exotic form, especially in the West, belies the intricacies of the hard grind of the dancing body – the sweat, the callouses, the aching limbs and constant readiness for performance, as well as the economic value of transnational labour (see Srinivasan 2012), of production and creation of audiences. Here I examine the production and control of Indian dance, looking at how the dancing body is understood as a cultural product laden with economic value.

As has been argued, the rise of nationalist agendas and the impending departure of the British colonizers was a significant rupture in cultural histories and practices, especially for Indian classical dance styles. Many changes were signalled and effected to the dance forms; one shift was the move to stage dance away from local environs, temples and homes to theatre spaces with proscenium stages. This necessitated transformations to the music, the lighting, costuming and the layout of the choreographic patterning as well as modifications to economic structures and the management of dance concerts. Gopal's career maps some of these variations as I go on to discuss. The normative pattern for support for the arts in India was patronage from 'Brahmins (the caste of priests and scholars), royal families, nobles, and Hindu temples or shrines' (Daugherty 2000: 238) – often local systems of support with their own intricate affiliations. Some of these systems were composed of complex relationships; for example in Rajasthan and other parts of north India, upper-caste groups were bound into a reciprocal bond with lower-caste groups, the lower-caste families providing the services, including music and dance, that the upper-caste families needed. This was called a *jajmani* relationship. Such local patronage structure is a hereditary one 'more specifically linked with ritual functions involving the genealogy of the patron's family and the conducting of different ceremonies, both social and religious' (Bharucha 2003: 218).

Rustom Bharucha (2003) oral history of music in Rajasthan in conversation with Komal Kothari lays out the power dynamics and intricacies of such local patronage, indicating that '[b]y asserting the power of retaliation through ritualized practices and threats, therefore, the musicians are capable of prevailing on their patrons and asserting their hereditary rights' (2003: 221). In this case, the control and economic power of the patrons are counteracted by those whom they employ. Because the patrons are obliged to patronize the musicians on hereditary grounds, they gain status from the patronage but are also dependent on the musicians. This example of the Rajasthani musicians, considered low caste, and patronized by the wealthy, demonstrates how power can be taken back into their own hands. Patronage, however, tends to rely on a monopoly, providing a route to the market. By controlling the platform, the price and the product are meticulously regulated. This is found in many spheres, such as in publishing, in the music business, and in sport and film production. Patronage always raises issues of power and constraint, as the patron/impresario can control access to the product, and therefore controls the finances and can dictate the way the art form is presented. Additionally, as noted, patronage can bring high cultural status and political power.

Gopal made use of different systems of economic power and cultural brokerage throughout his career. He experienced royal patronage when dancing as a young man at the magnificent guest events of the Maharaja of Mysore in his Lalita Mahal palace; he was then promoted and managed by Guido Carreras, La Meri's husband, during his first world tour (as his manager/impresario); and later he employed a wide range of managers and impresarios over his many years of international performing and touring. Gopal benefited from the revenue management work of Western impresarios such as Russian-born Sol Hurok, a promoter of stars of music, ballet and opera; Polish-born Julian Braunsweg, known for his work in ballet and the founding of the English National Ballet company and Hungarian Sandor Gorlinsky. These men opened doors for the dance artists, smoothing their passage into foreign territory and across political chasms, creating international audiences eager to see their performances. Alongside the promoters, Gopal's close friends and confidantes often became his tour managers. These friends included dancer Kay Ambrose, journalist Aleksanda Janta, Doris Barry (sister of dancer Alicia Markova) who worked as manager with Gorlinsky, and ex-army officer Michael Rouse. Gopal writes of Rouse that after the war, 'I asked him whether he would like to accept the work of being my company organiser and manager. Of all the people that have handled companies of Hindu dancers and musicians, Michael Rouse was easily the most tactful, alert and most beloved' (1957: 154).

Joan L. Erdman notes that in Jaipur in the eighteenth and nineteenth centuries, the royal household formalized the patronage of the arts by creating a kind of department of performing arts called *Gunijankhana* (Erdman 1992: 143). She describes how 'in Jaipur the *Gunijankhana* was the department which maintained artists for religious, social, and domestic services, as well as the cultural institutions which supported artists, professional musicians and dancers' (Erdman 1992: 145). Prior to independence, the establishment of institutions for dance, drama and music such as Rabindranath Tagore's Santiniketan,

Vallathol's Kerala Kalamandalam,[25] Rukmini Devi's Kalakshetra and Menaka's Nrityalayam as well as the Madras Music Academy began to take on the role of producing artists and their performances. They also provided possibilities for local supporters to offer financial support (Erdman 1992).

In India once the royal patronage from the Maharajas and their families and support for the arts from foreign governors dwindled with the onset of independence, artists became more dependent on state/government support or on their own family or friends' networks. Although not extensive, patronage from local temples continued to some degree, and this persists into current times, for example in London temples, where musicians are hired for large festival events (see David 2012b). There was a certain amount of patronage from wealthy individuals or families such as the Tatas, the Birlas, Bharat Rams and Charat Rams (Lowen 1992). Regula B. Qureshi writes that in this millennium period, hereditary musicians continue to perform 'but under conditions of reduced or fundamentally altered public patronage by the Indian state' (2009: 165), although they do receive support from overseas patronage. The overall economic picture across India for support for classical arts and folk genres is extremely intricate and warrants attention directed to specific areas – see for example Diane Daugherty's work on funding in Kerala (2000) or Veena Basavarajaiah's (2018) writing on the changes to arts and dance promotion in Bengalaru (Bangalore) where she articulates the rise of the new powerful middle-class and corporate sponsorship of the arts, especially after the Indian economic liberalization policies of the early 1990s. These scenarios include both formal and informal arrangements.

The system as used in the West of managers, agents and impresarios was almost non-existent, and as Gopal found during the 1940s when he was resident in India, government- and ENSA India-supported tours were frequently badly organized and not well managed. During this period of seven years in India, Gopal danced under the auspices of both NAAFI and ENSA India, effectively sponsored and commissioned by the Indian government. He complained about ENSA, 'I had been the first artist in India and Asia to offer my services for ENSA, and had untold difficulty dancing in this most disorganised "organisation" for bringing entertainment to the Indian and British troops' (1957: 171). Trying to get Indian government backing for his *Taj Mahal* ballet and an exhibition

[25] As discussed in Chapter 1, this school was set up through gifts of land from the local maharajas and Vallathol offered free tuition, board and lodging to young male students to keep the kathakali dance form alive. Now it is an established state-funded university.

of Indian art at the Edinburgh Festival later in 1956, Gopal's attempts were completely thwarted. Gopal was not alone in experiencing such discouragement. Sharon Lowen (1992) recounts similarly frustrating incidences of touring in India during the late 1970s and early 1980s, where bookings would be made and then not honoured, or timings would change on the day and often, changing facilities would be entirely inadequate.[26]

Erdman's (1983) detailed analysis of the development of state funding by the Indian government after independence, in her article that examines the case of the serious challenge made by a group of prominent dancers in Delhi in 1977 reveals how complex state support for the arts can be (see also Katrak 2011). Long-term problems with government institutions set up for the arts such as the Sangeet Natak Akadémi and the Culture Department of the Ministry for Education over their selection processes for dancers to perform overseas, those to receive grants, and for the ones getting support for their teaching all came to a boiling point at a press conference called by disgruntled artists. Erdman notes how they 'demanded an entirely new framework for culture' (1983: 249) and sought to have a voice in the government's funding and selection policies, accusing Sangeet of being 'utterly unresponsive to the needs of the performing arts community' (1983: 251). The Indian academies for the arts were set up in the decade after independence, institutions formulated on the French model of government support for the arts, to replace the private funding that the maharajas had provided.[27] Summarizing the outcome of such a widely reported protest, Erdman argues that 'the protest by Delhi's dancers in 1977 was a significant contribution to the development of a cultural policy for the arts in modern India' (1983: 269).

Gopal consistently mentions the Yuvaraja, brother of the Maharaja of Mysore, as being his first patron. It was he who appointed Gopal to dance at the palace and later for their garden parties and fetes, in temples and for late-night palace parties. In the early 1930s, the Yuvaraja commissioned Gopal to lead a European tour of dancers and musicians, paying him 2000 rupees towards costs of costumes, headdresses and instruments. Gopal scoured books on Indian iconography and visited various temples, copying designs and taking them to craftsmen to make the costumes and jewellery. He started training at the

[26] Lightfoot does mention that the Government of India gave Uday Shankar the land to establish his centre at Almora although the many buildings were paid for by American money (Lightfoot 2015).

[27] The Sangeet Natak Akademi for music, dance and drama was established in 1953; the Lalit Kala Akademi for the visual arts and the Sahitya Akademi for literature in 1954. At first and for some time after, all were run by government officials in the administrative and artistic positions, which became problematic (Erdman 1983).

famous KK, encouraged by the Yuvaraja who told him to 'never stop learning … promise you'll revive what has been nearly lost in Mysore State, in fact most of South India' (quoted in Gopal 1957: 26). The promised tour did not happen due to bureaucratic difficulties with travel and organization, leaving Gopal free to accept La Meri's invitation to tour with her in early 1937 (see Chapter 1). This tour was organized and managed by her husband Guido Carreras, who had originally been her agent.

Subsequently Gopal was to work with Sol Hurok, already well known for his work producing Uday Shankar's performances in the United States. In noting the change to commercial impresarios as the new patrons, Srinivasan writes that '[t]he emergence of Indian dancers in the 1930s, such as Uday Shankar, who was increasingly viewed as "authentic" (Erdman 1996: 89) disrupted the orientalist narrative previously constructed on the bodies of white women such as St. Denis, whose dances became "inauthentic"' (2012: 108). She continues

Figure 13 Ram Gopal and Aleksander Janta on ship MS *Batory*, May 1938, published in *Pamietnik Indyjski* (1970) by Janta.

stating that 'this twist empowered Shankar and disempowered St. Denis' (2012) not only by having powerful promoters managing bookings but also by using the promotional term 'authentic'. Perhaps too this was part of the reason for Gopal's success touring with La Meri and her subsequent dissatisfaction? As stated in Chapter 1, after leaving La Meri's tour, in January 1938 Gopal travelled to Hawaii and then to Los Angeles where he met Cecil B. de Mille and many Hollywood socialites. This first American tour was managed by his close friend (and probably partner) Janta who organized performance dates and handled press and publicity.

Janta subsequently managed later tours in Poland and India, performances in Paris and London, both pre- and post-war. One of the three performances Gopal gave in Los Angeles at the Wilshire-Ebell Theatre in West 8th Street (11 March 1938) was sponsored by De Mille and several of his famous friends, fashion designer Adrian, Max Reinhardt the filmmaker, and film star Mervyn Douglas, thus all of them becoming the new patrons. Whilst staying in Los Angeles, Gopal was introduced by Arthur Rubenstein to Hurok who then arranged Gopal's first very successful New York recital. This performance garnered rave reviews from critics John Martin and Walter Terry.

By 1932, Hurok had earned a reputation for being one of the top promoters in the arts; he had very lucratively managed the dance tours of Wigman, Shankar (as noted) and Spanish dancer Vincente Escudero, amongst other dancers and top musicians. Not only was Hurok talented on the artistic front, but he also played an important role in the highly political Russian American relationship, as Harlow Robinson states in Hurok's biography:

> By bringing Soviet artists to the West and American artists to the USSR from the mid-1950s through the mid-1970s, Hurok added an important measure of continuity and humanity to the fragile superpower relationship … Even at the height of the Cuban Missile Crisis, the moment at which the world came closest than ever to nuclear war, the Bolshoi Ballet was dancing across the United States under the 'S. Hurok Presents' banner.
>
> (Robinson 1994: xviii–xiv)

Impresarios such as Hurok were not only deft at handling the economic negotiations, and the production and mediation of values but also nurtured an intuitive sense of the political forces and monetary fluctuations worldwide. As J. P. Singh notes, '[c]reative practices and cultural politics are connected, but in complex and multi-faceted ways' (2010: 148). Specific skills are required for the art of promoting performances and organizing tours, and Finola Kerrigan, et al., point out that 'the impresario must know his audience. The best have a deep and instinctive understanding of what will sell, or what audiences will buy' (Kerrrigan et al. 2004: 50).

Gopal saw Hurok as the king of ballet impresarios (1957). Hurok was later to manage Gopal's second visit to New York ten years later for the Golden Anniversary International Dance Festival in 1948. This event 'marked the fiftieth anniversary of the unification of the city's five affiliated boroughs' (Kowal 2020: 167) and was a Golden Jubilee celebration which incorporated a dance festival. Hurok said of this event that 'Ram Gopal, brilliant exponent of the dance of India, accepted through his manager Julian Braunsweg, and, in this case, I was able to assist him in his financial problems, by bringing him at my own expense' (1953: 203). In fact, Hurok invited various countries around the world to send their state dance companies and Gopal was selected by Jawaharlal Nehru to represent India. Gopal performed with his group for four nights at the New York City Center theatre. The event brought dancers from all over the world, including La Meri and Rukmini Devi, and was deemed a great success, although Kowal suggests that 'the festival failed to live up to organizers' ambitious plans' (2020: 169), noting its clash with a three-week booking of the Ballets Russes in New York and the fact that many countries failed to respond to the invitation.[28] Martin wrote of Gopal in the *New York Times* of this later performance, 'He has much more authority and much more showmanship' (1 October 1948: 30) in a comparison with his earlier performance of 1938. Despite planning the festival as a vehicle to bridge cultural differences, encourage cultural diplomacy and promote the city's global cosmopolitanism, overall, the event revealed 'sociopolitical tensions between globalism and pluralism, on the one hand, and unity and diversity, on the other', argues Kowal in her analysis of the International Dance Festival (2020: 166).

Before the war, Gopal's 1939 French concerts and his sell-out season in London at the Aldwych and Vaudeville theatres in the summer and autumn of the same year were promoted by Russian impresario Eugène Grunberg who later in 1946 reformed the Nouveau Ballet de Monte Carlo. Australian dancer Louise Lightfoot, who had met Gopal at KK in 1939, was visited by Gopal in Bombay in 1940 when he was scouting for dancers for a tour. She tells how '[h]e suggested that I assist him in organising and very kindly offered me my expenses in Bangalore, as well

[28] Devi also danced at the Barbizon-Plaza Theater under the auspices of the Indian League of America and the New York Theosophical Society.

as free tuition in Indian dance and fifty rupees a month pocket money. The idea appealed to me very much and I told Ram Gopal that I would probably follow him to Bangalore a little later on', which she did (Lightfoot 2015: n.p.). Lightfoot wrote to J. C. Williamson's theatrical business in Australia with the idea of taking Gopal and his dancers and musicians on tour there but the company declined, thinking 'Indian music might not be appreciated' (Lightfoot 2015).[29]

From the autumn of 1947 when Gopal arrived back in England from India, his work was successfully promoted by Braunsweg. They had met at Covent Garden and after their lawyers had signed the business deal, Braunsweg promised Gopal seasons in London, Paris and America (1957). Braunsweg identified himself as an arts business manager, stating, 'I am an impresario. An impresario is, in essence, a versatile cultural juggler. For over fifty years I have juggled with personalities, talent and money; crises, scandals and money; temperaments, intrigues and money. Inevitably I have lost a fortune … Luckily I recognised very early in my career the importance of cigars, whisky and the ability to work out percentages' (1977 [1973]: 15).[30]

The autumn season was followed by a very productive and seemingly profitable tour of Scandinavia in 1948, organized by Braunsweg in conjunction with renowned Swedish dance expert Bengt Häger. The tour started in Copenhagen, Denmark, in April and then in May moved to the Cirkus Theatre in Stockholm, followed by performances in major cities of Sweden, Oslo, and locations in Norway, then Finland and a return to Sweden. After the first performances Gopal humorously noted that

> the rotund figure of Braunsweg rolled about with gleeful eyes and an increasing girth line. 'You make artistic "sings best … we make success, moo-ney plenty moo-ney, we make, then we go everywhere" … I knew then that the advance bookings must have been very good, for Braunsweg's gleaming eyes confirmed the fact as well as his throwing himself with all his great energy, enthusiasm and knowledge of theatre, into making this season a success. And as far as I had seen till then, he was the most energetic and kindly of European impresarios I had known'.
>
> (Gopal 1957: 175)

[29] Mary Lightfoot, Louise's niece, uses Lightfoot's diaries in her book, published as an e-book in 2015. Louise Lightfoot arranged several dancer's tours in India and Ceylon in the 1940s and went on to be manager/impresario for kathakali dancer Sivaram, taking him on his first tour to Australia in 1947, followed by tours to New Zealand, Fiji, London, Canada and Japan. She had watched performances in Australia in the 1920s by Rukmini Devi and Anna Pavlova, and Uday Shankar in Paris in 1937 (Sarwal 2014).

[30] As a young child, Braunsweg had loved going to music, drama and dance performances at the theatre and, when a teenager in Moscow, he was buying and selling tickets on the black market. As a student of economics, he was the one selected in his group of friends to arrange concerts to earn money and, by his twenties in Berlin, was becoming quite successful, including working for Diaghilev and the Ballets Russes (Braunsweg 1977 [1973]).

The programme for the 1948 tour featured Gopal in *Garuda, Hunter in the Forest, Cobra Devil Dance* and *Dance of the Setting Sun* as part of the eighteen items featured. Kumudini Lakhia joined the tour for the first time and danced a solo kathak piece, *Radha.* In fact, despite the apparent success of this extended tour, tensions between impresarios Braunsweg and Hurok in London meant that it almost did not happen. Lena Hammergren describes how Gopal's tour to Sweden in the 1940s was privately sponsored, and 'happened unscheduled after the company had been stranded in London, due to disagreements between two impresarios' (2009: 19). Häger's involvement in the tours is recorded by Nancy Westman where she records that Häger 'offered his assistance to the Indian company. Bengt had good contacts in Denmark, where no rules and regulations impeded his work as an impresario. He hired a theatre for a week, before knowing how he would be able to bring the Indians across from London' (2006: 89) and was joined by a Danish patron who provided income for the tour. Cleverly, Häger arranged

> the press conference at one of Copenhagen's most prestigious and elegant hotels – Hotel d'Angleterre – where plenty of smörrebröd and liquid food was served in anticipation of the arrival of the Indian stars. The assembled journalists grew anxious, however, whilst eating and drinking, as the exotic guests were late in arriving. Half an hour behind time, Ram Gopal entered the room wearing a dress of pure gold and with an Indian beauty on either side.
>
> (2006: 90)

So bewitched were the journalists by the beautiful, glamorous company that they wrote preview articles that drew crowds to purchase tickets.

As in London, the bleakness of the aftermath of war made such colourful and exciting cultural performances powerfully attractive and the bookings and performances were extended to accommodate the demand for tickets. Further tours to Sweden took place in 1949, 1951, 1952 and 1959. Theatre critic Karin Karlströmer wrote after performances at the Helsingborgs Konserthus (Concert House), Sweden, on 11 March 1949, that the dancers Simkie, Kumudini and Lilivati 'were enchanting in their incredibly beautiful dresses, which made the auditorium gasp in admiration. And, not only for the sake of the dresses. The gazelle eyed ladies shine in a beauty that almost takes your breath away' (cited in Westman, 2006: 92).

For Gopal's later performance work during the years of 1956–7, Gorlinsky promoted and managed his concerts and tours in Britain and Europe. Gorlinsky was successful in arranging Gopal's important performances in 1956 at the Edinburgh Festival and at London's Festival Hall (including the ballet of the *Taj Mahal*) as well as other London venues. Gopal writes of their discussion in London in 1956 when Gorlinsky stated:

> 'Well, let's see what I can do. I tell you what, Ram. I will conclude arrangements for the Nervi Festival in Italy, then you have August for rehearsal in London, Edinburgh for a week in September and I'll fix the Royal Festival Hall for two weeks later. Later, if we're a success, there is America and there is Europe.' So Sandor Gorlinsky instructed his travel agents to issue the necessary tickets by air from Bombay at £125 a head, in addition to the extra costumes and curtains and rehearsal that all mounted up in the final accounts to £10,000.
>
> (Gopal 1957: 201)

As a concert promoter, Gorlinsky looked after a variety of high-profile musicians and dancers such as Maria Callas, Montserrat Caballé, Natalia Makarova and Rudolph Nureyev.[31]

Other impresarios/promoters managing Gopal's tours in the 1950s and 1960s were Russian émigré Eugene Iskoldoff, known for his work with Opera Scotland and individual opera singers, U.M.A. Productions, Lynford-Joel Promotions Ltd and Barry O'Brien. In 1947, impresario Charles B. Cochrane and hereditary peer Lord Vivian sponsored some of Gopal's London Adelphi performances, and in the mid-1950s and 1960s, the Asian Music Circle organized performances for Gopal (see Chapter 6). Gopal's visits to Jacob's Pillow were arranged without the intermediary of an impresario or manager, causing frictions over finance and travel arrangements with Ted Shawn (as discussed in the next chapter). Even with the necessity of having a manager and/or an impresario to organize tours, bookings and advertising, patrons consistently were needed to provide the funding where box office returns were not enough or were not guaranteed.

Analysis of the economic structures for Indian dancers at the time reveals how several wealthy, upper-class cosmopolitan Western women were to play instrumental roles in these dancers' lives: Uday Shankar was supported by a wealthy Swiss patron and friend, Alice Boner;[32] kathakali dancer Sivaram was reliant on the patronage of dancer Louise Lightfoot; and Gopal was befriended by wealthy patron, and then close friend, filmmaker Claude Lamorisse. Dancer

[31] According to Otis Stuart (1995), the very savvy Gorlinksy helped Nureyev amass his fortune by creating offshore accounts in Luxembourg.

[32] Boner was born in northern Italy to Swiss parents and studied painting and sculpture, working mainly as a sculptor. She lived in India for over forty years and was awarded the *Padma Bushan* in 1974. Boner met Shankar in 1926 in Zurich and looked after his touring company for five years in the 1930s.

Kay Ambrose as noted above was Gopal's manager, close friend and facilitator in the early years of his touring. In the later period of his life, Gopal was looked after by Pamela Cullen and close friend Denise Iredell. Others such as Beryl de Zoete[33] and Eilean Pearcey[34] played strategic roles in his work. The presence of white, independent, often affluent women in the lives of these Asian dancers, facilitating the dancers' journeys internationally and interculturally, bringing their money, privilege and dance training/knowledge, remains a significant factor in such historical stories.

A scrutiny of the funding and economic complexities in the millennium years for young dancers negotiating the tortuous visa system for work in dance in the UK is set out clearly in the writings of Kedhar (see also Chapter 1). Kedhar argues, 'While the British nation-state has mobilized South Asian (dance) labor for cultural production and made the dancers' bodies increasingly flexible, it has also limited the ability of South Asian (dancing) bodies to stay, settle, and move freely within the space of the nation' (2014: 37). The dancing body as economic capital remains a highly contested, complex entity, subject to forces outside of its control and measured by an increasing volatile market. Gopal's freedom to travel back to India at the beginning of the war, after touring to the United States, Europe and the UK, and his subsequent return on the RMS Alcantara indicate both the power of the British passport to travel transnationally and Gopal's status as a wealthy, educated, cosmopolitan artist. It also reveals the stark differences that affect dancers in their ability to move freely nearly seventy years on.

33 De Zoete, born in London of Dutch descent, studied with Dalcroze in Hellerau in 1913, where she became friends with dancer Marie Rambert. She was a close friend of Boner and knew both Shankar and Gopal, travelling with Gopal in India and writing of his work. She was independently wealthy, a world traveller and a writer and journalist. De Zoete spent time at KK in 1935 and again in 1949 and did some training in kathakali.

34 Australian Pearcey specialized in drawings of dancers, often working from the wings during performances. Her archive that includes of sketches of Shankar is housed in the National Resource Centre for Dance (NRCD) at the University of Surry, UK. She was a good friend of Gopal and often sketched him too.

Plate 1 Ram Gopal's *Siva* headdress. © SADAA archive.

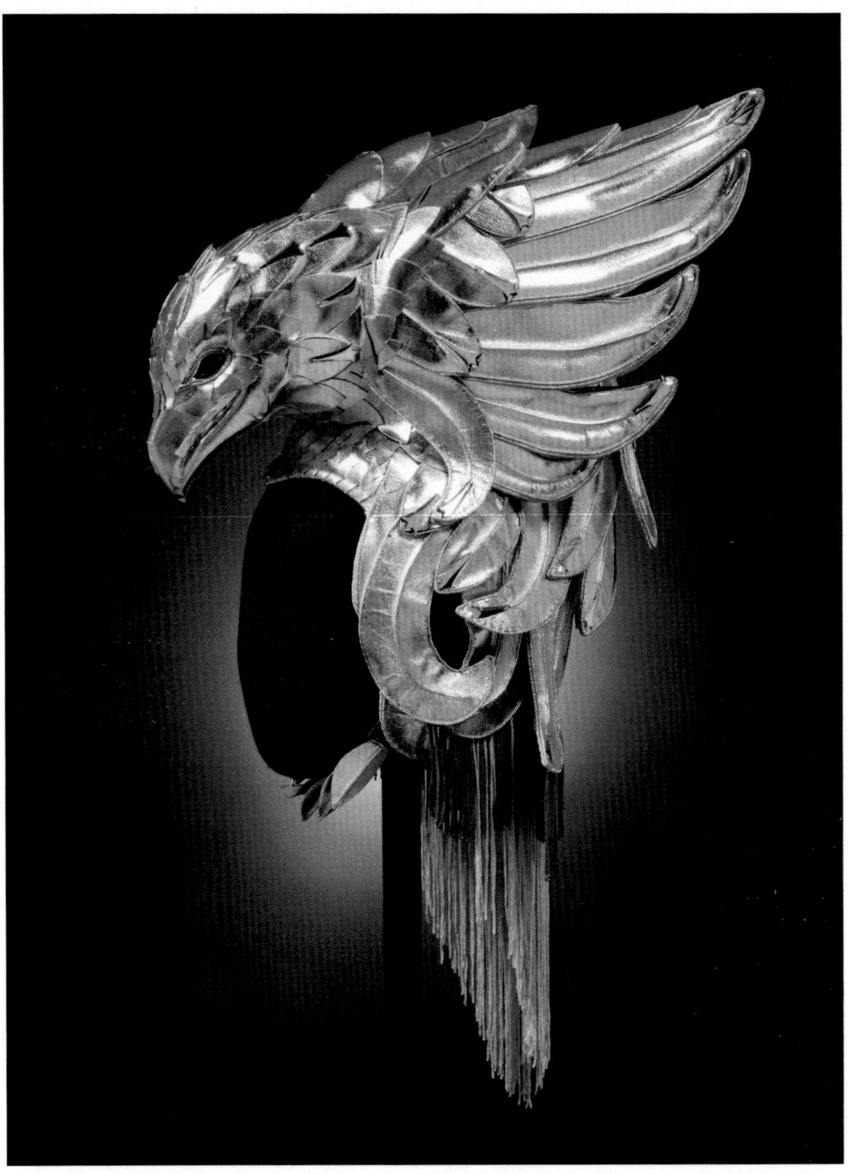

Plate 2 Ram Gopal's *Garuda* headdress. © V&A images.

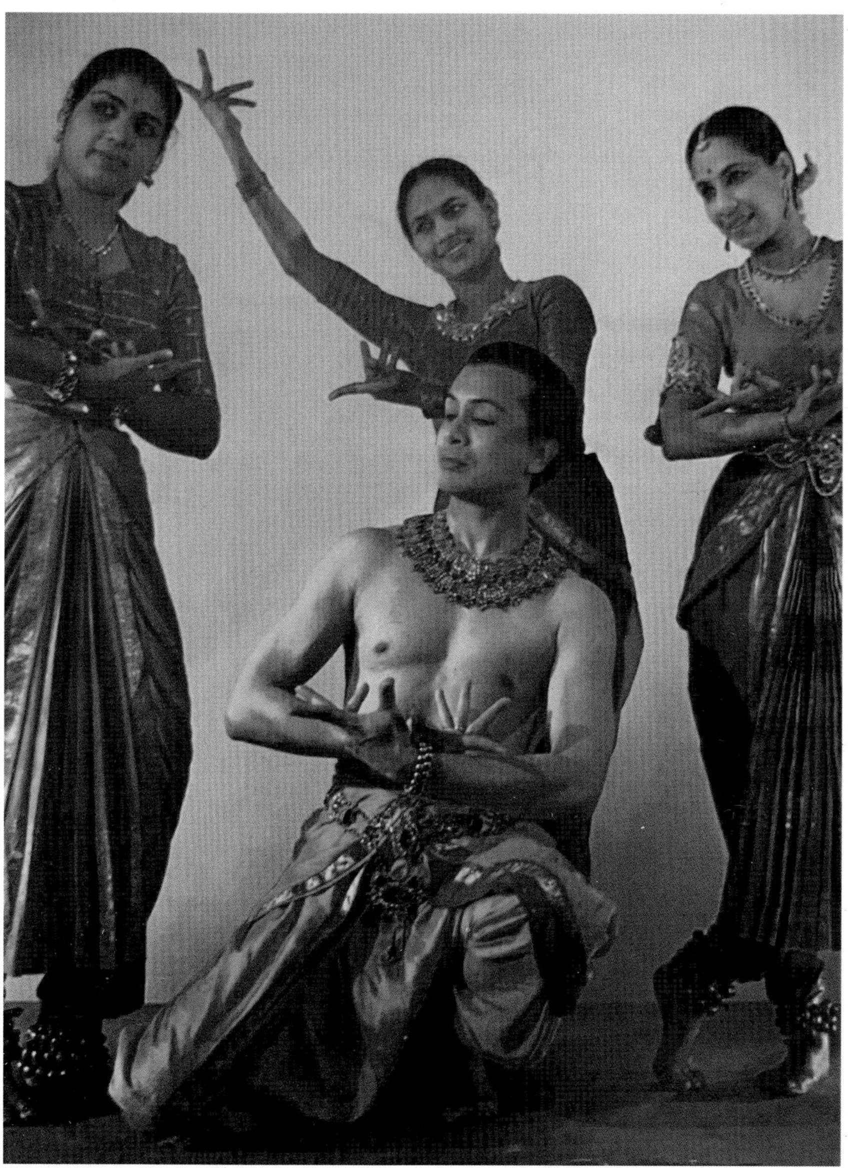

Plate 3 Ram Gopal and Kumudini Lakhia, c. 1948. Front cover of *Les Saisons de la Danse* magazine, 10 April 1976. Photographer S. Lido. Author's own collection.

Plate 4 Ram Gopal and author at Norbury Hall Residential Care Home, 2001. © Clive Boursnell.

4

Programmes of the post-war years

Gopal returned to a war-devastated, economically challenged and almost bankrupt Britain. These first years after the war were times of austerity, food rationing, housing shortages, power cuts and, in 1947, a very hard winter.[1] New initiatives by the Labour government to privatize the mining industry and the railway network went ahead, bringing strikes and difficulties. There was, however, at the same time, an optimistic spirit as the same government initiated new social welfare systems including free school milk for children and free higher education, and importantly, the creation of the National Health Service (NHS), as well as programmes to reform and reconstruct the damages to Britain's infrastructure.

The scene on the world stage was rapidly changing too. India's independence in 1947 thankfully began the dismantling of Britain's empire whilst the previously mentioned British Nationality Act in 1948 allowed movement of peoples to Britain from former colonies. In 1949, the signing of the North Atlantic Treaty created the North Atlantic Treaty Organization (NATO), an intergovernmental alliance consisting of over thirty European countries and North America. Simultaneously, there was the dark threat of nuclear weapons, the unexpected emergence of the Cold War and serious worries that the Korean war of 1950–3 might provoke the beginning of a third world war.

At least some events in Britain allowed for celebration. The international Olympic Games held in London in July 1948 were the first summer games since Berlin in 1936 and attracted a record number of participants. Despite being called the 'austerity games' as no new event buildings were constructed due to the economic climate, a crowd of over 85,000 people watched the opening ceremony and Britain won an overall twelfth position with 404 athletes competing. Fifty-nine countries participated, although Japan and Germany were banned and the Soviet Union declined to send competitors. In the autumn of the same year

[1] Rationing continued until July 1954, having commenced in 1940, and to some extent was worse after the war when resources were not available to expand food production and imports.

the wedding of Princess Elizabeth took place, a national event bringing a sense of unity and solidarity to austere Britain. It was for many a time of jubilation and romanticism after such a long period of the grim realities of war.

Three years later, London and the nation celebrated the *Festival of Britain*, an extensive outdoor and indoor event at London's South Bank, and other sites around Britain attracting 8.5 million visitors between May and September of 1951.[2] Costing £11 million to put on, and opened by King George VI, the Queen Mother and Princess Elizabeth, it promoted British science, technology, industrial design, architecture and the arts. The emergence of national festival events such as this was a recognized way for governments to demonstrate regeneration and 'recovery after a period of national danger and stress' (Hewison 1997 [1995]: 57). Those remembering the festival spoke of feeling an excitement, a sense of celebration and the promise of a new future (BBC documentary 2011) that brought colour, escapism and a sense of fresh beginnings to a bombed-out, dull and shabby London and country.[3] The *Festival of Britain* became a showcase for new young designers and architects who drew on ideas from European modernism to inspire their work and to create a sense of building for the future. Steel bands were bought over from Jamaica, there was open-air dancing along the South Bank to jazz bands in the evenings and the Royal Festival Hall, and a new extensive concert hall complex was opened by King George VI on 3 May 1951. Ravi Shankar played there for the first time in 1958, just seven years later. This was the Britain to which Gopal returned after his time during the war in India.

Setting the scene economically and culturally in England after the Second World War, this chapter investigates some of Gopal's many concerts of the late 1940s and 1950s, both at home and on tour internationally, discussing the dance items, the members of his company, critical reviews and audience reception, and the music accompanying his performances. I focus on one important and essential artefact – a copy of Gopal's first post-war 1947 printed programme – to mark this pivotal time of change globally and artistically and to note the start of Gopal's new fame as an international dancer, as well as the opening of a new interest in international artistic forms. I examine his iconic *Garuda* dance, included both in his pre- and post-war performances, analysing its choreography, costume and audience reception. At this post-war time, Gopal

[2] The festival took place at a range of venues including Battersea Pleasure Gardens, 'architecture in Poplar, science at South Kensington, industrial power in Glasgow, farming in Belfast, a travelling exhibition, and a festival ship, the converted aircraft carrier *Campania*' (Hewison 1997 [1995]: 59).

[3] Produced and directed by Julian Hendy, this one-hour documentary was first broadcast in 2011 on BBCTwo. It was titled *The 1951 Festival of Britain: A Brave New World*.

additionally showcased new culturally and historically woven material with his group of supporting dancers and musicians from India and the chapter looks at the dancers in the company and the musical performances. His interest and powerful connections with the world of classical ballet are noted, indicating his now assured place as performer of some note, shown additionally by his growing status as a celebrity icon.

Cultural impact

Did post-war audiences differ from those who had attended Gopal's sell-out debut performances in 1939? Were attitudes more open, more accepting, less dominated by colonial thinking that privileged the exotic east? Was there more accurate knowledge of India, its customs and its people? As discussed, the aftermath of war was very much in evidence; rationing was still in place; there were shortages of many items, and it was a time of drabness and severe austerity. Britain's role as a colonial power was drastically reduced, and the relief that war had ended was clouded by the realization that the country had virtually bankrupted itself in the effort of paying for the war. An account from audience member John White (my father) who attended Gopal's performances in January 1951 at the Cambridge Theatre, London, sets the scene:

> A new audience had emerged during the war that was enthusiastic and receptive. The new CEMA [Council for the Encouragement of Music and the Arts], later to become the Arts Council was the focus of the surge in interest in all the arts by people in the services. My recollection is that Gopal received favourable reviews and publicity and that his performances were well attended. They made a great impact on me. For me, the first thing was how different it was as an art form – and yet how powerful and moving it could be. A tradition, of which we were quite unaware, was revealed to the British audiences.
>
> (John White, interview with author, August 2000)

He described how the war had opened people's minds, creating a broader and more inclusive type of conceptualization than the narrow, confined atmosphere of pre-wars days. There was a fresh readiness to respond to artistic creations from abroad, shown for example in 1947 by the creation of the Edinburgh International Festival, and by inviting orchestras, dance companies and drama productions from overseas. Cultural expression in the forms of music and dance from all parts of the globe began to create a fresh and genuine interest. Men had travelled abroad, often for the first time, and women started to work outside the home; established social structures were dismantled, changing ordinary daily life dramatically and opening up revitalized horizons. Many Brits who had lived in India had now returned, establishing new audiences with a genuine interest in Indian performing arts. Jeanette Sidall (1999: 11) notes that the arts were turned to as a civilizing factor 'in their capacity to promote social cohesion and individual inspiration'.

CEMA was established by the Labour government in 1946 as an educational, participatory organization for public benefit. It received additional funding from the American Pilgrim Trust and initially awarded money for professional and amateur artistic work and allocated small grants. London was now seen as a focal point for international recitals, receiving foreign artists (as noted above) with a more receptive and interested attitude, in stark contrast to its previous role as a colonial metropolis at the heart of the empire. David Cannadine, discussing the dissolution of the British Empire, writes of how the new post-imperial regimes 'increasingly came to stand for national autonomy, open access, social equality, economic modernity, ethnic diversity and multiculturalism' (2001: 160). These were, however, complex and difficult terrains to negotiate.

One audience member of the time, training in architecture, recalls the feeling in London at that time as 'being the centre of the world in a great cultural surge. New orchestras and new music, as well as freshly discovered early music, was being played everywhere and most exciting of all, groups from abroad were bringing authentic music and dance from distant cultures' (Pam Turner, interview with author, August 2000). She described the impact of dance groups from Spain and China appearing in the concert halls, along with Ravi Shankar's performances that introduced Indian music to British audiences. Gopal was received in this context, performing to 'packed audiences [that] would be spellbound as he whirled to unfamiliar rhythms, or made the finest gesture with hand, eye, or just a ripple of muscle' (Turner 2000). My father remembers two particularly vivid memories of Gopal's dancing at the Cambridge Theatre in 1951: first Gopal in his eagle costume performing the *Garuda* dance, which he describes here, 'The costume itself was spectacular but had been fashioned with great beauty and artistry: the dance itself had enormous power and evoked the majesty of the bird in flight.' Another clear memory was of Gopal recounting a poem about the lotus and miming the flower opening with such subtlety and delicacy that 'it remains an unforgettable experience' (White, interview with author, 2000).

The glowing periodical reviews continued, and audiences filled the theatres as Gopal gave performances around the country, in London and internationally.[4] There were the occasional disparaging remarks, alluding to the performances appearing more stylized than before, that the music sounded monotonous, and that Gopal's introductory talks were too long. But more frequently the reviews indicated how welcome these dazzling performances were in the austere conditions prevailing after the war. Beryl de Zoete writing in *The Spectator* in 1947 describes the scene:

> There is no doubt that the war has had an extraordinary effect on the appreciation of dancing in this country. The love of ballet in England, the enormous audiences and vast enthusiasm strike every visitor from abroad. But the awareness of dancing extends to other forms than ballet. Many hitherto untravelled people made great journeys during the war, and some returned with a new consciousness … There is a new audience for our Indian dance and one very ready to be instructed.
>
> (de Zoete 1947a: n.p.)

Gopal rather idealistically spoke of that time that

> everything had changed in England, in beloved London. Everything but the spirit of the people of this great city. If it had been badly bombed, and the war had left its visible and invisible scars, these would heal quicker here than in other countries and people affected by the war, because of the incredible courage, humour and quenchless spirit of the English.
>
> (1957: 172)

Gopal's post-war performances

Having arrived on 23 July 1947 from India, Gopal famously danced at the opening ceremony of London's Victoria and Albert Museum's new Indian sculpture exhibition in September showing some of his new programme of dances (see Chapter 3). This was followed by a four-week season at London's Prince's Theatre which was, as before, sold out every night. This season garnered

[4] In 1947–8, Gopal and his troupe travelled extensively in Britain performing in Edinburgh, Cambridge, Leicester, Oxford, Bath, Cardiff, Buxton, Liverpool, Hull and Belfast. Their European performances included Paris, Copenhagen, Stockholm, Oslo, Berne, Zurich, Geneva as well as the New York (see Appendix 1).

more admiring reviews in the daily newspapers. Here is de Zoete again in *The New Statesman*:

> The large and enthusiastic audiences at Ram Gopal's programme of Indian dances at the Prince's Theatre are an encouraging sign of the great interest in dancing now felt by the general public … Ram Gopal himself makes very welcome concessions to his European audiences by his analysis and detailed interpretations of the South Indian mudras… . The *Setting Sun, Cobra Devil* and *Hunter in the Forest* dances, all in the Kathakali idiom, were, however, the most impressive, and the eloquence of his arms and hands is amazing.
>
> (de Zoete 1947b: 47)

The programme for the Princes Theatre, costing six pence, is a small A4-sized, printed front and back on four pages on thin, yellowing and fragile paper. The front page, with a border picked out in red ink, states the theatre's name and address and telephone number at the top. Underneath is the title, 'Ram Gopal and His Indian Dancers and Musicians', with the name Ram Gopal in red and the rest in black ink. The cover image of Gopal as *Siva the Hunter* is a black ink drawing by artist Kay Ambrose; he is depicted standing on his right leg with bent knee, the left leg outstretched on the heel and the arms held as if drawing back a hunting bow. He wears his Siva headdress, as well as arm ornaments, a necklace and his *ghungroo*, or ankle bells. Gopal is bare-chested and bare-legged, sporting a small garment round his loins. Inside on the first page is a written *Introduction to Classical Indian Dancing* that tells the reader about the dance styles of bharatanatyam, kathakali, kathak and manipuri. The facing page announces the performances, running every evening at 7.00 p.m. and matinees on both Wednesday and Saturdays at 2.30 p.m. Here the performance is titled *Ram Gopal and His Indian Ballet Company* and presented by Julian Braunsweg. Gopal's name is in bold and large type and the other eight members of the company are named: Shevanti and Rajeshwar taking main billing, with the others, Sarla, Leela, Banumati, Anura, Jaron Yaltan and Nataraj in smaller type. The bottom of the page notes that the Indian orchestra is under the direction of LAKHIA, with Babu Rae and others. The middle pages of the programme set out the seventeen items in two parts divided by an interval of fifteen minutes.

Part one starts traditionally with a bharatanatyam *alarippu* danced by Gopal and Shevanti. This is followed by a bharatanatyam *jethisvaram* [*sic*] performed by Rajeshwar. Each piece has the style of the dance named in brackets and italics after the title as well as a brief explanation. Two more solos follow: the

Figure 14a Princes Theatre, London programme, 1947. Author's own collection.

first by Shevanti in manipuri style, showing *Surya Puja* or *Sun Worship*; the second is Gopal performing the *Dance of the Setting Sun* (kathakali). Shevanti and Rajeshwar then offer a Manipur folk dance before a second solo by Gopal of his kathakali *Sarpa Asura Tandav* (Cobra Devil dance). Shevanti and Gopal perform two more solos – the first a *Gopi* (cowherd) manipuri dance and then Gopal showing *Deevali Puja* in kathakali style. The first half ends with the whole group dancing a joyful full moon dance in manipuri folk style, called *Golden Harvest.*

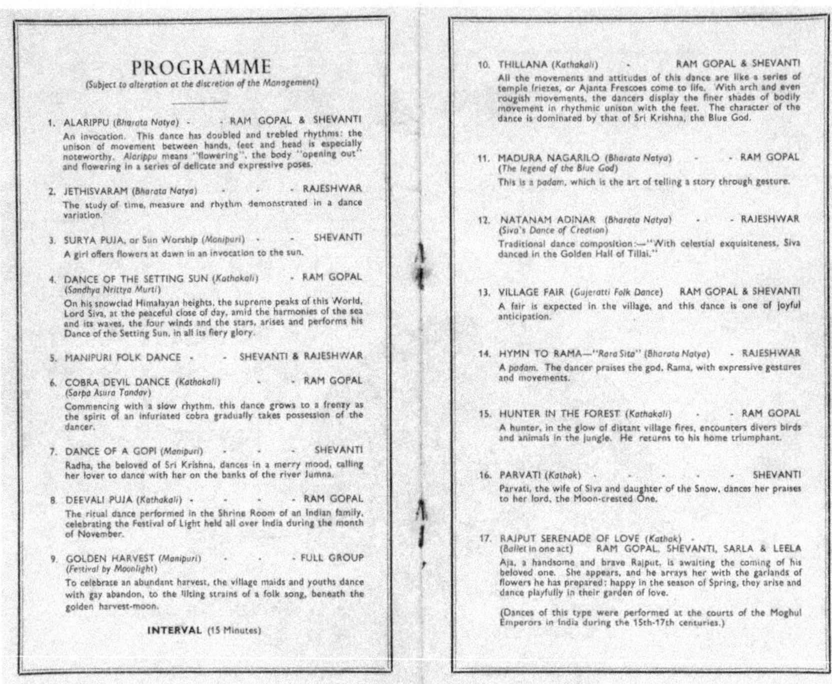

PROGRAMME

(Subject to alteration at the discretion of the Management)

1. ALARIPPU (*Bharata Natya*) - - RAM GOPAL & SHEVANTI
   An invocation. This dance has doubled and trebled rhythms: the unison of movement between hands, feet and head is especially noteworthy. *Alarippu* means "flowering", the body "opening out" and flowering in a series of delicate and expressive poses.

2. JETHISVARAM (*Bharata Natya*) - - - RAJESHWAR
   The study of time, measure and rhythm demonstrated in a dance variation.

3. SURYA PUJA, or Sun Worship (*Manipuri*) - - SHEVANTI
   A girl offers flowers at dawn in an invocation to the sun.

4. DANCE OF THE SETTING SUN (*Kathakali*) - RAM GOPAL
   (*Sandhya Nrittya Murti*)
   On his snowclad Himalayan heights, the supreme peaks of this World, Lord Siva, at the peaceful close of day, amid the harmonies of the sea and its waves, the four winds and the stars, arises and performs his Dance of the Setting Sun, in all its fiery glory.

5. MANIPURI FOLK DANCE - - SHEVANTI & RAJESHWAR

6. COBRA DEVIL DANCE (*Kathakali*) - - RAM GOPAL
   (*Sarpa Asura Tandav*)
   Commencing with a slow rhythm, this dance grows to a frenzy as the spirit of an infuriated cobra gradually takes possession of the dancer.

7. DANCE OF A GOPI (*Manipuri*) - - - SHEVANTI
   Radha, the beloved of Sri Krishna, dances in a merry mood, calling her lover to dance with her on the banks of the river Jumna.

8. DEEVALI PUJA (*Kathakali*) - - - - RAM GOPAL
   The ritual dance performed in the Shrine Room of an Indian family, celebrating the Festival of Light held all over India during the month of November.

9. GOLDEN HARVEST (*Manipuri*) - - - FULL GROUP
   (*Festival by Moonlight*)
   To celebrate an abundant harvest, the village maids and youths dance with gay abandon, to the lilting strains of a folk song, beneath the golden harvest-moon.

INTERVAL (15 Minutes)

10. THILLANA (*Kathakali*) - RAM GOPAL & SHEVANTI
    All the movements and attitudes of this dance are like a series of temple friezes, or Ajanta Frescoes come to life. With arch and even rougish movements, the dancers display the finer shades of bodily movement in rhythmic unison with the feet. The character of the dance is dominated by that of Sri Krishna, the Blue God.

11. MADURA NAGARILO (*Bharata Natya*) - - RAM GOPAL
    (*The legend of the Blue God*)
    This is a *padam*, which is the art of telling a story through gesture.

12. NATANAM ADINAR (*Bharata Natya*) - - RAJESHWAR
    (*Siva's Dance of Creation*)
    Traditional dance composition:—"With celestial exquisiteness, Siva danced in the Golden Hall of Tillai."

13. VILLAGE FAIR (*Gujeratti Folk Dance*) RAM GOPAL & SHEVANTI
    A fair is expected in the village, and this dance is one of joyful anticipation.

14. HYMN TO RAMA—"*Rara Sita*" (*Bharata Natya*) - RAJESHWAR
    A *padam*. The dancer praises the god, Rama, with expressive gestures and movements.

15. HUNTER IN THE FOREST (*Kathakali*) - - RAM GOPAL
    A hunter, in the glow of distant village fires, encounters divers birds and animals in the jungle. He returns to his home triumphant.

16. PARVATI (*Kathak*) - - - - - SHEVANTI
    Parvati, the wife of Siva and daughter of the Snow, dances her praises to her lord, the Moon-crested One.

17. RAJPUT SERENADE OF LOVE (*Kathak*) -
    (*Ballet* in one act) RAM GOPAL, SHEVANTI, SARLA & LEELA
    Aja, a handsome and brave Rajput, is awaiting the coming of his beloved one. She appears, and he arrays her with the garlands of flowers he has prepared: happy in the season of Spring, they arise and dance playfully in their garden of love.

    (Dances of this type were performed at the courts of the Moghul Emperors in India during the 15th-17th centuries.)

Figure 14b Princes Theatre, London programme, 1947. Author's own collection.

The second part of this programme at the Princes Theatre opens with a *tillana*, danced by Gopal and Shevanti. Strangely, it is named as being in kathakali style but this item is part of the bharatanatyam repertoire. Two bharatanatyam solos follow; the first is Gopal dancing *The Legend of the Blue God* and then Rajeshwar performing *Natanam Adinar* (Siva's dance of creation). After a folk dance from Gujarat shown by Gopal and Shevanti there are two further solos: Rajeshwar dancing a bharatanatyam *padam*, called *Hymn to Rama*, and then Gopal depicting a kathakali story of the *Hunter in the Forest.* Shevanti performs one more solo, a kathak dance of *Parvati* and the programme closes with a longer item, called a 'ballet in one act' – *The Rajput Serenade of Love* with Gopal and the three female dancers in kathak style.

The final pages of the printed programme name Michael Rouse as manager, stage director Ben Toff, and Kay Ambrose as artistic advisor. Prices of seats (dress circle from 7 shillings 6 pence to 15 shillings, orchestra stalls from 9 shillings 9 pence to 16 shillings 6 pence, and gallery 2 shillings unreserved) and announcements for the Christmas pantomime at the theatre follow.[5] On the

[5] These prices are in shillings and pence.

back page are adverts for drinks, food and restaurants. The nightly programme at the theatre revealed how Gopal was weaving together differing dance styles (manipuri, kathak, bharatanatyam, kathakali and folk dance), novel aspects of production (short items that included solos, duets and group pieces; two halves of a programme with an interval; live music with musicians onstage) to tailor his shows for the mainly Western audiences. Gopal used the term 'bharatanatyam' for the first time in his post-war concerts; prior to that, pieces were said to be taken from the 'Tanjore temple dances'. Importantly, Gopal did not undertake formal training in bharatanatyam until his return to India in 1939. The programme discussed above does not include musical interludes, although later this was to become a standard in the programmes, foregrounding the musicians almost as much as the dancers. Gopal's work as an innovator, producing pioneering intercultural work that wove together contrasting cultures without erasing difference, grew in this post-war period, establishing him as one of the leading artistic icons of the time.

In 1948, further seasons followed at the Saville and Adelphi theatres in London, the Oxford Playhouse and the Théâtre des Champs-Elysées, Paris. Gopal continued to tailor his programme to Western audiences by introducing and explaining each dance before its performance, just as he had experimented with in India during the war. Occasionally Ambrose would take this role in the evening's production. His programmes as discussed above included some of his most popular dances familiar to London audiences (*Setting Sun, Garuda*), but also many new items in bharatanatyam style such as *alarippu, jatisvaram, tillana* and a *padam* titled *The Legend of the Blue God.* He brought over from India dancers trained in manipuri dance. As before and as noted above, the items were short and varied including solo dances, duets and group choreography in addition to the musical interludes, and there were at least two and sometimes three intervals in the programmes.

Extensive tours to Scandinavia followed in 1948, 1949 and 1952 that included Norway, Sweden and Denmark (see Chapter 3 for further discussion on the Swedish tours) and in Switzerland during August–September 1948. In 1949, Gopal went to Turkey on a government of India–sponsored tour, where he performed in Istanbul and Ankara. Of this trip, he noted, 'The only places, after America, to move me with their age-old traditions and beauty were Istanbul and Ankara. In 1949 Turkey was as beautiful as a fairy-tale city and our [Indian] ballet made there a deeper impression than in any other country in the Middle East' (1957: 182). Later in 1952 they performed in Berlin. Lakhia remarked, 'Germany was very drab after the war. Berlin was bombed and there was no colour anywhere, so Indian dancers seemed so colourful and exotic' (interview with author, December 2017).

After his US debut in 1938 (see Chapter 1), Gopal returned to New York in 1948 for the Golden Anniversary International Dance Festival (which celebrated the Golden Jubilee of the City of New York) from 21 September to 3 October that year.[6] Sol Hurok managed his appearance and he had been requested by Nehru to represent India. Gopal and his troupe performed at the City Center, receiving a review from Cecil Smith, who noted the vigour and 'dramatic impact of Ram Gopal and his dancers, their magnificent, wide use of space and their unhesitating use of devices to startle the observer, to move his emotions and to keep his attention fresh' (quoted in Gopal 1957: 180–1). It was advertised (wrongly) as Gopal's first time in the United States. His next two trips to the United States were to dance at the Jacob's Pillow summer dance festival in 1954 and 1958, invited by director Ted Shawn. Gopal writes of these visits:

> Jacob's Pillow was a revelation of concentrated work, in an ideal woodland setting, with the white spirit of Shawn. Here dancers of all the known and created styles taught, learned, danced and lectured, side by side … All nationalities mingle, all arts are seen, discussed and dissected, and all in the friendly, natural setting of the unforgettable Jacob's Pillow.
>
> (Gopal 1957: 181–2)

Rebekah Kowal's careful analysis of the correspondence between Shawn and Gopal over the arrangements of this visit reveals the complexities and tensions over arrangements for his contract to perform at Jacob's Pillow, indicating as she argues the cultural differences in understanding between these two dance giants. Despite the success of both visits, Gopal was not happy about the financial provisions made or the offer by Shawn to provide dancers trained by La Meri (Kowal 2020: 186–7) to dance in Gopal's performances.[7] In the end, Shawn compromised; Gopal did receive a higher payment and brought his companion (and lover) Serafin Kycia with him. He did not use La Meri's dancers.

[6] Kowal notes how Grover Whalen who had been president of the 1939 New York World's Fair was tasked with programming the Golden Anniversary festivities. He asked Hurok to organize a world dance festival as part of the event, both men wishing to use this as a 'globalist project' for America (2020: 1–5).

[7] I am grateful for this clear explanation of their correspondence (housed in the archives at Jacob's Pillow) by Kowal as my planned visit to the archives there was cancelled due to the Covid-19 pandemic (2020).

Iconic Garuda

The spectacular dance of *Garuda: The Golden Eagle* that drew audiences was a shortened excerpt of a longer kathakali piece representing the mythological golden eagle, believed in Hindu lore to be the vehicle of the deity Visnu. As the programme description in 1940s India narrates:

> Garuda steals the Amrita, the food of the Gods [from the Nagas, or snakes]. From his crouching position he surveys his prey and with darting movements of the eye, and quick movements of the head, he soars into the air and overcoming the guardians of the ambrosia snatches it away. As a reward for not having drunk it, Vishnu makes him his steed and he becomes the immortal carrier of Lord Vishnu.

These same notes were repeated in other programmes, such as at the Theatre Royal in Brighton in December 1950. Movements in the dance depict these aspects carefully and the visual impression is of a bird in flight.

The only film remaining of Gopal dancing this piece was made at Jacob's Pillow, Massachusetts, USA, by Carol Lynn in September 1954 and is held in the archives there.[8] Running at just over fifteen minutes and including five of Gopal's items, the film reveals that the *Garuda* dance is just less than two minutes. Lynn included his *Poem*, *Tillana*, *Dance of the Setting Sun*, *Rajput Serenade* and *Garuda* which were interspersed with other dancers' items (as well as further dances by Gopal) in the mixed bill programmes. Filmed in black and white and roughly edited, three of the dances are cut before their final endings and the quality of the film remains poor. Neither is there sound (although the written programme records that Gopal was accompanied by percussionist Eyrick Darby for the *Garuda* dance). It is, however, possible to get a sense of the dance performance. Gopal appears on stage right through the wings, showing one outstretched eagle's wing, with his back to the audience. Vigorously shaking the wings, he moves quickly, with fast footwork, back and forth across the stage, ending in the centre, wings outstretched. Facing upstage, he exuberantly moves his wings up and down several times and then repeats to the front. Gopal depicts the bird

[8] It is unclear whether it was filmed in rehearsal or at the one of the four performances as part of that year's dance festival on either 3 or 4 September (both days had matinee and evening performances). Gopal also performed at Jacob's Pillow in August that year from 11 to 15 but did not include the *Garuda* item. The complete film may have been recorded at several performances in August and September and edited together. I am deeply indebted to Norton Owen, chief archivist, and director of preservation at Jacob's Pillow for allowing me access to the film when Covid-19 restrictions meant I could not travel or visit the library in person.

pecking by moving his head forward and back sharply and then transfers from side to side with extended, deep lunges. Suddenly, with a giant leap, the eagle disappears into the wings stage left creating a dramatic exit and sudden end to the dance. No other film of this dance exists; the only other photographic records are mainly black and white, in addition to some sketched notations by Ambrose in her book *Classical Dances and Costumes of India* (1951), as well as her stunning scraperboard drawing of Gopal in action as *Garuda*. Photographer Baron (known for his work in ballet) produced one full colour photo of Gopal as *Garuda*; he kneels, one wing folded into the centre and one wing outstretched, looking sideways, gleamingly resplendent in gold (Baron 1950).

The costume for *Garuda* was remade in the early 1960s. Costume designer and maker Jenny Levy Casperson told me about Gopal approaching her to copy and reproduce the existing, well-worn costume (interview with author, August 2016). They were both good friends of Ambrose who introduced them at one of her infamous Sunday evening dinner parties. Casperson already knew

Figure 15 Sketch of Ram Gopal as *Garuda* by Kay Ambrose. Author's own collection.

of Gopal and had seen him dance in the 1950s. Gopal was so delighted with her costume that he commissioned a second copy.[9] The wings are fabricated out of twenty-two carat gold kid leather stitched as feathers and held in place on each arm and hand with three arm bands. More kid leather feathers sit round the neck, back and shoulders secured to a type of short bolero and worn on a bare chest. This top piece and the loincloth-type lower garment have bright turquoise blue corded tassels hanging down the front of the chest and between the legs. At the front of the loincloth are more gold leather feathers, and a large piece of jewellery. Apart from this small garment, Gopal was bare-legged wearing just his ankle bells. The headdress, constructed like a helmet and made in moulded rubber, with the same gold leather on top, has the beautiful and powerful head of the bird with a large beak and bright red jewelled eyes, sitting at the front of the headdress on the forehead of the dancer. Thin gold tassels hang down the back. As the lights shone on the costume, it gleamed and dazzled. Dance critic Cyril Beaumont noted (*Sunday Times*, 22 October 1950), 'His first entrance dazzles with the superb beauty of his Eagle costume,' and the reviewer in *The Spectator* in 1948 commented that 'Gopal's second programme at the Saville Theatre is almost entirely new and even better than the first ... Ram Gopal has a splendid new Garuda dance with flexible golden wings, which he wields marvellously' (18 March 1948). The first critical reviews of Gopal's pre-war 1939 Aldwych performances had noted that '[w]e have rarely seen a more exciting solo dance than "Garuda", the golden eagle, with its wonderful suggestion of flight' (*The Times* 1939: n.p.) (See headdress in Plate 2 of colour insert).

Lionel Bradley (see Chapter 1) describes in his penned account that 'what was so marvellously impressed upon one was the strong winged bird, springing into flight. Gopal had long, narrow wings fastened along the whole length of his arm and a headdress suggesting a beak. Some people have declared his representation in flight to be far superior to [Serge] Lifar's in his ballet "Icare"' (1939: n.p.). Bradley goes on to wonder whether Gopal had seen Lifar's famous piece and whether it had influenced him but concludes that Gopal 'had equal mastery' as Lifar in the representation of flight (1939).[10]

Generally, post-war audiences were very appreciative and were beginning to gain a more knowledgeable interest in Indian dance. There were, of course,

9 The costume was carried in two specially made boxes and was insured.

10 The 1935 solo that Serge Lifar danced was depicting Icarus; he also donned wings and 'flew'. Clement Crisp writes of this piece that Lifar 'affirmed his beliefs about the primacy of choreography ... about the significance of male dancing and about himself as a dancer ... Like Icarus, Lifar aspired, sought to fly' (2002: 8).

still inexperienced critics who did not fully comprehend the dance form and continued to write ill-informed, condescending reviews, replete with old colonial attitudes. The *Daily Herald*'s reporter, writing of Gopal's troupe's performances on 13 August 1948, described the company as performing 'ritualistic dancing and fussy, repetitive music from weird instruments' yet concluding by saying that a visit to their performances was 'a unique and satisfying experience'. The critic for *The Stage* (10 July 1948) used pejorative, imperialist terms such as 'native musicians', and a monthly publication, *Musical Events*, published a review calling the performance 'a novelty; something as far removed from our normal conception of ballet as can possibly be imagined' (May 1948: n.p.). Most professional reviews, however, were superlative in their praise.

Music

Gopal and his company not only performed successfully again in London but also toured the UK, Scandinavia, Europe and travelled again to the United States in 1948. Some of these post-war tours featured now-famous dancers Kumudini Lakhia who had joined Gopal in 1948 aged eighteen and Mrinalini Sarabhai.[11] Musical director Rajanikant Lakhia (usually known as Rajani and later to marry dancer Kumudini) played *tabla*, *mridangam*, violin and *sarod* and was additionally trained in Western music. He had also studied law at Lincoln's Inn, London, and was a practising lawyer. Lakhia went on to compose the score for Gopal's newly commissioned ballet of *The Legend of the Taj Mahal* in 1956. Gopal wrote, 'I was fortunate to get Rajani Lakhia as musical director. His genius in creating the most lyrical and exquisite melodies always surprised me, and the music he created for the Taj Mahal Ballet, the first full-length, two-hour ballet ever to come out of India is a masterpiece of Indian music, in mood, theme and rhythm' (Gopal 1957: 186–7).

The Legend of the Taj Mahal premiered at the Edinburgh Festival in August and moved to the Royal Festival Hall in September 1956. It garnered mixed reviews, with *The Times*'s critic noting that 'the music by Rajani Lakhia has piquant moments, and some commonplace ones, as the western ear judges them' (1956: n.p.) and Peter Williams, writing in *Dance and Dancers*, stated that he found it

[11] Sarabhai, discussed in Chapter 3, joined Gopal's company in India during the war. Lakhia, whom I go on to discuss, joined in 1948.

'difficult to say anything about Indian music apart from the fact that it is Indian. The present "score", however, not only inevitably sets the right atmosphere, with its markedly varying rhythms it also gives the choreographer considerable scope' (Williams 1956: 19).

An EMI 12" LP made in 1958 of the songs and dances of India by the Ram Gopal company featured many of the musicians who toured with the *Taj Mahal ballet*.[12] It was recorded in conjunction with the influential Asian Music Circle (formally the Indian Music Club), founded in 1946 in London by Indian writer Ayana Deva Angadi and his English wife, Patricia Fell-Clarke, a painter and novelist. They established Indian dance and music classes in London in the 1960s and offered extensive support to Gopal. Their foundation was extremely influential in the establishment and appreciation of Indian culture in post-war Britain, working with musicians such as Ravi Shankar, the Beatles, Yehudi Menuhin, Ali Akbar Khan and dancers Gopal, Shanta Rao, Krishna Rao and Chandrabhaga Devi. Despite the growing public appreciation of Indian culture, critics continued to reveal their lack of understanding and awareness and their cultural biases. Although apparently visually compelling and 'exotically' pleasing, the performances seemed to them to be alien and incomprehensible. The *Daily Telegraph* reviewer again, in 1956, noted that 'the music provided by the Indian orchestra with its myriad repetitions of a single phrase and insistence on virtuoso percussion rhythms, only emphasises the irredeemably alien and fundamentally incomprehensible character of this whole art for the westerner' (cited in Shah 2005: 51).

Gopal continued to programme the musicians not only playing for the dance pieces, but additionally in their own items, often starting the evening's performance with a musical piece and performing an instrumental interlude in the first or second half of the programme. Again, he foregrounded the musicians as professional players, rather than just accompanists to the dance movement. I note how the programme used Western terminology, calling the musicians an 'orchestra', who were playing an 'overture' and an 'interlude'. It may have been deemed more acceptable to the British, European and Americans who made up Gopal's audiences to use these more familiar terms. Gopal may have followed Shankar, who was producing the same type of programmes of short, danced items, an interval and musical interludes in his British and European tours in the early 1930s.

[12] This recording included items such as *Alarippu, Jatiswaram, Natanam Adinar, Thillana* and other folk dances and was released on the Columbia label.

Gopal's dance company

The lead dancers in the 1947 programme were Shevanti and Rajeshwar, who later married. Gopal describes Shevanti as not only 'my favourite pupil but from 1944 onwards my leading partner and soloist. She has a superb technique, with an unbroken fluidity of movement I have not seen equalled' (1957: 184–5). Both Shevanti and Rajeshwar danced with Gopal at the sculpture exhibition at London's V&A museum (part of which is captured on silent film) and described in Chapter 3.

Not all of Gopal's company were Indian by birth and trained in India. British-born, ballet-trained Marianne Balchin, dancing under the pseudonym of 'Mrinalini', had studied at the Arts Educational School in London, danced in the Anglo-Polish Ballet company and went on to understudy Diana Gould in ENSA performances. She joined a ballet company run by Elsa Brunelleschi and, during this time, learnt two Indian dances in the repertoire from an Indian teacher trained under Shankar. This fuelled her interest in Indian dance. Kathakali dancer Sivaram was appearing in London in June 1948 and Balchin undertook training in kathakali with him, later dancing with him. She was introduced to Gopal who auditioned her for his company and she continued to train in bharatanatyam with him. Balchin also took lessons from Gopal's kathak teacher, Radhelal Misra, who was working with the company; she remained with Gopal for about eighteen months but was eventually tired of what she saw as internal politics and Gopal's financial difficulties. Critic Judith Makrell, interviewing Gopal in 1989, commented that 'ultimately the struggle to maintain a company of 50 dancers and musicians defeated him' (1989: 17).

Balchin's memory of the time was still vivid, and she described to me the power of Gopal's stage presence and his charisma as a dancer. She recounted how the audiences were full of dance lovers, the majority of whom were followers of the ballet; just a handful of Indians would attend performances. The Indian community at that time in Britain was still small, as the significant immigration of the Indian population to Britain from East Africa and India did not take place until the 1960s. When asked about her own reception as a Western dancer performing classical Indian dances, she replied, 'Well, the Indians I met loved you to take an interest in their art but did not like you to get too good. At the beginning of performances people would say "She can't be good if she's English". Then at the end (because she *was* good) their comments would be "She can't be English, she's really Indian"' (interview with author, June 2000). Balchin continued her career as an Indian dancer with Krishna Kutty and then with Shirin Vajifdar and her New Indian Ballet Company in the early 1950s, dancing folk, manipuri and kathakali dances. She joined Krishna Rao's company in the 1960s when they toured in Ireland and danced in their performances in London at the Queen Elizabeth Hall. Later, she gave recitals and lecture demonstrations all over the UK, India and the United States.

From a contemporary point of view, Sitara Thobani notes how when non-Indian dancers 'are celebrated for "looking Indian" in their dance performance, this celebration simultaneously references racialised *and* culturalized ideals' (2017: 184) creating a sort of racialized aesthetics and reconstructing essential notions of race. In Andrée Grau's important report *South Asian Dance in Britain* (2002), she writes how white bharatanatyam dancer Magdalen Gorringe, performing in an Indian restaurant as part of the Edinburgh international arts festival in 2000, received comments such as '"My children hoped for an ethnic dancer" wrote one woman. "We expected native dancers" complained another. Throughout the month she received a constant stream of jokes about which part of India she came from' (Grau 2002: 46).[13] This was notwithstanding the fact that Gorringe grew up in south India and speaks fluent Tamil.

The fact that Balchin was expected to assume an Indian name, Mrinalini, for performances followed the pattern set by the Western oriental or interpretive dancers before the war. She was presented as an Indian dancer, even though she was known by onlookers to be English, just as Uday Shankar's French partner Simkie was introduced in the 1930s. At that time, this practice was deemed acceptable. But later in 1956, Fernau Hall did write that Balchin 'is tired of having to pass herself off as an Indian: from now on she will dance under her English name' (Hall 1956: 21). Anne-Marie Steenhuis-Hesterman, a Dutch kathak dancer who performed in the 1940s–50s, took the name Damayanti and wore a black wig to cover her fair hair.[14] But the changing of names to construct new (and exotic) identities was not limited solely to the world of Indian or oriental dance. Ballet dancers frequently changed their

[13] The report came out of a three-year, Leverhulme-funded research project that set out to investigate the significant role 'that the South Asian dance profession plays in British cultural life' (Grau 2002: 6).

[14] Steenhuis-Hesterman was a professional ballet dancer in Pavlova's Company (after Pavlova's death), who was taught kathak in Holland by Indradev Prasad. I studied with her intensively on several occasions.

names to create a more Russian or French image and they were often under pressure to do so. Famous examples include dancers Margot Fonteyn, whose original name was Peggy Hookham; Alicia Markova, originally Alice Marks; and founder of the Royal Ballet, Ninette de Valois, born Edris Stannus. Even ballerina Darcey Bussell commented in a documentary *Looking for Margot* (BBC 1, 2016) that she was asked as recently as 1990 at the Royal Ballet to change her surname. Quite rightly she refused.

The use of language as a tool in creating illusion is familiar within the theatrical world as indicated above, yet these examples of transformation of names serve to remind how language is used to effect power and control. Ania Loomba comments on the power of discourse, underscoring the existence of 'a whole field or domain within which language is used in particular ways. This domain is rooted … in human practices, institutions and actions … Discursive practices make it difficult for individuals to think outside them – hence they are also exercises in power and control' (1998: 38–9). Loomba discusses 'the attention paid to language as a tool of domination and as a means of constructing identity' (1998: 41), clearly shown in the above examples.

As noted, Gopal and his company travelled to Scandinavia in May–June 1948 to perform.[15] Lakhia, accompanying him as dance partner spoke to me about their tours there, saying,

> We toured to Scandinavia, travelling by ship. We started in Sweden, and performed in Gothenburg, Stockholm and Uppsala. The public loved us and the press gave great reviews. In Stockholm, there was a huge government event, and no rooms left to stay in, so Braunsweg announced the dancers needed rooms and people offered their homes generously. Performances took place at the Cirkus Theatre in Stockholm. People wanted us back but it didn't happen that time. Nehru's sister was married and living in Sweden, and she came to see the show and then hosted a big reception and feast afterwards.
>
> (interview with author, December 2017)

Lakhia joined Gopal's troupe as a principal dancer in kathak and stayed with the company from 1948 to 1952. Gopal loved her dancing, stating that is the 'very qualities of soul and expression that make Kumudini a great dancer' and that 'her superb line, lightening spins and great purity' of the classical Kathak schools

[15] See details in Appendix 1.

of 'Jylal and Radhelal (leading maestros)' were matchless (Gopal 1957: 185). In 1950, a review in *The Scotsman* of their London Adelphi theatre shows alluded to her star quality:

> Apart from Ram Gopal, who danced with the ease and virtuosity to which we have become accustomed in the past … the outstanding performer of the evening was Kumudini; even to the Western eye, not versed in the subtleties and allegory of the dances of the East, it was obvious that she is an artist of great quality and her performance made apparent to the spectator the universality of movement as an art, apart from any particular and local meaning it may have in its country of origin.
>
> (18 October 1950)

Lakhia danced a duet with Gopal called *Moghul Miniatures* in his programmes and duets with him in the ballet of the *Legend of the Taj Mahal.* She had kathak solos such as the story of Draupadi and learnt manipuri dance to perform items with the rest of the troupe.[16] Gopal also taught her some bharatanatyam and they performed *tillana* together. They respected each other and a great fondness developed between them. Lakhia told me how well Gopal looked after her as young teenager, performing in the company aged eighteen; Lakhia described their close connection, saying 'he was like an elder brother to me' (interview with author, December 2017) (See Gopal and Lakhia in Plate 3 of colour insert).

Art and politics

Gopal was rarely on record commenting on politics or the turbulent world affairs, although in writing he invokes the battlefield in the text of the *Bhagavad Gita* to philosophize about the Second World War. He left India on 2 July 1947 just a few weeks before the sudden and fateful decision to partition India into two states, that of India and the newly formed Pakistan. His father had been involved in his later years with political parties such as the Arya Samaj and the Brahmo Samaj (see Chapter 1) and supported Indian nationalism. A reaction to his father's political commitment may have been a factor. Gopal's performances in Britain attracted an aristocratic, moneyed clientele and as a guest or invited

[16] My father's 1951 Cambridge Theatre programme shows Lakhia dancing in five group items – a manipuri *Rangapuja*, a kathak *Moghul Miniatures*, *The Cloud Messengers*, *Ras Leela* and *Village Fair*; three solo pieces – one kathak setting of *Draupadi*, a bharatanatyam *Thillana* and a manipuri *Surya Puja*; plus a trio with Sarabhai and Sesha called *Malabar Temple Dance*.

speaker he often mixed with ex-Raj personnel at events and receptions. These events included garden parties at the Hurlingham Club, Fulham, hosted by the Earl of Inchcape, President of the Royal India, Pakistan and Ceylon Society who supported some of Gopal's performance in 1948 and 1950 so it is not surprising that the discussion of politics was off the agenda. These wealthy people partly played a type of patronage role for Gopal, and he would necessarily need to be circumspect in his dealings with them.

Yet considering the time he was living through, one of the most turbulent world periods in addition to the withdrawal of Britain as a colonial power in India and the subsequent devastating partition of the land, this seems somewhat surprising. It raises questions about whether Gopal was apolitical in some way, or whether as a colonial subject, he did not feel free to speak out, perhaps silenced by the enforced power dynamics. Rebekah Kowal highlights an incident where Gopal, in his correspondence with Ted Shawn in negotiating a contract for his performance at Jacobs Pillow in 1954, states that neither he nor his companion/partner Kycia was communist. Kowal writes, 'It is interesting that in his correspondence with Shawn, Gopal went out of his way to underline his and Mr Kycia's political neutrality, signalling the pressure of Cold War realities and Mr Kycia's Polish ancestry' (2020: 186).

I suggest another factor problematizing the argument is the reticence about his sexuality and his relationships, as in the 1950s India, Britain and the United States were places where intolerance of homosexuality was rife. Orchestrated purges via the police in Britain and the McCarthy government in the United States led to arrests of public figures and to a new repression of any overt (and sexual) behaviours that might be considered suspicious. It is certainly problematic to look back to a period eighty to ninety years ago and view it through a lens of current attitudes towards gender identities, politics, morality and inclusivity. Millennial expectations of behaviour, social mores and cultural expressions stem from entirely changed worldviews and conceptual understandings that create challenges in perceiving nuances of decisions and actions of the earlier period. Distinctive forms of culture had discrete values, and there was certainly, for example, in the United States, a fear of speaking out and being affiliated with Communism if you were part of the creative, leftist arts scene during the McCarthy era (late 1940s–early 1950s).

Artists have been vociferous at various times about their work being apolitical or being 'above' the world of politics, yet that may often conceal unspoken political views. In the interwar years, tensions were apparent in the German modern expressionist dance groups in relation to support of the country's Fascist regime. Susan Manning's (1993, 1995) and Marion Kant's (2004, 2011) excellent writing on this subject reveals some of the multi-layered and multi-valent reasons for known artistic collaborations. Kant argues that although Mary Wigman considered her art above politics and as apolitical, as a kind of presumed universalism, her work was in fact symptomatic 'of a particular class of people – the educated bourgeois intellectual leaning to the right' (2011: 124). Artists and their work can never really be apolitical.

This was also the time of the Cold War, where two powerfully different ideological systems of thought – the Communism of Russia and the eastern bloc and the capitalism of the United States and the West – were in direct confrontation. Because this war was more ideological and psychological than military, culture and in particular the performing arts played a powerful role on both sides. 'Governments and their institutions, such as the CIA … took the performing arts very seriously' (2018: 5), note Tony Day and Maya H. T. Liem in their work on the Cold War and culture. Funding for culture was increased in 1954 by President Eisenhower with the creation of an Emergency Fund, and dance companies such as that of Mexican-born José Limón were sent to Latin America – Rio de Janeiro, São Paulo and Montevideo – and jazz musicians to the Soviet Union (2018). In a counter-move, Soviet ballet companies including the Moiseyev and the Bolshoi begin successfully touring the world in the mid- to late 1950s. It was global movement of cultural performances both ways that helped break down such prohibiting factors and barriers of the Cold War, the Iron Curtain, the Berlin Wall and problematic visa requirements imposed by governments. Day and Liem argue that there is a 'curious counter-tendency on the part of culture generally and theatre in particular to counteract the stasis and impenetrability of the various blocs' (2018: 6).

Considering these worldwide factors, Gopal wove a relatively successful path through the politics of the national agenda in India and the tensions of colonial heritage which was eased by factors such as his family wealth, his education and his settling in Britain after the Second World War (not liked in India after the tensions of partition). As a gay artist, negotiating his gender preferences was the more difficult terrain, and he never came out publicly or privately to family, not unsurprisingly given the sexual politics and illegal status of homosexuality in both India and in Britain at that time. But he performed his dances during a period of critical change where the unspoken presence of the *devadasi*, the powerful and devastating effects of colonial rule, and India's independence all contributed to an uneasy re-contextualization of the dancing body. Gopal 'presented the classical form to an international viewership' (O'Shea 2007: 59) and enjoyed larger acclamation outside of India, whilst paving the way for generations of Indian dancers to follow him.

Star persona

The decade of the 1950s and early 1960s was a period of acclaim for Gopal and his work. Performance tours continued around Britain as well as trips to the United States, Trinidad, Europe (the Netherlands, France, Italy), Scandinavia, East Africa and Ceylon. Such was his popular appeal and fame that in 1950 a racehorse was named after him that ran at Newmarket racetrack on 30 March 1950, on 10 April at Birmingham racecourse, and on 10 June at Worcester.[17] The horse *Ram Gopal* was owned by a Mr T. Lowry and was noted in the *Times* racing selections. Gopal's television appearances also boosted his popular appeal. He and Shevanti gave a twenty-minute programme shown on Saturday evening TV on 27 November 1948, presented by Christian Simpson and featured in the *Radio Times*, accompanied by two photos. They performed *Garuda, Ajanta Frescoes* and *Rajput Serenade of Love.* Anura did his Kandyan drum dance and music was played by 'Ram Gopal's own company of Indian musicians' (*Radio Times*, 19 November 1948).

On 17 February 1951, Gopal was in a fifteen-minute broadcast again at peak viewing time on Saturday evening and on 4 September 1955 he appeared on the televised *Commonwealth Show.* These post-war TV appearances followed an earlier broadcast on London Television from Alexander Palace in August 1939 (another Saturday evening) of 'Ram Gopal and his Hindu Dancers and Musicians'. Sherril Dodds (2001: 8) records how in the early 1930s 'the BBC set up an unofficial broadcasting service' that showed ballet performances. It became an official station in 1936. Ballet was the primary dance form broadcast, although occasionally international dancers, such as

[17] Noted in the Beginnings chapter.

Shankar, Gopal and Spanish dancer Argentinita, were shown. The service closed during the Second World War. Filming was notoriously difficult as recordings conditions 'were primitive. The studios spaces were small and, once they were filled with the bulky television equipment, this left little room for the dancers' (2001). Poor-quality images also required the costumes to be basic and heavy make-up to be worn.

Films featuring Gopal as an actor were also on release supported by extensive publicity and I discuss these in more depth in Chapter 5 (also see Appendix 2), but the showing, for example, for seven nights at the Picture Theatre Academy, Oxford Street (London's West End) of *Lord Siva Danced* – Sarah Erulkar's 1948 film of Gopal dancing (introduced in Chapter 2) – and excellent reviews in the film press indicate the level of interest in Gopal's dancing. During the early 1950s, *The Planter's Wife* premiered in London's Leicester Square cinema. In California, three more films with Gopal in non-dance roles (*Outpost in Malaya*, *Elephant Walk* and *Purple Plain*) were shown. Gopal's first book on Indian dance (co-written with Serozh Dadachanji) was advertised and reviewed in the national press in 1951, and as was his autobiography and its book launch party, published six years later in 1957 (*Manchester Guardian*, December 1957). After Gopal's debut at Jacob's Pillow, USA, in 1954, a well-known children's writer, Regina J. Woody, wrote a book, 'Janey and the Summer Dance Camp' (1956) that told a fictional story of Janey visiting Jacob's Pillow and meeting the 'famous Indian dancer, Mr Ram Gopal' (1956: n.p.) who teaches her kathakali hand gestures. Beautifully illustrated by Arline K. Thomson, the book indicates the level of fame that Gopal had achieved in the United States as well as in Europe. In all these ways discussed above, Gopal not only accrued celebrity status in his own right but was becoming part of the popular imagination and culture. Through the critical coverage in the press, the promotion of performances and his films, interviews, public and television appearances, and what others say, a star persona (now understood as celebrity culture) emerges. As Richard Dyer notes, a 'star phenomenon consists of everything that is publicly available … star images are always extensive, multimedia, intertextual … Images have to be made' (2004 [1986]: 3–4). Star status is shown through an ability to transcend spatial constraints, an access to mobility with transnational travel and performances to international audiences and which brings social prestige and social and economic capital (Thiagarajan 2012).

Ballet connections

Gopal's knowledge of world cultures was extensive, and he took particular interest in the world of Russian ballet, a passion that led him to build an extensive collection of Russian dance sketches and lithographs.[18] He made annual pilgrimages to Diaghilev's Venetian grave, and he later worked with the Harlequin Ballet company in London in the 1960s. The world of dance is relatively small, so dancers working in different genres often were acquainted, valuing each other's expertise and friendships. Gopal mixed with many ballet stars and was good friends with Alicia Markova and Anton Dolin, for example. He knew those running significant ballet companies such as Ninette de Valois, and Marie Rambert and was recognized by all of them not just as an Indian dancer but an outstanding dancer per se. His fame during the late 1940s, 1950s and into the 1960s enabled him to mix with fruitfully in the word of arts and with those wholly involved in the dance scene.

The result of this is that Gopal appeared in many books on world dance and ballet in the 1940s and 1950s: Kay Ambrose's *Balletomane's Sketch-Book* (1941) displays several pages of photographer Baron's shots of Gopal, as well as her sketches in the wings of his 1939 performances. The *Ballet Annual* (1949) features Gopal as *Garuda* and Arnold L. Haskell's *Going to the Ballet* (1950) showed Gopal posing in his *Garuda* costume in black and white, whilst *Baron at the Ballet* (1950) has a full-page, colour photo of Gopal as *Garuda* (noted earlier). Cecil Beaton's book *Ballet* (1951) describes meeting Gopal with a black-and-white photo dancing on a Bombay beach. Further books and periodicals depicted Gopal in his other famous dances: Gordon Anthony's *Dancers of the World in Colour* (1953) featured Gopal in a Siva pose in colour, and in *Every Child's Book of Dance & Ballet* (1957) he is shown in his kathak costume for *The Legend of the Taj Mahal.* Houston Rogers's black-and-white photo occupies a whole page. Fernau Hall wrote four pages on Gopal and his company in *An Anatomy of Ballet* (1953). In 1959, photographer Mike Davis's book *Ballet in Camera* (1959) featured a written piece by Gopal on 'The Dance in India' with two black-and-white images from *The Legend of the Taj Mahal.* As late as 1980 Gopal appeared in ballet photographer Gordon Anthony's book *Dancers to*

[18] The collection was significant enough to be sold at Sotheby's on 13 March 1980 and suggested prices ranged from £50 for the smaller items to £25,000 for an oil painting of Marie Taglioni in *La Sylphide.* Included were caricatures and drawings of Diaghilev by Mikhail Larionov signed to Gopal, original costumes designs for Anna Pavlova, as well as lithographs of Fanny Elssler, Carlotta Grissi and Taglioni.

Remember: The Photographic Art of Gordon Anthony (1980) in a full-page black-and-white photo as *Siva*, as well as a short biography.

Ballet magazines also showcased Gopal. The *Dancing Times* (DT) reviewed all his main British performances and Gopal wrote several articles for DT and for *Dance & Dancers*. In the *Ballet* magazine, Gopal was regularly featured: in 1939 he scripted a two-page article on 'Training for the Hindu Dance'; this was followed in 1947 when he wrote a six-page article that included loosely crafted sketches of him by Milein Cosman and a photo of him in a Siva pose by Roger Wood. A three-page article 'Ram Gopal in Madras' was written by Bernard Peacock (January 1947). A further edition in April 1948 included 'Thoughts on Fokine and Ram Gopal', penned by Alfred W. Gent, and in 1951, Gopal appeared on the front cover again in Siva pose. The issues on 27 November and 11 December 1947 of *World Ballet News* ran front-page photos headlining 'Ram Gopal opens at the Prince's Theatre' and a feature titled 'Ram Gopal, an Ambassador of Indian Art' by Bernard Peacock. US magazine *Dance* ran a three-page article, 'Ram Gopal. Classic Hindu Dance' written by Leon Bruce. This extensive coverage indicates the extent of the general dance interest in Gopal's performances and his status in the world of arts during this time. In 1952 and 1953, Gopal published two articles in *Ballet Today*, 'Hindu Themes Have Influenced European Ballet – and Dancers' and 'Indian Dancers Should Learn European Teamwork', and in 1962, he wrote 'Eastern Dances for Western Dancers' for the DT.

Gopal's publications encapsulate his fascination for the classical forms of Indian dance and of ballet and his ideas of the advantages of a shared training, using the discipline of the ballet barre for Indian classes and the training in hand gestures and breath control from Indian dance for the ballet. Gopal cherished a vision of an East-West dance collaboration since the days of his first successful performances in 1939 and his return after the war. His love of ballet and appreciation of the great Russian dancers as noted meant he spoke at regular intervals of how he saw ballet and Indian dance working together. In 1947, newspapers reported on his desire 'to see the greatest authorities of the various schools of dancing in friendly discussions at the same table' (*Theatre World* November 1947). Gopal spoke to reporters then about his hope to establish a permanent centre of Indian culture in London and his decision to make London his base. He had always been happy to train Western dancers for his company, saying 'emphatically that British dancers and Europeans can not only learn the dance of India, but even surpass many aspirants in India itself' (Gopal 1962: 16).

Gopal's links to the world of ballet are numerous and I discuss his connections with Harlequin Ballet company and his famous partnership with Markova in Chapter 6. Gopal had watched Markova at the Metropolitan Opera House in New York dancing *Giselle* in the 1950s, and they had then discussed ideas for a collaboration, but only in 1960 was their visions for the *Radha-Krishna* duet realized. Both Markova and Anton Dolin were visitors to his 1939 London performances, and Nijinsky to the later London season in 1948, a meeting described in some detail by Gopal (1957). Gopal bought a book on Nijinsky in 1937 at station bookstall in Calcutta, which inspired him so much that he met with Nijinsky in his private box during the interval of the show. Knowing that Nijinsky was in the audience that night, Gopal remarked that he would dance especially for him, stating it was like dancing for Siva, the god of the dance. Gopal attended Nijinsky's funeral in London in April 1950 (he is named as one of the dance stars attending the graveside, *Leicester Evening Mail*, p. 12, 14 April 1950) and would regularly put flowers on his grave.[19] He describes the scene: 'Nijinsky was interred with the usual ceremony. The crowd departed. I had withdrawn a little distance under a tree. After the throng had disappeared, I approached and threw in a few handfuls of earth and softly laid flowers I had brought for his grave' (1957: 122). He speaks a heartfelt prayer to Nijinsky and leaves, later dreaming of him that night.

Gopal's love of ballet as described above, particularly the Russian ballet, was a powerful force in his creative thinking and inspiration in his dancing. He was taken to the Ajanta film studios in Bombay in the early 1930s to watch some Russian dancers filming there and was introduced to Victor E. Dandré, impresario and husband of Anna Pavlova. Dandré encouraged him to visit their lead dancer, Olga Spessiva, the next day at the Taj Mahal hotel where she was rehearsing in the large ballroom and she danced for him there. He was obviously somewhat enamoured by this beautiful ballet dancer, describing, 'And then she danced in her practice costume. Suddenly she became another woman. Her soul seemed to emerge from every movement and it seems to me that she smiled and danced with some invisible being with whom she moved with the most exquisite grace' (1957: 115–16).

[19] Nijinsky was buried in St. Marylebone Cemetery, Finchley, north London in 1950, in an unmarked grave, but after a fund was set up in Paris by dancer Serge Lifar, his body was exhumed in 1953 and reburied in Montmartre Cemetery, Paris.

Later in Paris in 1938 he met Princess Krainsky Kshesinskaya, a prima ballerina assoluta of Russian ballet at her studio there.[20] Gopal states that she had danced with Nijinsky. Further Russian ballet connections in 1954–5 are evident when Gopal made several visits to the London Diaghilev exhibition at Forbes House, Hyde Park, with Ballets Russes dancer Tamara Karsavina and was invited along with other dancers Dolin, Markova and Karsavina to give one of the exhibition talks.[21] Gopal's presentation was 'The Dance as Yoga' (*Observer*, 9 January 1955: 8). Gopal writes of how he and several Indian dancers, Shankar, Menaka and Devi, took inspiration from Pavlova's dancing, stating that Pavlova 'wove her enchantment in India and the Far East as far as Japan, in addition to conquering the entire Western world' (1957: 118). *The Times* newspaper carries information about a tribute performance on 23 January 1955 at the Stoll Theatre, London, to commemorate the twenty-fifth anniversary of Pavlova's death and the proceeds distributed to dance charities. Organized by Gorlinksy, who invited Gopal to perform along with Margot Fonteyn, Markova and Dolin, Michael Somes, and many other international ballet dancers, the programme also included a talk by Dame Ninette de Valois on 'The Art of Anna Pavlova'.

Karsavina became a good friend. Gopal recounts (1952: 7) how she came backstage after a performance in 1948 and told him that when she and Nijinsky were dancing Fokine's *Le Dieu Bleu* (1912), a ballet of Krishna and his consort, that she wished that they had been able to see Gopal dancing the role, as they 'had to work out from photos, museums and their own imagination, the various attitudes and movements of their dance'. In 1950 Gopal visited the Legat School of Russian Ballet School in Tunbridge Wells, Kent, to talk with Madame Legat, the owner and director of the school, whom he knew well. He writes of how he believed Nijinsky had had some training in breath control from his teacher Nicholas Legat, because of Nijinsky's famous jumps and seeming suspension in the air (1952: 7). The year 1959 saw Gopal perform in a programme titled *Trio de Ballet* with classical ballet dancers Alex Rassine and Marina Svetlova, touring for over four weeks to Liverpool, Edinburgh, Glasgow and Newcastle. The evening

[20] Known in the West as Mathilde Kschessinska or Matilda Kshesinskaya, she was born in Poland in 1872.

[21] Mounted by Richard Buckle and attracting 140,000 visitors with over 40,000 catalogues sold. It ran in London and then transferred to the Edinburgh Festival. See https://www.vam.ac.uk/blog/diaghilev-and-ballets-russes/diaghilev-1954-again-times-change (accessed 16 August 2021).

was a compilation of ballet duets and ballet solos, interspersed with Gopal's Indian solo items, including *Rajput Serenade*, *Hunter in a Forest*, *Krishna Tillana* and *Dance of the Setting Sun.*

Gopal also met ballet dancer Serge Lifar during his first trip to Paris in 1938 (see Chapter 1) and he was asked to perform at a special gala benefit performance for Nijinsky in Paris on 28 June 1939 at the Louvre that Lifar was organizing. The *Gala de Danse* was part of a grand retrospective exhibition on the Ballets Russes and Diaghilev at the Musée des Arts Décoratifs and amongst the list of dancers appearing alongside Gopal were Lifar and Dolin.[22] Later Gopal featured in the *Illustrated London News* when he attended the opening night of the Bolshoi Ballet's performance in London in October 1956. He is pictured looking glamorous in a gold silk Nehru jacket standing next to elegant film star Vivien Leigh, sporting a fur stole. The *Illustrated London News* reported that the 'distinguished audience, which included the Prime Minister and Lady Eden, gave the great ballet company an almost overwhelming reception' (13 October 1956: 599). Present too were dancers Beryl Grey, Pamela May, Moira Shearer, Margot Fonteyn and Alicia Markova amongst many others, dressed in dazzling evening dresses and fur stoles.

Illustrated by Gopal's presence at these grand openings and his growing fame in popular culture outside of the dance world, the 1947 printed programme underscores Gopal's significant place as a performer in the years after the Second World War, exemplifying his numerous programmes of British and European tours of this period. As Reginald Massey wrote, '[m]oreover Ram Gopal, throughout his long stay in Britain, has done much towards spreading the interest in Indian dance' (1969: 369).

[22] Patrizia Veroli writes how this was the 'first significant celebration of the impresario. No fewer than 532 objects were assembled, including 362 watercolours, gouaches, drawings, paintings and engravings, eleven décors and backcloths, twenty-eight sculptures, twelve playbills, sixty-one books, thirty-six scores, and twenty-six letters'. The patron for the event was the Prince of Monaco and the French Ministry of National Education (2014: 118).

5

Film and static images

Artists' impressions

What remains as a rich legacy of Gopal's dancing is captured on film, in photographic images, paintings, sculpture and his own written notations. Images of him abound in the archives of many leading society photographers from Britain, the United States and Europe – an extensive list that includes the well-known names of Cecil Beaton, Carl Van Vechten, Angus McBean and Baron amongst others. This chapter takes as its starting point one of the lively, fresh, sketched watercolours of Gopal, drawn in the wings and dressing rooms of his shows in London in 1939 by artist Feliks Topolski, and investigates the extensive range of artistic images made of Gopal in the various mediums named above.[1] Questions about representation through images are addressed by interrogating the manipulation, exoticization and representation onstage of the racialized body. I examine the impact of such imagery by artists on Gopal's career as well as the way he exploited its effect and question how it may have influenced audience perceptions of Gopal. Created imagery is of course essential to a performing artist in constructing the public, performing persona. As noted earlier, Gopal took great pride in his appearance both on and off stage, and it is evident that from the onset of his career in 1936, photographic imagery and film were to play a significant part in his huge success as an artist.

The twelve delightful watercolour sketches created by Topolski in 1939 are held in the collection of the British Museum (BM), London, although not on public display.[2] Topolski later created a life-size oil painting of Gopal, flamboyant

1 Almost certainly these were the performances at the Aldwych Theatre, London, during late July and early August in 1939, made over several performances and possibly at rehearsals.

2 My sincere thanks to Richard Blurton, former assistant keeper, Department of Asia at the British Museum, for allowing me to view these artefacts. Blurton was instrumental in their procurement for the museum in 2006 from an art dealer who purchased them from Gopal's estate at his death.

and colourful, now on show at the National Portrait Gallery, London. Polish-born Topolski, who studied at the Warsaw Academy of Art, arrived in London in 1935 to illustrate the Silver Jubilee celebrations of King George V for the Polish newspapers. He was never without a sketchbook, drawing rapidly in pencil, crayon or pen at every opportunity, with barely a glance at the paper. His son Dan Topolski, speaking in 2010 at Gresham College, London, about his father's work, noted his 'true and honest depictions were stunningly accurate, infused with movement, humour and compassion and performed with deceptive ease'.[3] Topolski loved London life and, as war broke out, decided to stay and became an official war artist for the British government and the Polish government in exile, travelling all over the world for his work. He then took British citizenship in 1947 at the end of the war.

The small watercolours are drawn in a swift, flowing, impressionistic style that brings a lively vigour, capturing the essence of the moments of performance without being concerned with detail. Sketched in pen with an additional loose wash of watercolour, predominately using grey, black and sepia, and occasional dramatic magenta and delicate pale blue for some of the costumes, the paintings evoke backstage and frontstage views. Four of the sketches reveal Topolski's place in the wings, looking onto the stage where Gopal is performing. These particular ones illustrate the drummer sitting on stage left, the large standing spotlights in the wings and Gopal's close friend and manager, Janta, watching. Four more focus on Gopal as he is performing on stage, facing the audience and are drawn from the stalls or in rehearsal. The images reveal Gopal's costumes, depicting his solo kathakali dances of *Sandhya Nrittya* (*Dance of the Setting Sun*) and the *Cobra Devil Dance*, as well as the kathak *Moghul Court Dance*. Another three of the small drawings create the intimacy of the dressing room, where Gopal is shown relaxing between items, sitting looking into a small hand-held mirror, in another tying on his ankle bells. A final sketch depicts Gopal wearing a smart Nehru jacket and gazing pensively away from the artist. Topolski wrote, 'I simply have a passion for experiencing my life with a pencil. I try to submit myself to the events I witness, and my hand starts doing the work.'[4]

All twelve watercolours are delightful. For discussion, I have selected one that expertly and brilliantly captures Gopal's projected persona of a certain fluid

[3] Gresham College was founded in 1597 and has been providing free lectures within the City of London for over 400 years. Dan Topolski's lecture 'Feliks Topolski: Eye Witness to the 20th Century' was given on 22 March 2010. It can be watched here: https://www.gresham.ac.uk/lectures-and-events/feliks-topolski-eye-witness-to-the-20th-century (accessed 11 August 2019).

[4] Quoted on https://culture.pl/en/artist/feliks-topolski (accessed 11 August 2019).

sexuality and studied attractiveness. He sits in his dressing room, costumed for his dance of Siva, headdress in position and earrings dangling, jewellery on his arms and round his neck and bare chest. The small, short loin-cloth-type costume is softly drawn and shows the decorative belt around his waist. Gopal leans back, his hand placed carefully on his thigh, gazing into a hand-held mirror and absorbed in his own reflection. His head, make-up and headdress are drawn in careful detail; the rest is quickly and lightly sketched in brown sepia pen. A wash of dark grey background accentuates his sitting figure, poised before performance, immersed in his thoughts. Signed with a simple F. T., the drawing conjures a seductive figure, self-confident and self-contained in the world of the dancing deity, the *Siva Nataraj*, knowingly conscious of his beauty and power of allurement.

Figure 16 Sketch of Ram Gopal in his dressing room by Feliks Topolski, 1939. © British Museum.

Gopal's relationship with visual artists continued throughout his career. Not only was Topolski present in the wings at the Aldwych, but also artist Kay Ambrose, who joined him for these performances and later appearances at the Vaudeville Theatre. Ambrose was already working with Haskell on a book, *Balletomane's Sketchbook* (1941), and was a familiar figure backstage at dance performances in London.[5] She had studied art at Reading University and had been fascinated by dance from a young age. Ambrose became a close friend, taking on the role of Gopal's tour manager and artistic director between 1947 and 1948 on several British and European tours, and accompanying him to India in 1949. In this early period, another artist American Thomas Handforth made several drawings and posed photographs of Gopal in Tokyo in 1937. Selected drawings by Handforth were used for Gopal's publicity and printed programmes on the first US tour in Hawaii and New York. Janta mentions that Handforth was instrumental in the decision to go to the United States, stating,

> And it was Tom who has thrown a suggestion into the dilemmas I had at the time … [He said] 'Instead of going on a trip to India with uncertain outcome, show Rama in America. If he makes it there, you will conquer the rest of the world.' He also supported his idea with a promise of connecting me with influential friends he had in Hollywood and New York.
>
> (1970: 6–7 [transl. Garapich])

Janta called him 'a master of master of pencil and stylus. Anyone interested will find his copperplates with urban scenes from Peking, portraits or artists, street performers, athletes, riders, jugglers and soldiers from Mongolia, the world discovered and drawn by his skilled hand' (1970: 6 [transl. Garapich]). Handforth had been staying with Janta in Tokyo and lived for some time in China which had influenced his technique and style.

Ambrose published drawings of Gopal's dance movements in the book she wrote with Gopal, *Classical Dances & Costumes of India* (1950). They are loosely drawn figures, full of life, but capturing the movement and detail, some in ink and some in pencil – a kind of graphic, visual notation. In these line drawings Ambrose records items from Gopal's bharatanatyam repertoire – a whole sequence of *alarippu*, some *adavu-jethis*, the first part of Gopal's *Natanam Adinar* and the choreographic floor patterns of his *tillana*. She features his kathakali work in carefully executed drawings of basic postures, in the *Sari dance* and in

[5] This was followed by *The Ballet-Lover's Pocket-Book* (1943) and *The Ballet-Lover's Companion* (1951a) amongst others.

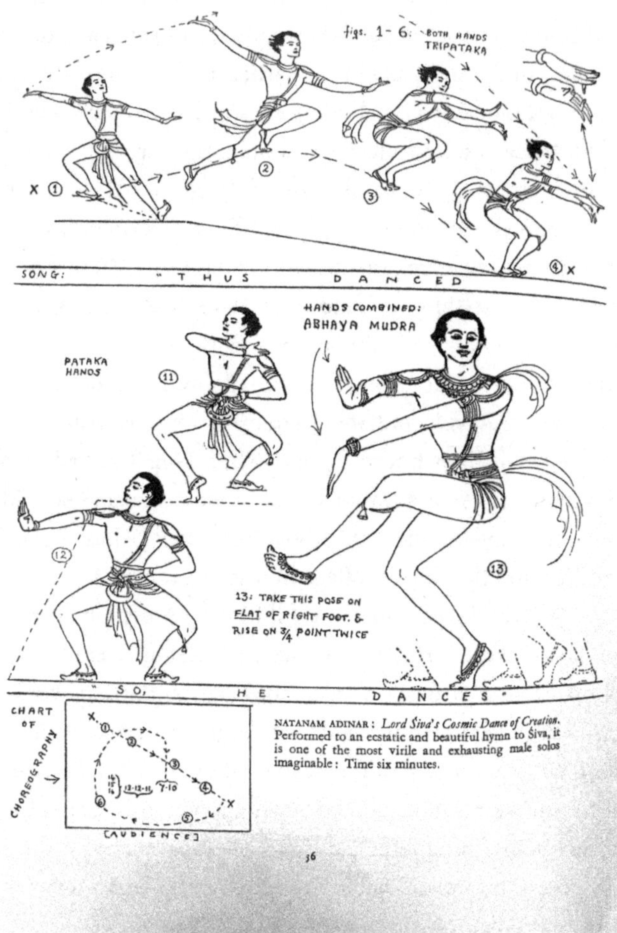

Figure 17 Drawings of Ram Gopal as Siva by Kay Ambrose, *Classical Dances & Costumes of India* (1950).

a small section of his famous *Garuda* piece showing his huge, airborne leaps. Sketches of Gopal's hand gestures, his depiction of the nine *rasas*, costumes, musical instruments and other Indian folk styles dance out of the pages of the book. Other quick drawings are deliberately witty, offering a wry take on London's dance audiences. A pencil drawing titled 'Bangalore meets Bayswater' shows Gopal peering out of his dressing room door to a long queue of people waiting to see him, dressed in suits, tiaras and fox furs.

Supplementing Ambrose's rich and artistic records in this book are four black-and-white photos of Gopal and one of Retna Mohini by dance photographer Baron, several black-and-white photos by Denis de Marney as well as other photos by unnamed photographers. Several of Ambrose's sketches of Gopal in his *Cobra Devil Dance* and his Javanese duet with Mohini appear alongside drawings of other dancers in the company in her earlier book on the ballet (1941). As well as Ambrose's notations of Gopal's dances, some of Gopal's own hand-written notebooks of dance notation survive, although they are not publicly available.

Many other artists drew, painted or sculpted Gopal during his career, in addition to Topolski, Ambrose and Handforth. German-born artist Milein Cosman (born Emilie Cosmann) came to Britain in 1939 to study at the Slade School of Fine Art, settling in London in 1946. She drew sketches of Gopal's performances in London in 1939 and her work was used for the cover of his Princes Theatre programme in 1950. Small bronze sculptures of Gopal in his famous roles of *Garuda* and *Siva* were made by artist Annette Rowdon (née Fischer of the publishing house family) when Gopal stayed at her house in Fulham, London. Her sculptural pieces of other dancers (Alicia Markova) and well-known musicians are now in private collections, and at the Royal Opera House, London, and the Royal College of Music, London.[6] *The New York Times*, 18 February 1947, carries notice of an exhibition by American modernist sculptor Richmond Barthé at the 57th Street branch of the Grand Central Galleries, which featured Gopal amongst other dancers and actors. Barthé's work is housed in the collection of the Smithsonian and was exhibited at major sites including the Rockefeller Center and the World Fair in Chicago in 1933. He had many public sculptural commissions in the United States and in Jamaica after he moved there in 1950. Other artists producing paintings of Gopal included French artist and fashion designer Jean-Denis Maillart and Russian-born Marevna.

Through the camera lens

In Gopal's debut American tour of 1938, Hollywood photographer George Hurrell captured studio photos of him, and the fact that Hurrell wanted to shoot Gopal revealed the iconic status he had already attained there. Hurrell was one of the creators of the Hollywood glamour portrait that abandoned the conventional soft focus and replaced it with a sharp, dramatic look and his signature black-and-white photos include film stars such as Bette David, Joan Crawford, Jane Russell and Marlene Dietrich. It was a bold new style in which movie stars and dancers were idealized, glamorized and ultimately turned into icons. Firstly a

[6] Thanks to Rowdon's friend Peter Hartley who sent me this information (2019).

painter, Hurrell became head of the portrait photography department at MGM in the late 1920s giving him access to all the Hollywood film stars; he stayed for a few years and then left to set up his own studio on Sunset Boulevard. Hurrell took images of Gopal in Los Angeles and a decade later in New York in 1948, where he was then working. These included the *Dance of Siva*, with its original headdress, languid reclining shots of Gopal in costume as well as his *King Klana* Javanese dance piece (see Beginnings chapter for image). There are some photos of Gopal in his first *Garuda* eagle costume.[7] During his time in Hollywood, Gopal was also painted by well-known German-born actor and portrait artist Martin Kosleck. Kosleck's painting of Gopal in his Siva costume is on the front of Janta's 1970 book *Pamietnik Indyjski* [Indian Diary].

American photographer and writer Carl Van Vechten undertook a two-day shoot of Gopal on 21 April and 11 May 1938 in his apartment/studio in New York, producing some stunning, suggestively homoerotic photos of him. Van Vechten, renowned for his nude photographic work of African American men and whose collections of photographs are now in the Yale Beinecke Rare Book and Manuscript library, and the Library of Congress, took over 100 shots of Gopal and several of Janta in those two-day sittings. His makeshift studio in his New York apartment served as his professional setting, using a variety of background drapes and his precious Leica camera. Ven Vechten began his photography work in the early 1930s so at this time was still experimenting with style, setting and modes of capture. A dance lover who frequented performances, Van Vechten was also an established critic and author, writing reviews for the *New York Times* in the 1920s–30s of performances by Loie Fuller, Isadora Duncan, Anna Pavlova and the Russian Ballet. He attended Gopal's New York debut performance and wrote, somewhat romantically, 'Ram Gopal … bears us away with him from the untruths of everyday life into the reality of his mystic visions' (cited in Gopal 1957: 63) – a comment that was to predict the exoticized lens through which his camera turned to view Gopal.

Ajay Sinha's contemporary project (2017, 2022) on Carl Van Vechten's collected work held in the Yale Beinecke collection examines the type of gaze placed on subjects such as Gopal, a gaze that was without doubt homoerotic, as well as a glamourous and mysterious one. Sinha artfully describes one of the poses:

> Standing in front of the camera, Ram Gopal produces an arrangement of decorative outlines, accented by bold armbands, chest ornaments, and a wired

[7] Four of these photos are held in the collection of the National Portrait Gallery, London. Gopal's *Garuda* costume had several iterations.

> tiara that curls out into tendrils on either side of his ears. What eroticizes the decorative silhouette is the photograph. Raking light sculpts out the musculature of the youthful dancer. On the right, the figure melts into the glow of the background curtain. The satiny fabric reflects the softness of his skin; shadows flicker across the columnar folds like a ghostly double of the body. The camera brings the luminous, pulsating composition into a tight focus.
>
> (Sinha 2017: 3)

Sinha concludes that the gaze is one that is mutually constructed, with Gopal seemingly complicit in the homoerotic undertones, stating that 'the Yale photograph is "particularized evidence" of a brief moment when the Indian dancer's self-presentation and the interracial, homoerotic gaze of the American photographer meet and activate transcultural fantasies of each other' (Sinha 2017: 6). Van Vechten included several carefully posed shots of Gopal and Janta in their formal suits and physically sitting close with bodies touching. In some they are looking at the camera, with Gopal sitting slightly in front. One photo shows Gopal looking back at Janta, eyes shining and smiling whilst Janta holds his gaze tenderly, lovingly. Further photos of Janta, dressed in Gopal's costumes, add to the collection.

The series taken by Van Vechten of Gopal is eclectic, illustrating how experimental his work was at this stage. In several photos he plays with the image, in one double exposing the shot, so Gopal's legs are repeated at the top of the frame as in a mirror image and obscuring the body; in another, Janta's arms are seen protruding through a draped curtain giving Gopal the appearance of four arms like a sculpted deity. Several photos are taken of Gopal in double-breasted suit, white shirt and tie; some are solo, and others as noted are with Janta. Van Vechten also took three solo portrait shots of Janta. The remainder of the collection contains photos of Gopal posing in different costumes, some with elaborate Siva headdresses and others without, and much dramatic jewellery on show.

Two photos are especially conspicuous: one is a close frame of Gopal's feet and legs on a pedestal. It is either a static pose in *kuttanam* or is part of a movement, *kuditta mettu adavu* where in a small jump onto a half-toe position, the heels are raised off the ground and then brought down. Gopal wears metal snake ankle bracelets on each leg, the photo emphasizing the strength of his lower body. The second depicts Gopal looking down, hands in prayer position (*anjali*), dressed his Siva costume and a thin, gossamer, transparent scarf draped across his arms and body creating a delicate and androgynous look. Only the top half of Gopal's body is shown. Mystery, fluidity and beauty shout out from the camera's

Figure 18 Photo of Ram Gopal Carl by Carl Van Vechten, New York 1938. © The Carl Van Vechten Trust.

gaze. As Sinha points out, Gopal 'thus, through cross-dressing, … accentuates his androgyny toward a veiled, feminine, Salomé-like figure, borrowing from American women dancers such as Isadora Duncan and Ruth St. Denis' (2017: n.p.). The creative, somewhat transgressive atmosphere of these photographic shoots is described by biographer Edward White, who writes of Van Vechten,

> At apartment 7D his shooting space was small and quickly became hot under the studio lights. In coming years he moved to larger premises, but in all his studios there was a closeness, an atmosphere of emotional intimacy. All around lay the clutter of Van Vechten's props and backdrops – crumpled sheets of colored cellophane, posters, rugs, African sculptures, floral wallpaper. To the sitters who arrived this was clearly neither an artist's workroom nor the studio of a commercial artist but the den of an obsessive hobbyist.
>
> (White 2014: 263)

Other celebrity photographers keen to capture Gopal followed. Cecil Beaton, commissioned during the Second World War as a war artist, and later very prominent as a celebrity photographer, took hundreds of photos in India and Burma. In 1944 during a two-day shoot, he photographed Gopal on the shore close to Bombay, near Government House. From this he selected twenty-eight black-and-white shots to be part of the British Official photographs of India during the war. Placing Gopal within such a significant photographic war record endorses the notion of his being the 'jewel in the crown' of Britain's empire, or as Naseem Khan rather wryly pointed out, 'he was the acceptable face of the empire' (interview 2017b). Housed now in the Imperial War Museum archives in London, the prints made from Beaton's negatives are 150 centimetre square, with no frame or border. All are captioned and dated with the year (although some captions have been lost).

Of the selected Beaton photos now in the archive, eight are of Gopal in dance poses. Although the colour is not shown, Beaton records that he is wearing a 'traditional costume in magenta and gold' (photo captions). Gopal has a bare chest and is costumed in a printed silk dhoti, pleated in the front and worn to his ankles. His dance bells peep out from the folds of the silk fabric. He has on a triple layered jewelled necklace, connected to a decorative chest piece, a large ornate belt, and bracelets on his wrists and upper arms. Large rings adorn his fingers. Unusually, Gopal is not wearing a headdress, so his full head of longish hair blows luxuriously in the breeze. One close-up taken on the beach and showing Gopal's full body in bharatanatyam dance pose is featured on the front cover of this book. In it, Gopal stands with his left foot crossed over his right. Both hands are outstretched, taking *alapadma hasta* (open lotus), with the right hand down by his side and the left held high, creating an aesthetic line of powerful static movement through the arms and outstretched fingers. Clearly here is a type of hypermasculinity, trained onto his beautiful, biracial body by the hereditary teachers. Gopal stands erect, looking down at the lotus flower on his right. The light plays on his right side whilst the rest of the body is almost in silhouette. It is a sculptural, extended, regal pose. Taken from below and revealing the expanse of sea behind, the photo captures a sublime, serene moment.

Nine photos in this collection of Gopal on the beach are framed by the presence of a young boy, a pupil from his Bangalore dance school. In some shots, they move in unison, with Gopal foregrounded, positioned for the start of *alarippu*. In others, the boy takes an alternative static pose in contrast to Gopal. He wears a simple, plain white tied dhoti with ornate belt, necklace and body ornament. Six of the photos feature Gopal, the boy and one of Gopal's musicians, who plays cymbals and is singing the rhythmic dance syllables (*nattuvangam*). These images reveal the symbiotic relationship of music, dance and rhythm. Beaton wrote of this photo shoot,

> In Bombay I was fortunate enough to meet Ram Gopal and on several occasions he organised a private performance for me in which he and his assistants evoked the traditional dances that are based on the poses in the sculptures of the Caves of Ellora. One of the most beautiful sights I could ever see was staged when Gopal and his young accomplices performed their ritual dances on the flat rocks at the edge of the Arabian Ocean.
>
> (Beaton 1951: 63)

In Beaton's *Indian Diary and Album* (1991 [1945]), one photo of Gopal and one of his students are included but with Gopal's name misspelt and no commentary. The same photo of Gopal's student appears on the cover. Another shot of Gopal is included in *Beaton Portraits* (2004), with the same photo appearing again in the Imperial War Museum's publication, *Theatre of War* (2012). Beaton, additionally famous for his film and stage designing, worked extensively in dance with ballet dancer and choreographer Frederick Ashton. He created sets for Ashton's *Apparitions* (1936) for the Vic-Wells Ballet and for the Royal Ballet and designed Ashton's *Les Sirènes* (1946) and *Marguerite and Armand* (1973). His other collaborations with Ashton included *Illuminations* (1950) and *Picnic at Tintagel* (1952) for New York City Ballet and *Casse Noisette* (1951) for Sadler's Wells Theatre Ballet (later Birmingham Royal Ballet). Beaton also worked on *Turandot* (1961) for the Royal Opera (originally produced by the Metropolitan Opera, New York).[8] This significant work in ballet indicates the sensitivity Beaton had for capturing and designing for dance movement.

Gopal's own extensive collection of images from performance also exists. Some of these images are now in individual holdings, others are in private archives and the rest in accessible archives such as the one created for South Asian Diaspora Arts Archive (SADAA).[9] The many photos of Gopal featured in ballet material and taken by ballet photographers were discussed in the previous chapter. Controlling the public image was an essential part of his artistic aesthetic sensitivity, so photos in this collection are retouched to enhance his body, making

[8] For further details of these design commissions, see http://www.roh.org.uk/people/cecil-beaton (accessed 6 May 2019).

[9] SADAA at https://sadaa.co.uk (accessed 18 March 2020). I was instrumental in helping establish this Ram Gopal archive at SADAA.

the lines slimmer or clearer, as many artists would do. Photographers specializing in the world of dance, ballet, fashion and performance who took shots of Gopal's performances who are not discussed in detail here include Gordon Anthony (brother of Dame Ninette de Valois, founder of the Royal Ballet), Baron, Henri Cartier Bresson, Mike Davis, Sture Ekstrand,[10] Francis Goodman,[11] Frank Herrmann, Stanley Jepson,[12] Angus McBean, Houston Rogers and Roger Wood. Contemporary photographers Clive Boursnell and Vipul Sangoi captured Gopal in his later years. Many professional studios were involved in photographing Gopal over his years of performances and include Studio Vivienne, London; Madame D'Ora, Paris; Studio Iris, Paris; and Erica, London.[13] The photographs, drawings and sketches discussed above provide further sources of legacies for today's dancers, teachers and dance historians, with Gopal's own body and the diverse images providing a rich repository of information. They create a greater sense of the reality, immediacy and dynamism of the dancing body that sadly in performance remains quite ephemeral.

Filmic evidence

Several professional films were made of Gopal dancing.[14] Some early, undated 8 mm film footage in poor quality showing Gopal dancing on the rooftop terrace of his family home, Torquay Castle, was salvaged by Bangalore filmmaker Ayisha Abraham.[15] Recorded on one reel by amateur filmmaker Tom D'Aguiar the eight-minute clip was spliced into two. D'Aguiar's film of Gopal, on rusty spools and in a plastic bag, was fungus-ridden and had badly deteriorated but were found by D'Aguiar's children when he died and was given to Abraham. Abraham tells how she had met Anglo-Indian D'Aguiar when he was in his nineties, still with a very clear memory of the past. D'Aguiar, an amateur photographer and

[10] Swedish photographer Ekstrand has one photo of Gopal in the National Portrait Gallery, London, and many more in archives in Sweden. Photographer Sune Sundhal took a series of photos of Gopal and company whilst touring in Sweden. These are held at the Arckitekhur-och designcentrum, Stockholm.

[11] Goodman's images of Gopal at the 1947 performance at the V&A, London, are held in National Portrait Gallery, London.

[12] There are two black-and-white shots taken in India by Jepson, undated and part of the Newsome-Glenn Collection in the British Library, London.

[13] The lists of photographers and studios are not exhaustive.

[14] See also Appendix 2.

[15] Abraham suggests it was filmed in 1938. Examining the footage, I propose it could be slightly later, perhaps filmed during Gopal's return to Bangalore during the war period, in 1940–1 when he had started his dance school.

filmmaker was one of the first to produce colour prints which Gopal saw at a national exhibition in Bangalore. He asked D'Aguiar to film him dancing as he had never seen his colour images on screen.[16]

D'Aguiar's silent film concentrates on Gopal's performance of different hand positions (*hastas*) in kathakali style. Dressed in a kathak-style costume (Mughal coat and loose trousers) and wearing a turban, necklace, rings and earrings, Gopal is accompanied by two of his male dancers, mostly there to frame and highlight his movements. Chests bare, they wear tied dhotis with jewellery and large decorative headdresses. For most of the film, they are kneeling either side of Gopal, with hands in *anjali* (prayer position). Gopal mimes the lotus opening and then shows a bee taking pollen from the flower. D'Aguiar edits in shots of butterflies flying and a lily opening from his own fishpond to indicate the movements Gopal is making. Next Gopal illustrates a fish swimming and then depicts in mime a beautiful woman with large eyes, long hair and curvaceous figure. He shows an elephant waving its trunk and ears, which D'Aguiar follows with a shot of a small elephant model, placed imaginatively in front of some foliage.

Next comes the *hasta* for birds flying; after this, Gopal looks seductively at the camera, arms folded in front, demonstrating his neck and eye movements. All the hand movements are clear and expressive; he has, without doubt, beautiful *abhinaya*. The camera pans to six male musicians sitting in the sunshine, lingering in close-up over their instruments which include the *jaltarang*, flute, *tabla*, *sarangi*, harmonium and *nattavangam*. It is unclear whether this is a film of Gopal's orchestra at his house or whether D'Aguiar has edited this in. The film returns to the balcony where Gopal now performs certain kathak movements with the dancers on each side. Other local bungalows and trees can be seen behind the wall of the roof terrace as the three dancers start to move together, the men making serpentine arms as Gopal completes his kathak arm positions. There is some hint of the colour that must have been there in the original.

When Abraham first viewed D'Aguiar's film, she recalled how 'age marks the film and makes it fragile and faltering as the light falls upon it' (2013: 173). She interspersed the Gopal film fragments with his recorded voice, with other photos and film (especially parts of Claude Lamorisse's *Aum Siva*) and

[16] D'Aguiar was an engineer with the Colonial British Post and Telegraph Department (Abraham 2013). He belonged to the Mysore Photographic Society, enjoying photography more than film-making. He edited his films and made his colour prints at home (Abraham 2008). There appear to be two different spelling of his name – Ayisha uses D'Aguir, but he is usually found under D'Aguiar.

comments from dancers, playfully constructing *I Saw a God Dance* (2012), a 'more linear documentary style biopic' (2013) that runs for just under twenty minutes. Writing about her experimental creative techniques she stated, 'In my practice, I try to collate disparate shards of found footage together to see how they work side by side. The categories of time, movement, memory, reflect the trajectories in which the films made from this found footage can be interpreted' (2013: 169–70).

Later, in 1947 Gopal was filmed dancing at the opening of a new sculptural exhibition in the revamped Indian section of the V&A Museum in London on his return to Britain after the war. As noted in Chapter 3, there is some Pathé News footage of the event, but it is in black and white and without sound. The edited excerpts run for 4.16 and 1.34 minutes respectively and only show short pieces of different dances with some repetition. Gopal is dressed in his Siva costume (see Chapter 2), with the spectacular headdress. The longer section begins with Gopal performing kathak movements, followed by dramatic kathakali eye movements and posed in front of the large sculpture of the dancing Siva Nataraj. Next two female saree-clad dancers perform a folk dance and then Gopal and Rajeshwar dance *alarippu* in front of the Nataraj. An excerpt of his *Dance of the Setting Sun* follows, and the film ends with Gopal and Shevanti in a Siva/Parvati pose, again in front of the Nataraj, whilst the two female dancers continue their folk movements, framing the standing pair. The camera pans to the Indian sculptures in the gallery to complete the final shot. The second, much shorter clip includes movements from Gopal's *tillana*, and some kathakali hand gestures depicting the lotus and the bee and a bow and arrow. In these close-up shots Gopal is wearing the extended, dramatic kathakali finger coverings on his left hand. The short film clips and the press photos indicate how Gopal played with a sense of exoticism and of his own beauty, reclining languidly, one leg over the other in front of one of the sculptures, eyes cast down pensively, as if one of the sculptures was alive and breathing.

The following year, film director Sarah Erulkar created a twenty-three-minute documentary on Gopal, *Lord Siva Danced* (1948), filmed at Central Film Studios in Bombay with additional shots in London (see Chapter 2); some of the dance clips from this documentary are utilized in the later documentary made in 1989 noted below. Reviewed favourably in the film magazine *Look and Listen* (1951) and in *Documentary Film News* (1958) this 1948 film was shown at the Edinburgh Festival. *Look and Listen* described, 'Ram Gopal and his company, presents a short introduction to Indian classical dancing. It was most praiseworthy to begin by revealing the religious origin of the dances, but the film does linger rather too long on figures of the Hindu gods, while a clear exposition would have been much more instructive than the abstruse lyricism of parts of the commentary' (Moore 1951: 257).

Dance ethnologist Allegra Fuller Snyder wrote later of this same film, 'Ram Gopal and company, with Shevanti, in one of the great ethnic dance documentaries. Six dances illustrate the major dance techniques of India. One of the highlights of the film is the appearance of Gopal's aged guru, Chandupanikar, in a Kathakali dance depicting a jungle fight between an elephant, a cobra and a tiger' (1980: 109). I have viewed this film twice, once at a showing and discussion with Erulkar at the Nehru Centre, London (2004), and later at the British Film Institute where it is held in the archives. None of the supporting cast are named in the credits for the film but certain artists can be recognized. Rajeshwar is featured in the opening dance, performing *alarippu*, followed by a demonstration of bharatanatyam steps and the Siva dance of *Natanam Adinar.* For these pieces, he wears a costume similar to Gopal's, a gold coloured, short, loin-cloth-type garment with pleated front, large necklace and armbands and bells. Dances of Manipur are performed by Shevanti and kathak by Kumudini. As a finale, Gopal performs his Siva *Dance of the Setting Sun*.

Film footage of Gopal performing at Jacob's Pillow in 1954 made by Carol Lynn is held in the archives at Jacob's Pillow as well as a videotape copy in the collection of the New York Public Library Dance Collection (see Chapter 4).[17] Lynn, a former Jacob's Pillow student and later associate director of Jacob's Pillow dance school and festival from 1943 to 1960, was given permission by Ted Shawn post–Second World War 'to begin filming performances in the new Ted Shawn Theater, at her own expense', records archivist Norton Owen (2002: 64). Between 1945 and 1962 she captured the US debuts of Ballet Rambert and the National Ballet of Canada as well as rare footage of Gopal and Pearl Primus amongst others (2002). Lynn recorded the sixteen-minute-long film of Gopal in black and white, with no sound, on 16 mm film stock.[18]

Chapter 4 examines the *Garuda* footage from this film and notes the other items that Gopal danced: *Poem*, *Tillana*, *Dance of the Setting Sun* and *Rajput Serenade*. In the first piece (just thirty-eight seconds) Gopal is seen reciting a

[17] Gopal performed in a mixed bill running from 11–14 August. He gave a lecture/demonstration on 6 August and then further performances on 3–4 September that year. He appeared again at the Jacob's Pillow summer festival in 1958 during 15–19 July.

[18] It is likely that this was filmed either at dress rehearsals or in a dedicated session rather than at a live performance. This film was digitized a few years ago (personal communication between author and Norton Owen, 4 September 2021).

poem and depicting through hand gestures bees flying, fish, water and Krishna playing the flute. He wears a large open shawl over his costume, a pleated silk dhoti. It is followed by *tillana*, a fast bharatanatyam item that often closes a programme, described here in the programme as '[a] pure rhythmic dance of Shri Krishna who does this dance of love for Radha and the Gopis' and running for two minutes in the film. Next is his famous *Dance of the Setting Sun* (three minutes length) but is unfortunately cut before the final end position of the performance. The recording may also have been edited as this dance was usually four and half minutes long. Before the final *Garuda* dance, Gopal performs his kathak *Rajput Serenade*, a delightful, short piece showing kathak turns and steps, described simply as '[a] Prince awaits the arrival of his Princess'. He wears a turban, leggings and a belted, flared Mughal style coat/dress. The ending to the dance is cut and so finishes rather abruptly. Despite the poor film quality and the unfortunate editing, it is remarkable to have some footage of Gopal's dances at Jacob's Pillow, filmed almost seventy years ago.

Gopal's close friend, the filmmaker Claude Lamorisse created two films of him, *Aum Shiva*, alternative title *The World of Ram*, released in 1970 and a second film in 1973 called *Nataraj: King of Dance*. Both were created by her own Aristo production company and are regrettably no longer available, although excerpts from these films have been used in a later documentary as I note below.[19] The films were made on 16 mm film stock and in colour. *Aum Shiva* (eighty minutes) features Gopal's choreography and narration by actor Patrick Allen and Gopal; it was screened at London's Commonwealth Institute in the early 1970s. Filmed when Gopal was in his late fifties, the dance clips show him as a stouter figure, costumed to no longer reveal a bare chest and without the energy or finesse of his early performances. Through their friendship Gopal made use of Lamorisse's apartment in Venice on Via Giudecca overlooking one of the main canals and attended the film festival there annually. Pam Cullen, a close friend of Gopal and who looked after him in his later years, describes him being well known in the local neighbourhood where he would regularly eat out at the nearby restaurants. Lamorisse also owned a large chateau and grounds (Chateau des Meaulx) in Claviers, southern France where Gopal would stay.

In 1989, British TV Channel 4 commissioned a new thirty-minute TV documentary featuring Gopal, which incorporated part of Erulkar's 1948 film and Lamorisse's later film showing clips of Gopal dancing. Broadcast on the UK's

[19] They are listed in the archives of the British Film Institute (BFI) but are not available to be viewed.

Channel 4 on 5 September at 9.00 p.m., it was titled *Bandung File: Ram Gopal, Dancing to the Music of Time.*[20] This documentary interspersed clips of his dances with an extensive interview at Lamorisse's Venice home. Gopal, in his seventies at the time, covers much of the detail of his life that is in his autobiography; there is some focus on his brief dance partnership with Alicia Markova and their friendship, as well as his avid interest in the world of ballet. The film offers a rich source of information and record of Gopal's work, providing a rare opportunity to hear his voice and see his dancing body on screen.

More recently in 2016, SADAA created a twenty-five-minute documentary film focusing on Gopal's dance of the golden eagle, *Garuda*. Titled 'Remembering Ram Gopal, a Documentary', it formed part of a large project funded by the UK Lottery Heritage Fund (see Beginnings chapter) and includes extensive and informative interviews with Jenny Levy Casperson, costume designer and maker of one of the *Garuda* costumes; Jane Pritchard, curator of dances at London's V&A dance and theatre collection; myself and audience member from the 1950s, John White, as well as Gopal's long-standing friend, Pamela Cullen and Gopal's niece Joy Jones. The documentary features the late Naseem Khan, writer and arts commentator, and Mira Kaushik then director of Akademi. Interviews are cut between still photos of Gopal, shots of his printed programmes, Ambrose's drawing of his *Garuda* role, and a focus on the *Garuda* costume and its recent conservation at the V&A. The complete film is sensitively handled and provides valuable discussion and vivid material on his life and work.

Gopal's fairly extensive work as a film actor and choreographer in the 1940s and 1950s in several feature films and on television is generally not well known. He even played in an early Bollywood film made in Calcutta by New Huns Pictures, titled *Draupadi* (1944). Filmed in black and white and directed by Baburao Patel, it includes a four-minute sequence of Gopal and Janaki in a group dance. The films shot in the 1950s that involved Gopal as an actor include *Hindustan Hamara* (1940), director Paul Zils; *Outpost in Malaya* in 1952 directed by Ken Annakin;[21] *The Purple Plain* (1954), directed by Academy award-winning Robert Parrish; *Elephant Walk* (1954) with William Dieterle as director; and *Navy Heroes* (1955), director Wolf Rilla. In 1955, Gopal played in one episode of a British TV show *We Do It Differently*, directed by Joan Kemp-Welch (3 November) followed in 1956

[20] This documentary film was part of a series that focused on issues affecting Britain's Asian and Afro-Caribbean populations, with specific interest in the fields of sport, politics and culture. The production company was Bandung Productions and series editors were Darcus Howe and Tariq Ali, directed by Zoe Hardy.

[21] Original title *The Planter's Wife*.

Figure 19 Advert for the film 'The Planter's Wife' (alternative title 'Outpost in Malaysia') with Ram Gopal, in *Picturegoer*, Saturday 20 August 1952.

by *Leave to Die*, a film episode for TV directed by Derek Twist. Gopal featured in another TV documentary that year, *Russian Ballet – Bolshoi and Kirov* (1956), produced by John de Vere Loder. The next year 1957 was a busy one with Gopal taking part in three further TV shows (see below). I discuss the feature films noted above in more detail in Appendix 2 as this still remains a somewhat hidden aspect of Gopal's working life.

Gopal appeared as himself in two television talk/variety show formats in 1957; firstly, *Chelsea at Nine*, a weekly international cabaret filmed at the Chelsea Palace Theatre, King's Road, London, for Granada TV and directed by Corby Ruskin. This show ran for an hour on Monday evenings between 1957 and 1960 and hosted comedy skits, jazz performances, dance and contemporary theatre and included well-known stars. Gopal featured in one episode. The second, *Alan Melville Takes You From A-Z*, a Friday night entertainment show on BBC TV, selected its contributors for each week all named under the same letter of the alphabet. It ran weekly for forty-five minutes from 1956 to 1960. Hosted by Alan Melville, guests included famous entertainment personalities including dancers Alicia Markova, Ninette de Valois and Gopal (in different episodes). Also in 1957, Gopal appeared as a dancer in one episode of the TV series *McCreary Moves In* that aired on 30 November, titled 'Dance of Death' as well as arranging all the dances for this particular section. Fifteen years later, when he was in his sixties, Gopal appeared on the talk show, *WIB-Schaukel* (originally *VIP Swing*) made for German TV and starring Margret Dünser as host. Directed by Edgar von Heeringen, the series ran from 1971 to 1980. Guests included celebrities from film and television, singers and members of royal families. Famed for its glamour and insights into VIP lives, the series has a cult following and is available still now in boxed DVDs.

The descriptions given above indicate the celebrity status that Gopal achieved in the 1950s and 1960s, stepping out from the world of dance to become an actor and TV personality in his own right. Working in Hollywood (and Bollywood) films with such famous actors as Elizabeth Taylor, Peter Finch and Gregory Peck and appearing regularly for a period on television, through such extensive publicity and exposure, Gopal became known not just as an Indian dancer but as a kind of superstar. Public visibility is key to such success, keeping the public 'collective preoccupation with the famous' (Cashmore 2006: 3) and stars worked hard to achieve this in an age before social media and smart phones.

Gopal was keen to make his own films and in 1955 began corresponding with Sir Michael Balcon, the eminent film producer who ran Ealing Studios from 1933 to 1955 and who was Chairman of the British Film Institute (BFI) production board. They discussed the production of potential films on various topics that were to be specifically shot in India and Ceylon.[22] Film script synopses written by journalist and writer Derek Patmore were sent to Balcon, one of which was titled *Interlude in Ceylon*, and in which Gopal would star. Patmore knew Gopal and Balcon well, writing to Balcon as 'My dear Mick'. After several attempts to meet to discuss further arrangements, Balcon penned the following letter to Gopal, which I quote in some detail as it is indicative of the complexity of the business undertaking required for this type of venture:

> We have met on more than one occasion to discuss the possibility of film production in India. I am now writing to confirm to you that we are, under certain conditions, very interested indeed in producing one or two films in India. The prerequisite of any project is of course a subject or theme which in our opinion is likely to obtain the widest possible distribution throughout the world. We think our personnel here are best equipped to deal with contemporary subjects and we have in mind stories dealing with British and Indian characters against the Indian background, so that when it comes to actual production of a film, the exteriors could be made in India and the interiors in this country. The final stages of film-making should also be carried out in this country.

[22] See correspondence file at the BFI, Rueben Library, London. There are several typed and handwritten letters.

> We do not believe we can undertake any venture of this sort without advice, and we feel that such advice could be forthcoming from you. We also feel very strongly, for reasons we have discussed, that anything we undertake should be in the nature of a joint venture with Indian interests on some financial basis agreeable to both parties, providing of course that once we were agreed on such a formula and the project settled from a story and script point of view, the actual production is left in our hands. We would also want to handle the questions of world distribution through our own contractual arrangements with distributors. It is very difficult to state this in our preliminary letter all the points we have discussed in our various conversations, but with goodwill on both sides, there would seem to be no great difficulty in coming to an arrangement, providing you can get the requisite support during your forthcoming visit to India.
>
> The object of this letter is merely to reaffirm our interest and we shall look forward to hearing from you on your return.
>
> (Balcon, 1 December 1955)

Balcon clearly expresses his interest and sets out the business requirements for their potential partnership. It is unclear whether after this, any proper contract for filming followed; however, Gopal started his own production company, Ram Gopal Productions that owned the film rights of J. R. Ackerley's famous book, *Hindoo Holiday,* and another story by popular novelist, Ethel Mannin.[23] Gopal wanted to film *Hindoo Holiday* but as Peter Parker notes in his biography of Ackerley, despite Gopal and Ackerley's close friendship and plans for Ackerley to 'be involved at every stage, not only with the script but on location in India … the project never came to anything' (1990 [1989]: 400). Zahid Chaudhary writes of Ackerley's book that '[t]wo of the most prominent colonialist travel writers of India, E. M. Forster (*Hill of Devi*) and J. R. Ackerley (*Hindoo Holiday*), practiced sexual relations with other men, and their experience of the Indian Orient was filtered through their own sexual identifications. The homoerotics of Ackerley's *Hindoo Holiday* are less coded than Forster's *Hill of Devi*, which suppresses homoerotic tension' (2004: 85). Ackerley worked on several of Gopal's scripts; some of these are still in existence in privately held archives. Clearly Gopal and Ackerley shared interests in this type of subject matter being portrayed on film.

[23] First published in 1932, *Hindoo Holiday* was a fictional account of Ackerley's stay in India in the 1920s, working for the Maharajah Vishwa Nath Singh Bahadur for five months. It contains homosexual themes.

Representation of the racialized (dancing) body

It is widely acknowledged how film of the dancing body is problematic (see Beginnings chapter) yet is essential for retaining some element of ephemeral performance as well as for analysis through repeated viewing. Sherril Dodds (2001) explains how film and television since the 1930s have had a close relationship with dance but argues how much technical and aesthetic limitations and editorial decisions affect what the viewer receives of the actual reality of the live dancing body. Contingencies of medium (quality and type of film), of budget (more than one camera is without doubt essential), of lighting, of place of viewing (large or small screen) and of the director's decisions on what is shown and what is edited out conspire to make film a challenging recording method for dance.

It is essential when analysing the work of Gopal on film, on TV, in photographic records and in artist's representations of him that the way he is presented, and the way he is viewed, is critically interrogated. In Jennifer Patrice Sims' work on mixed-race identity in the United States (2012), she reminds the reader how in popular culture and in some research literature, individuals who are racially mixed are perceived to be more beautiful than others (2012: 64).[24] Underscoring this view, Maxine Leeds Craig argues that the 'racialized body is a political, cultural, and material body. It feels and appears. It is a gendered body. It is a performing body' (2012: 323). She remarks how current theories of race omit the real sense of the body and therefore there is a need for '*embodied* theories of race without essentialism' (2012; my emphasis). It is marked how Gopal's dancing received this kind of racialized view, with critics rhapsodizing about the 'beauty' of his part Burmese, part Indian ethnicity. As a dancer, Gopal's body on stage became the locus of views and assumptions from the mainly Western audiences. His 'exotic and exquisite beauty' was a constant point of reference as indicated in the cited critical reviews in this book's discussion.

The presence of the pleasurable gaze of the audience (scopophilia) was without doubt part of the objectifying of the oriental other – a gaze not only eliciting enjoyment but also creating a relationship of power between the observer and the observed. Developed in contemporary feminist film theory by Laura Mulvey

[24] The term 'mixed race' is problematic, but I use it following the writings of scholars who address mixed-race identity politics. Mixed race is of course a social construction and today it is widely accepted that individuals should be free to self-identity their own heritage. In the UK, David Gilbert points out the 'significant scarcity of discussion about mixed-race identities', noting that the 2001 Census was the first time the category of mixed race was included (2005: 55).

(from Freud's psychoanalysis) in relationship to a pleasurable male gaze on a female body, here it is reversed, the gaze fixated on an idealized male dancing body, and particularly in pre- and post-war Britain, an (exotic) Indian one. Kumudini Lakhia, filmed by Abraham in 2012 talking about her dance partnership with Gopal, recounted how

> all the twice weekly matinées were full of elderly ladies, only there to see this Indian god with his beautiful skin colour and his spectacular headdresses and his figure. There was such a long queue at the stage door. All the girls used to say, 'I don't know why we dance at matinées, they only come for Ram!'

I argue that Gopal played with this racialized lens and haptic scrutiny of his body and his performances, knowingly counteracting the gaze and utilizing it to his advantage. Like most performers, he used the superlative reviews from critics in his publicity material and in his books and deliberately created a dramatic, exotic and beautiful figure on and off stage, playing with the trope of the glamourous, Asian other.[25] For many of his solo items, Gopal wore revealing, short costumes, his sparsely clothed body knowingly exuberant and consciously planned for audience response. As previously noted, his love for colourful caftans, silk turbans and large pieces of jewellery for his everyday dress meant he was always ready for the cameras and maintained this persona in both public and private. In this way, Gopal created what Sudhanva Deshpande has described as 'a consumable hero' (2005: 197), his body and personality an object of longing and consumption, reinforced by the way he impressively played with performative and creative space on stage and in his life, and played with the boundaries of heteronormativity (David 2015).

Audience desire and appeal was managed through Gopal's own control of his image, something he took particular care with. The artists discussed in this chapter helped create a star image for Gopal, many using a potential homoerotic lens in their work that depicted a stunningly beautiful but racialized body on stage that audiences and followers bought into. The fresh, lively watercolours captured by Topolski nearly ninety years ago allow Gopal to dance out of the historical past, recreating for today's dancers and researchers a sense of the alluring potency of his performances.

[25] Bharatanatyam dancer Vena Ramphal confirmed she too likes to play with the exoticization of her body and the dance form, using it as a tool to empower her performances (personal communication with author, December 2021).

Endings: The concluding years

London dance classes

In 1962, Gopal spoke to reporters about his hope to establish a permanent centre of Indian culture in London and his decision to make the city his base. He had always been content to train Western dancers for his company, stating emphatically 'that British dancers and Europeans can not only learn the dance of India, but even surpass many aspirants in India itself' (Gopal 1962: 16). Marianne Balchin (see Chapter 4), Sheila Cove (Shakuntala) and Marianne Schneider (Mallika Devi) were some of several Western dancers who worked with Gopal in the post-war period. In the early 1960s, Gopal joined forces with Harlequin Ballet Company, run by John and Barbara Gregory, and became one of their patrons. He taught the company Indian folk dances and some joined him for classical classes, but his efforts to effect some collaborative works with the company were unsuccessful. Financial resources were constrained and artistic temperaments on both sides did not lead to an easy relationship. During this period of teaching in the 1960s, he collaborated not only with Harlequin Ballet but also with the Asian Music Circle and taught privately, which I go on to discuss.

Efforts were made by Gopal to start a 'School of Classical Indian Dancing' in London. Full-page advertisements were placed in the *Dancing Times* monthly and announcements in *The Times* newspaper from October 1962 to September 1963, during which the name of the school morphed from the above to 'Ram Gopal's Commonwealth School of Pakistan, Ceylonese and Indian Dances' and then finally to 'The Ram Gopal British Commonwealth School of Dance, Drama and Music'. The fact that Gopal used the term 'Commonwealth' was significant. This was a loose and flexible association of states that grew out of the colonial British empire that were self-governing but still dependent on Britain. The new Labour government of 1945 supported the growth of the Commonwealth, encouraging new concepts of nationhood, shared economic wealth, aid, mutual interest and co-operation. Despite the fact that details of the existence of this school appear obscure, I focus on the adverts placed in the *Dancing Times* and *The Times* as significant artefacts and indicative of this later period of Gopal's long-held ambition to have a London centre of Indian dance. Gopal did not comment when I questioned him about it, and Balchin told me that several attempts were made to establish such a school but that they all 'fizzled out and that Gopal himself was more of a performer than a teacher' (personal communication with author, September 2000). Gopal's papers reveal legal evidence of him establishing a company by guarantee under the title 'Ram Gopal's British Commonwealth School of Dance, Drama and Music Ltd', incorporated in 1963. The chapter begins by discussing attempts to

Figure 20 Advert for the Ram Gopal School of Classical Indian Dancing, 1962. Author's own collection.

fulfil this desire for an established school of Indian dance and then surveys the last years of Gopal's performances and later life beyond the stage. It concludes with Gopal's death and some final musings on his extraordinary life.

Although daily classes for Gopal's school were advertised at the Harlequin Studio, St Andrew's Hall, W.14, where Harlequin Ballet Company had their base, Barbara Gregory had no recollection of classes being held there regularly, although there is evidence they existed for a period (personal communication with author, July 2000). Correspondence between Gopal and John Gregory reveals Gopal paid rent for four months' hire of St Andrew's Hall, September to December 1962, and again for the following term in January 1963 (NRCD archived papers). They also discussed Gopal's wish to equip the hall's stage and auditorium with drapes, lighting, good flooring and better seating. For this Gopal needed to raise money and in exchange, Gregory offered him a low rent for the space and invited him to become a patron of the Harlequin Ballet Trust, which Gopal accepted. He was invited to make a guest appearance in their spring season in 1963.

Dancer and actress Zohra Segal contacted Gopal when she arrived in London in 1962 (see Chapter 3) and began to teach at Gopal's school in the church hall. She is named as principal of the dance school in adverts in June, July and August 1963 in the *Dancing Times*. Segal had trained in German modern dance with Wigman in Germany in the early 1930s (as noted) and had subsequently been Uday Shankar's main dance partner from 1935, touring with him globally. She then taught at Shankar's school in Almora, India, in the late 1930s and early 1940s before it closed in 1942. Segal recounts her memories with Gopal in the 1960s:

> Classes at Ram Gopal's school were held at the Harlequin Ballet's headquarters at St Andrews Hall on Vereker Road, W.14. This was a magnificently large church hall rented by Barbara and John Gregory, the talented directors of the Harlequin Ballet, who together with their children, Paul and Paula, and a batch of devoted dancers carried on their courageous work under very difficult circumstances… . The second hour of my training at his school was devoted to holding a class with his pupils which, together with the members of the Harlequin Ballet, amounted to over a dozen students, at times going up to twenty.
>
> (Segal 2015 [2010]: 196–7)

Some private classes were held in Gopal's residence in London, at 12 Cadogan Court, Draycott Avenue, Chelsea, London, as Naseem Khan recounts below. She described attending classes in 1962 in the front room of the terraced house. It was cleared of furniture and housed mirrors, barres and a large statue of Siva Nataraj in the corner, surrounded by flowers. She commented:

> He is a presence, no question … His stance is marvellously upright and he looks wonderful, in a silk turquoise kurta and white churidars. 'Let's get going. Let's do our namaskar' … He is the man that brought Indian dance to England before I was born, and who has danced before royalty. And now he is teaching me, in a private studio behind the King's Road.
>
> (Khan 2017a: 63)

She adds, 'He is a marvel. When he demonstrates an *adavu* its sheer disciplined beauty takes my breath away. He is, after all, the equivalent of Nureyev' (2017a: 64). Khan later remarked that his role was as an ambassador for Indian dance in the UK, noting that he was meticulous, expansive but unpredictable (SADAA film 2016). Other teachers employed along with Segal for the classes included Rina Singha for kathak and Anura teaching Kandyan dance. Khan notes that classes had about 8–10 students, taking place several evening a week.[1]

Khan argued that the school 'failed ultimately because Gopal had no organisation or administrative base backing his efforts' (1976: 26) later adding in her obituary on him that his attempts to establish a teaching base in London 'were impeded by Ram's distaste for dull and prudent long-term management' (2013: n.p.). Finance was clearly a difficulty, with a lack of governmental Arts Council support that performers enjoy today causing pioneering ventures such as this to struggle to survive. Khan explains the difficulties of the time:

> A number [of dancers], like Shanta Rao, Krishnan Kutty, and Ram Gopal himself had seriously tried to put down roots and make a place for themselves in Western culture. But time was not on their side. There was no Arts Council until the late 1940s to help cushion the risk and, even if there had been, it is doubtful that it would have regarded Indian dance as a fit subject for British patronage. Survivors of those early years remember them as years of struggle and huge financial uncertainty.
>
> (Khan 1997: 25)

During the 1960s–70s, a new influential organization in London, the Asian Music Circle, began to put on classical and folk Indian music and dance

1 Khan later worked for the Arts Council and became a cultural advisor. Her seminal report *The Arts Britain Ignores: The Arts of Ethnic Minorities in Britain* (1976) drew attention to the mainly unseen range of arts practices taking place in what were termed at the time ethnic communities, and she argued for them to be recognized and funded.

performances. This arts group was founded in 1946 by Indian writer Ayana Deva Angadi and his English wife, Patricia Fell-Clarke, a painter and novelist, and was first called the Indian Music Club.[2] They not only promoted concerts (in Birmingham as well as London) but additionally offered classes in music and dance and extensive support to Gopal, who was named as their artistic director. In 1960, their printed programmes for Gopal's dance performances had adverts for classes taught by Gopal at 248 Earl's Court Road, London, on Wednesdays from 8 to 10 p.m. and Saturdays from 3 to 5 p.m. The Asian Music Circle was instrumental in the establishment and appreciation of Indian culture in post-war Britain, working with such musicians as Ravi Shankar, the Beatles, Yehudi Menuhin, Ali Akbar Khan and Indian dancers Shanta Rao, Krishna Rao and Chandrabhaga Devi. An LP made in 1958 by EMI and produced by the Asian Music Circle featured songs and dances of India by the musicians of the Ram Gopal company, many of whom were the same musicians on tour with Gopal's *Taj Mahal* Ballet.

But it took until the early 1970s to fully establish recognized classes in Indian performing arts in London. This happened with the opening of the Bharatiya Vidya Bhavan (Institute of Indian Culture, now the Bhavan Centre) in 1972 and the Academy of Indian Dance (now Akademi) in 1979.[3] Up to 1979 dance had always existed under the umbrella of music within the Arts Council and it took till then to create a separate funding department for dance. Similarly, it was only in the early 1980s that a small percentage, 4 per cent, of the Arts Council dance budget was allocated to 'ethnic minority groups'. It was distributed first to Black dance groups and then to South Asian performers such as Shobana Jeyasingh and Pushkala Gopal (bharatanatyam), Unnikrishnan (kathakali) and Nahid Siddiqui (kathak) who received a certain level of funding for their work in performance, touring and education. Jeyasingh began her performance work in the UK as a solo bharatanatyam dancer. Later she developed her company and moved to more experimental contemporary dance work drawing on South Asian classical dance styles as well as martial art forms. Pushkala Gopal and Unnikrishnan, whilst retaining a classical base, also choreographed dance dramas and innovative items of dance. Siddiqui likewise maintained her classical kathak but produced creative

[2] Its main object was to foster 'the appreciation and study of the Music and Dance of all Asian countries, thereby creating greater understanding of Asian peoples and cultures' (1960 St Pancras Arts Festival programme in collection of author).

[3] Tara Rajkumar, founder of the Academy of Indian Dance, received a grant of £500 in 1979 from the Racial Equality Commission to start the organization. Tara also writes, 'We were also extremely fortunate to have the legendary London-based dancer Ram Gopal as an incredibly supportive Patron' (2021 Facebook).

and innovative choreography within a kathak idiom. This led to a marked increase in awareness and appreciation of South Asian dance. In 1991, another new initiative heralded further support and funding for dance; this was the establishment of National Dance Agencies in various centres throughout the UK, following recommendations in Graham Devlin's hard-hitting report on the development of dance (Devlin 1989). This enabled the setting up of *ADiTi*, a national organization for South Asian dance based in Bradford, north England, and allowed more funding to be allocated for different forms of dance, including South Asian.

1960s performances

Gopal continued giving national and international dance performances till the mid-1960s. Segal joined his company as a dancer and choreographer in this period and the 1965 March programme of their two-week season at the Queen's Theatre, London (costing one shilling) with seven shows a week, recorded that the opening dance piece, *Chandamama*, a group folk dance for the whole company, was choreographed by Segal. Also dancing was her daughter Kiran (aged twenty) and later in the first half, they performed a duet together. In the second part, Segal had a *Radha* solo. Segal wrote:

> I would work with Ram, choreographing duets for him in the Uday Shankar style of dancing. He himself is a classical dancer, yet wanted to add yet another style to his many items. We were to perform these duets at a forthcoming show, but when the performance actually materialised at Queen's Theatre in May '64 [*sic*], Ram did all the duets with his old partner, Mallika Devi (Marianne Schneider) who had arrived from Paris for the occasion.
>
> (2015 [2010]: 196–7)

Several of the students at Gopal's school taught by Segal appeared in the group numbers, as she notes rather wryly, 'Apart from the daily exercises, I choreographed a number of group dances with these students which we *did* include in the Queens Theatre show' (ibid).

In the 1960s, there were appearances in Italy at the Nervi International Festival, a trip to perform in Israel, a second short tour to Trinidad, performances in the UK in London and Manchester, and festival shows in 1960 at the Eisteddfod, Wales, and in Edinburgh as well as visits to Greece and Spain. The highlight of this period though, celebrated with some enthusiasm by press reports and reviews, was Gopal's collaboration with ballet dancer Alicia Markova in a newly choreographed duet, *Radha-Krishna*.

Radha-Krishna

Gopal's desire for an East-West fusion came to some fruition in 1960 when he worked with Markova in this partnership – one that was somewhat reminiscent of Shankar and Pavlova in 1923.[4] Markova had seen Gopal dance in London in 1939, and he had been backstage to see her after watching *Giselle* at the Metropolitan Opera House, New York, in 1953. He garlanded her with marigolds after the performance and told her about the Shankar-Pavlova duet, stating it would be very nice if they could do that one day. She agreed but it was not till 1960 that both were available and for Markova to have the time to learn Indian technique from Gopal. Although Markova described it being difficult to learn, Gopal praised her speed in absorbing the hand movements, commenting on her expressivity and sympathy with the gestures (Leonard 1990: 317). Their *Radha-Krishna* duet, one item in a full-length Indian dance programme, played at the Princes Theatre in London for two weeks in March 1960 and then toured to the Edinburgh Festival in the summer of that year. Dance critic Peter Williams wrote:

> Markova/Radha awaits the blue god Krishna in the person of Ram Gopal. He appears playing on his flute with a mischievous expression on his face. He dances, she is rather coy but is eventually persuaded to join him and they move together in ecstasy ... It was altogether charming and given with sincerity and style by both artists, who seemed to inspire each other.
>
> (Williams 1960: 13)

Markova related how Gopal would fill her dressing room with incense and insist that she ate in the break between the matinée and evening performance, when he had large quantities of the most delicious Indian food delivered. She recalls, 'It was guaranteed to keep you anchored to the floor' (interview *Bandung File* documentary, 1989). Gopal's friend and dancer John Gregory wrote of their duet, 'Markova's classical serenity brought a marvellous contrast to his brilliant Krishna. The performance was acclaimed' (2013 [1996]: n.p.). As stated in

4 Pavlova's programme had a section on 'The Oriental Impressions' that included Dances of Japan, followed by *A Hindu Wedding* and *Krishna and Rhada* [*sic*]. Both Indian pieces were choreographed (or 'arranged' as the programme stated) by Uday Shankar and music composed by Comolata Banerji, played by a Western orchestra. This was part of a four-week programme at the Royal Opera House, Covent Garden, London, with seven shows a week, from 8 September to 4 October 1923. Shankar danced this item with Pavlova in New York at the Metropolitan Opera House later in October that same year.

Figure 21 Ram Gopal and Alicia Markova in *Radha-Krishna*, 1960. © PA – Reuter Photos.

Chapter 1, Gopal had already created a *Krishna-Radha* duet with La Meri in 1937 for their Eastern tour together which they restaged in Trinidad in 1958. It is a recurring theme featured in classical Indian dance and is taken from Hindu mythology, telling the story of the deity Krishna dancing with his beloved friend, Radha, and so has inspired many artists.

Markova's costume for this duet is held in the archives of the V&A Museum. There is a cream satin *choli* (short blouse) with gold braid and woven gold decoration, cream satin loose, baggy under-trousers of the same material, plus a pink chiffon, gathered and full long skirt with gold braid around the hem. Silver sequins are stitched in patterns on the skirt and on the decorated cream waistband. The long veil (206 cm × 57 cm) worn by Markova is made of pink chiffon, with the gold braid and silver sequins as in the skirt and the complete costume was designed by Madame Manya, Markova's long-time costumier.[5] Kumudini Lakhia, when asked about this duet of Gopal, said to me that it was mainly a kathak piece and she thought he had based it on Shankar and Pavlova's original *Krishna-Radha* duet. Whilst Markova's costume could be seen as a kathak one, Gopal's was not.

There are later examples of such cross-cultural fusion with male and female artists trained in different dance styles marked through creative duets, as seen in Akram Khan's work with ballet-trained Sylvie Guillem (*Sacred Monsters*, 2006) and Vidya Patel's piece with contemporary dancer Connor Scott (*About the Elephant*, 2018).[6] Gopal and Markova remained good friends and were asked to become patrons of the newly formed Academy of Indian Dance. They visited the annual Yorkshire Ballet Seminars as guest artists and Gopal was invited to take part in a surprise television programme on Markova's life in 1995, called *This Is Your Life*.[7] Their good friendship was strengthened when Markova's sister Doreen Barry became Gopal's stage manager for some of his tours (see Chapter 3).

End of performing

The period described above saw the last of Gopal's dance performances. During the years of the 1970s and 1980s, although not dancing, he remained invested in the dance world attending events such as the 1975 Film Festival of Classical Indian Dance in London, where he gave a talk on dance, and taking part in events run by the Academy of Indian Dance, to which he gave his whole-hearted support when it was initially founded by Tara Rajkumar in 1978. He visited the Bhavan Centre, London, to see performances and meet students and attended performances of other Indian dancers such as Rathi Karthigesu and Rajkumar.

5 Madame Manya had also designed and made costumes for Pavlova.

6 Khan's company website notes, '*Sacred Monsters. Monstres Sacres.* The term was used for the first time in France in the 19th century as a nickname for the big stars of the theatre, such as Sarah Bernhardt. It marks the birth of contemporary stardom in which the icons of the arts and sports world are given divine status by their audience and the media.' See https://www.akramkhancompany.net/productions/sacred-monsters-2006 (accessed 18 October 2021).
The Guardian gave *About the Elephant* a four-star review stating, 'The blurb says this is a piece about looking for clarity in a world of noise, and yes, you can see that clarity, for sure. But more simply it's a conversation between two styles and two people, a palpable meeting of energies between two bodies' (Winship, 8 June 2020). See https://www.theguardian.com/stage/2020/jun/08/about-the-elephant-review-connor-scott-vidya-patel (accessed 18 October 2021).

7 *This Is Your Life* was run by Thames Television then by ITV from 1992; this was the 36th series and Markova's second time on the show. Using a reality format, its success was premised on a celebrity being 'surprised' by the host who proceeds to take them through their life, meeting former friends and colleagues live on stage and on camera.

Figure 22 Ram Gopal and Rathi Karthigesu (author's bharatanatyam guru). © Madan Aurora.

Gopal met up with dance colleagues Shala Mattingly, Raja, Indrani and Baskar Roy Chowdhury in New York in 1985 and made several trips to India, often with Claude Lamorisse where he would meet dancers, scholars and friends and regularly watch performances (Kothari 2000). He participated in the East West Dance Encounter conference in Mumbai in 1982 along with dancers and former partners, Kumudini Lakhia and Mrinalini Sarabhai. In the early 1990s he stayed as special guest of V. P. and Shanta Dhananjayan at the inauguration of their new performance space and returned to visit them in 1995. A six-month sojourn in Bangalore with Wing Commander Alec Richard Hindley in 1998 was Gopal's last visit to his home country giving him a chance to catch up with old friends. The Hindley's connection to Gopal was through Lylah, Hindley's wife, who was the sister-in-law of Lt. General Thimayya. Nina, Thimayya's wife, had studied at Gopal's school in Bangalore in the 1940s and danced with his company during the war. Gopal's close friend and fellow dancer U. S. Krishna

Rao wrote about this last visit that 'we felt he was not his old self, having lost so many of his old friends who used to look after him. His health too was failing and he needed help to walk. On his earlier trips, he would visit us regularly and watch the classes … but during this last visit … he was mainly homebound' (Rao 2003: 28). Critic Leela Venkataraman also remarked on his frailty on that final, poignant trip telling how her 'last memories of Ram Gopal are of a very frail old man, resplendently clad in brocades and turban sitting slumped in his wheelchair, watching a dance performance in Bangalore. Age might have sapped his physical vitality – but not the mental resilience', she commented (2003: n.p.).

But this time was also one of financial difficulties as Gopal was no longer performing nor touring. He sold his large collection of Russian dance lithographs and paintings at Sotherby's (fine art auction house) in 1980, presumably to raise funds. Although he appeared on television during the 1980s and 1990s – his film of *Purple Plain* on BBC 1 (1981), his Channel 4 documentary (1989) and *The Planter's Wife* repeated on BBC 1 (1996) – he would only have been paid royalties for these. Gopal was notoriously generous but was known not to be very savvy with financial affairs. In 1989, his interview with dance critic Deborah Mackrell was published in a UK national newspaper (Judith Mackrell 1989: 17). Importantly, Gopal was finally honoured in 1990 by the Indian government for his services to dance through the Sangeet Natak Akademi where he was made Fellow of the Akademi. He was bestowed with the title of Pandit 'for his extraordinary services in the field of dance' (Kothari 2000: 23) at a special reception which was held for him at the Indian High Commission in London in 1999. In July 1999 in the UK he was awarded an Order of the British Empire (OBE) by the Queen for services to dance. Both these honours came long after his dancing prime. That same year he moved into Norbury Hall Residential Care Home in south London where he was to remain until his death four years later. Prior to this, in the mid-1990s his nephew Peter Ramgopal looked after for him for a few years.

The last period

In 2000, three years before his death, Gopal, now very frail, was a special guest at Akademi's Coming of Age special millennium performance at the Royal Festival Hall, London. Magdalen Gorringe writes how the performances in the site-specific event

> had taken over the front of the building, with bharatanatyam dancer Mavin Khoo dressed to resemble one of the pioneers of South Asian dance in Britain, Ram Gopal, standing like a beacon on the top of the building. Reflecting this image of his younger self, Gopal himself, elderly and in a wheelchair, but with undiminished elegance and presence, presided over the occasion on a stage in front of the building, framed by the newly instated Millennium Wheel, which encircled him like the ring of flames around the dancing Nataraja.
>
> (Gorringe 2021: 277–8)

Mira Kaushik, director of Akademi at that time, spoke about Coming of Age being a 'metaphor of the existence of Indian dance in this country for fifty years'. She continued, 'It was an ultimate moment for us, for the whole of the dance community. Ram's legacy is yet to be matched in this country by any of the contemporary South Asian dancers' (SADAA film 2016).

Whilst in the nursing home, Gopal was visited regularly by dancer friends, family and other acquaintances, and I made frequent visits. We would talk, look at his dance books and discuss the performances of the past (See Gopal and author in Plate 4 of colour insert). On one occasion we spoke about his oldest dance friend U. S. Krishna Rao, and Gopal regretfully mentioned how he had lost touch with him. So together we penned an email that I sent to Krishna Rao. Rao's son, Jayadev, read it out to Rao and said his father 'was overcome with emotion and thrilled beyond belief' to hear from Gopal (email to author 29 August 2002). It elicited the following emotional response a few days later from Rao which I quote here in full:

> My dearest Sono, thank you very much for your lovable and warm letter through Ann David in London. I have been expecting your letter since we parted company some two years [*sic*] ago in 'Maha-Maya'. But you have been in my thoughts all these years. Both of us have gone through many vicissitudes of life to attain a certain level of respectability and grandeur, you in your universal way and I in my small national way. We have now come to the end of our lives, expecting ultimately to be at the feet of Almighty God to serve him. It is a nice feeling that I have been responsible to do some good to our Dance Art and I am sure you have the same feelings. We are both in our 90th year living our old age with infirmities with sang froid. Though we are separated from each other by thousands of miles, we have kept up our

> friendship through thick and thin and have felt the same warmth which we felt in our 20s, 30s, 40s, 50s and so on. I greet you with all my heart and May the Almighty Lord bless you with Peace and Harmony. With undying love for you too, yours Krishna.[8]

During these last years Gopal was supported and cared for by close friends Pam Cullen, Denise Iredell, Nani Bhatt and Lamorisse's family, as well as the Royal Ballet Benevolent Fund. Sunil Kothari described a visit to the nursing home:

> [H]is room which is clean and filled with flowers, has a beautiful view of the garden … Even now, Ram dresses like a prince with his exquisite Mysore turban and flowing silk robes. He wears rings and shows off precious stones. Though advancing age has taken its toll, his spirit is irrepressible and he is full of beans, laughing, gossiping, joking and recalling the wonderful days of his early career.
>
> (2000: 21)

This upbeat, positive condition was sadly not to last. In October 2003, Gopal became seriously ill and was hospitalized.

Closing moments … or not?

A small chapel at Croydon crematorium. 20 October 2003. About forty people are gathered to commemorate and bid farewell to legendary dancer Ram Gopal who died, aged ninety-one, the previous week. As the coffin is carried into the chapel, the sound of recorded sitar music plays; all the gathered mourners carry a single red rose to place lovingly on the coffin. Gopal's friend Nani Bhatt and daughter Leela recite a Sanskrit *sloka* and the female priest welcomes the congregation. All sing the hymn of 'Abide with Me'. Spoken personal tributes follow from Naseem Khan, writer Reginald Massey, myself and Gopal's niece Joy Jones. Further hymns and Christian prayers follow before we file out into the winter sun to talk, to view floral arrangements, share remembrances and support each other. Afterwards, we reminisce further over supper at the local Indian restaurant where Gopal loved to eat. Dancers from Italy, Lamorisse's family from France, representatives from the care home, close friends and

[8] This was written in August 2002. Rao died two years later in 2005, aged ninety-two.

acquaintances are all gathered to pay respects to this beautiful, creative dancer who touched so many hearts. Later his ashes are taken to France, to Chateau des Meaulx, to be interred by the side of the grave of his great friend and support, Claude Lamorisse. Obituaries fill the papers all over the world, with Naseem Khan remarking that the 'coverage of his life was actually on a par, ironically, with the coverage in 1939 when he first came as a visitor. But of course, in this case, it was a greater recognition of the amazing quality of his work. He'll go down in the history of dance as one of India's greatest dancers' (SADAA film 2016).

Interweaving themes within the histories of Indian dance have been foregrounded by the pioneering intercultural performance work of dancer Ram Gopal, who, I have argued throughout this book, disrupted notions of gender, identity, and classicisms in dance and art forms. In bringing his modernist, culturally interwoven programmes to audiences in the United States, Europe, Britain and beyond, Gopal challenged normative thinking about the display of the male dancing body on stage and brought new re-imaginations of Indian dance that questioned and played consciously with well-trodden colonial tropes of exoticized and racialized bodily performance. Many dancers have commented on Gopal's courage in taking such risks, in performing such acts of resistance. Kumudini Lakhia described how Gopal 'was such a strong person inside. He could face anything' (Facebook Live interview: 2020). The way Gopal played with his sexuality in a knowingly homoerotic way, yet retaining a mysterious, hidden dimension to his exuberant on- and offstage character was remarked upon by Sunil Kothari, when he noted that 'somehow, he did not want many of those things in his life to be known' (Facebook Live interview: 2020). What were the perceived moralities of the performing, dancing body, especially an Indian one, in colonial and post-colonial times? Gopal faced these uncertainties – the unknown and rapidly changing sociocultural landscape in India and worldwide, the reconstruction of classical dance forms with their underlying nationalist agendas, the pull of European modernist thinking and the interweaving of different histories of dance from Asia, India, Europe and the United States – meeting them head-on with his innovative, comprehensive and extensive world performances.

Success drew him into the world of celebrity culture, a very different scenario to that of today's social media, but where rave reviews, television performances, film roles and mixing with aristocracy and the wealthy brought fame and, at times, some fortune. Gopal's generosity and lack of financial acumen meant that these fiscal successes were often short-lived. Naseem Khan commented that 'Ram's own volatility may not have been good for managing dance schools, but it was part of his charm. He was vivid, generous and unpredictable. When money was around, he spent it lavishly. His friends, and those in distress, could be sure of instant sympathy' (2003: n.p.). Dancers Lakhia and Segal talked at length about his care and generosity with his friends: instances such as Segal's worry about bringing her children to Britain in the 1960s when 'Ram Gopal was tremendously helpful, giving me testified letters and documents to prove my employment with him, even offering to stand as guarantor for the children' (2015 [2010]: 196). Lakhia recalled their post-war tours in Germany describing how

> he would treat us very, very nicely. Hotels in Germany after the war had no bathroom, just a toilet. You had to go to the general public baths if you wanted a bath. So Ram would take a more fancy, expensive room with a bath and then we would all use it. He was a very sweet man, a very nice man.
>
> (Facebook Live interview: August 2020)

Ashish Khokar, who knew him well, summed up Gopal by stating, 'He was a generous soul, not a business person and had strong likes and dislikes' (personal communication with author, December 2017).

The complexity of his character was also evident through his volatility and sharp tongue. He honed cutting remarks to be ready when faced with racist comments, stating,

> [Q]uite often in London I would be approached at parties, and in galleries and someone would come up to me and say, 'Can you speak English?' I'd say, 'Yes, I can, can you?' And they'd say 'What a lovely tan you've got'. I'd say 'I'm sorry, I can't say the same for you. You look such a horrid, pallid white'. I have a very quick, triggered reaction to these comments.
>
> (*Bandung File* 1989)

His directness was recalled by Pam Cullen on first meeting him when he said, 'I'm just going to meditate before I go onstage, so you'd better bugger off!' (SADAA film 2016), and friends in India at the East-West conference remembering his comment 'she's fat' in earshot of most of the audience at the appearance of a famous dancer onstage who was somewhat overweight.

Despite the paucity of existing moving images and the fading of public memory, Gopal continues to dance out of the archives, enlivening in this digital age such media platforms as Flickr, Tumblr, Pinterest and Foursquare where he resplendently captures our imagination in sumptuous photos from the early period, mounted by today's contemporary digital influencers, bloggers and vloggers. Ephemera from his performances are on sale on the e-commerce platform of Ebay. His presence in these curated, visual mediums raises certain questions. Did Gopal really outlive his fame? Has he been forgotten in the writings and expressions of dance history? Or is this new, current pictorial sharing of older material creating a fresh audience, eager to learn and understand the early pioneers? Certainly the power of his presence on and off stage is noted by many today: costume-maker Jenny Casperson when first meeting Gopal described how 'the presence and magnitude of the man just took your breath away' (SADAA film 2016) and his niece Joy Jones spoke similarly of 'his presence and magnetism' onstage (SADAA film 2016).

Gopal's performances span the collapse of empire, illustrated through the moment of his early reception by Queen Mary in 1939 almost as a symbol of the 'jewel in the crown' and concluding in 1990 with his award of an OBE where the freedom of the empire is given (ironically now representing the defunct empire). Through the British honours award system, Gopal was given the freedom of the (expired) empire. His dance of *Garuda*, the piece that so represented his fame, remembered by many and shining out from all his other solos is of a bird that is characteristically a symbol of power and empire. Gopal's story reflects these issues of power and belonging; if seen through the lens of the empire, his disappearance into a semi-obscurity is like the collapsed empire, forgotten, frail and alone. Yet his legend lives on, like the empire, whose underlying structures of its heyday continue to (silently) act.[9]

South Asian dancers when asked about Gopal's legacy raised several considerations about his significance in the world of Indian dance, emphasizing his pioneering cross-cultural work and his interweaving of different performance cultures as well as his outstanding and aesthetic showmanship. Chitra Sundaram noted how Gopal 'made the art of dance accessible. He embodied it as a kind of medium. He was a master of being aware of the audience, giving his performances a porosity that moved away from the essentialist ideas of classical forms'. Hari Krishnan spoke movingly about how he found Gopal's book *Rhythm in the Heavens* in his library in Singapore, one of the few books there on Indian dance. As a ten-year-old boy, he pored over the book, loving the representation of the

[9] I acknowledge the input of this conceptualization of empire from Magdalen Gorringe in discussion of Gopal's place in the interweaving histories of Indian dance.

spectacular and the theatricality displayed. Krishnan said, 'The book conjured up for me images of an alternative reality showing different possibilities of what I could do as a moving, dancing body coupled with a male figure. Ram Gopal was really a beacon of hope for me that marked one of my first entry points into me seriously becoming an Indian dancer.'

Despite not learning about Gopal's legacy during his training in the UK, Shane Shambu talked of Gopal bringing an intercultural aesthetic and 'creating a new language using all styles of South Asian Dance that was really exciting. His story telling was inspirational and he seemed to be more interested in the visual and the aesthetic'. Like Sundaram, Shambu acknowledges Gopal's ability to put on a compelling show and to market the dance effectively, deliberately using the tool of exoticism. Gopal was not so important as an inspiration or role model for Shambu's own work that has taken a different trajectory but is respected a dancer and producer that can teach those that follow through the processes he used. Other dancers, such as Anusha Subramanyam, also saw Gopal as a figure

> who really made Britain/the West aware of the richness of Indian culture. Gopal's programmes gave detailed descriptions of styles and dances (which we don't do now). The dance he brought was not just for connoisseurs but for everyone – he made it accessible. He really understood the workings of a touring company and what audiences needed and expected. He taught what it meant to be a performer with a real love for what he did. At that time there was a growing movement where everyone was genuinely interested in each other's cultures, away from the politics.

And Gorringe recounted poetically how

> Ram Gopal rests in the imagination of South Asian dancers in Britain as a slightly mythical figure. Tall, handsome and bejewelled, wrapped in the glamour of tête-à-têtes with royalty and duets danced with Dame Alicia Markova. Stories of his sell-out success in the West End and tales of Londoners queuing around the block to watch classical South Asian dance rest in the collective memory of the sector as both something extraordinary, and as an aspiration for what we might, at some point, achieve again.[10]

As a pivotal figure playing a central and decisive role in the interweaving histories of Indian dance and their presentation to new audiences across the world, Gopal destabilized binary representations of gender, disrupted the way audiences perceived unfamiliar bodies, challenged the colonialist tropes of

[10] Interviews carried out in May/June 2022 and March 2023 with the author.

exoticism, of East–West binaries and brought a type of modernism that drew inter- and transcultural threads from classical forms, folk traditions, European sensibilities and cosmopolitan views. Feted by many, honoured for his services to dance only towards the end of his long life, Gopal, as Kowal writes, 'was confronted by double standards springing as much from shifting cultural notions about what authenticity in ethnic dance looked like as from evolving expectations of audience members and critics for artistic positioning within and relative to an artist's treatment of movement materials and cultural content' (2020: 188). Gopal's position as a transnational, transcultural pioneer performer is now being recognized in the millennium period and his significance in creating a modern, international form of Indian dance that was enjoyed by global audiences is here recorded and memorialized.

Appendix 1: Performances by Ram Gopal (solo and with other dancers) worldwide 1937–66

Note: This chart is not a comprehensive list of all of performances that took place. It captures those where information can be found. Some information is detailed; much is incomplete. Question marks indicate where no dates are specified.

Dates	Venue	Title of show	Dancers	Musicians	Management 1	Management 2	Description/ info
1937 November?	Tokyo			Recorded music		Aleksanda Janta	
1937 November–December?	Tour to Yokohoma, Osaka & Kobe			Recorded music		Aleksanda Janta	
1938 January 19 & February 2	Dillingham Hall, Honolulu, Hawaii	Ram Gopal, The Hindu Temple Dancer	RG	Taped music		Aleksanda Janta	
1938 January 25	Academy of the Arts, Honolulu, Hawaii		RG	Taped music	Invitation from cultural director of Honolulu Academy of Arts	Aleksanda Janta	
1938 March 11 & April 4 & 11	Wilshire Ebell Theatre, Los Angeles	Ram Gopal, Hindu Temple Dancer	RG	Taped music	First performance sponsored by Cecil B. De Mille & others	Aleksanda Janta	
1938 May 1	46th Street Theatre, New York	Ram Gopal, Hindu Temple Dancer	RG	Taped music, plus drummers?	Sol Hurok	Aleksanda Janta	A recital of the dance of North and South India and authentic Hindu temple dances
1938 June	Grand Theatre, Warsaw			Recorded music		Aleksanda Janta	

1938 June/July	Tour to Lviv, Krakow, Katowice, Poznan, Tonin			Recorded music		Aleksanda Janta	
1938 November 26	Theatre de la Gaité Lyrique, Paris	Concert de Gala avec RAM GOPAL, danseur de Temple Indou	RG (mixed programme with Western classical music items)		Eugene Grunberg		
1938 November	Musée Guimet, Paris		RG (solo)				No prog evidence to be found
1939 March–April	Globe Theatre, Bangalore		RG, Retna Mohini & troupe			Aleksanda Janta	
1939 March–April	Regal Theatre, Delhi		RG, Retna Mohini & troupe			Aleksanda Janta	
1939 March–April	Regal Theatre, Bombay		RG, Retna Mohini & troupe			Aleksanda Janta	
1939 June 28	Musée des Arts Decoratifs, Palais du Louvre, Paris	Gala de Danse for Nijinsky	RG (solo)			Director Serge Lifar	

(*Continued*)

Dates	Venue	Title of show	Dancers	Musicians	Management 1	Management 2	Description/ info
1939 July 6	Salle Pleyel	Grand Gala (Charity event). RG et sa Compagnie de Danseurs et Musiciens Hindous	Maya Rani, Retna Mohini, Sohan Lal	Keshan Dordra & company	Eugene Grunberg	Aleksanda Janta	
1939 July–August for two weeks (extended to four). 8.45 p.m. Matinees Tues & Fri 2.30	Aldwych Theatre, London	RG & his Hindu Dancers & Musicians	Retna Mohini, Sohan Lal, Maya Rani, Anuradha, Rukmini	As below	Presented by Eugene Grunberg (Paris)	AD-Aleksanda Janta	Genuine Kathak and KK & of the classical school of Southern India
1939 November 13, for three weeks (extended to four)	Vaudeville Theatre, London	RG & his Hindu Dancers & Musicians	Retna Mohini, Sohan Lal, Chandra Vali,	Dir: Keshan Dorda, Bupen Mukerjee,	Presented by Eugene Grunberg		
1939 December 1, special charity matinee	Vaudeville Theatre, London	RG & his Hindu Dancers & Musicians				Proceeds of which were to be given to the Hindustani Social Club	Special charity matinee to mitigate the distress caused by the war among Indian sea-men and pedlars

WAR YEARS	IN INDIA	(incomplete)			
1941 August 21	B. R. V. Theatre, Bangalore	Dance Recital	Gopal and Mrinalini, assisted by Kunchunni and their company of dancers and musicians		Organized in aid of the District Commander's Red Cross Fund
1941 December 9–11	V. P. Hall, Madras	Ram Gopal with Mrinalini, assisted by Kunchunni			
1943 January 29–31	Capitol Theatre, Bombay	Bharatanatya and Kathakali Dance Recital by the Celebrated International Dancer Ram Gopal	Haridas, Satyanaran, Gopinath, Kochappan, Smt Janaki, Ammani Devi, Thangam Devi, Smt Kumari & Saroja	Saraswati Orchestra	
1944	Bombay	All India Dance Festival			
1945	Delhi	All India Dance Festival			

(*Continued*)

Dates	Venue	Title of show	Dancers	Musicians	Management 1	Management 2	Description/ info
1946–47	India tour: Regal Theatre, Delhi	The Celebrated International Dancer Ram Gopal with Krishna Ubhayakar and Chandrabhaga Devi	Kunchunni, Jankai, Padmini, Mohini, Roopmati	Saraswati Orchestra	V. D. Govindaraj		
1947 September 17	V&A, London		RG, Shevanti & Rajeshwar		Introduced by Arnold Haskell	Opening of V&A Indian section & exhibition	
1947 November 3–8	The Playhouse, Oxford		Shevanti, Rajeshwar, Lakshmi				
1947 November (6 matinees only)	Adelphi Theatre	Ram Gopal and the Hindu Ballet			Charles B Cochran & Lord Vivian		
1947 November 14	Film Theatre, Imperial Institute, London	Ram Gopal on 'The Dance in India' (illustrated)			Royal India Society		
1947 November–December for three weeks	Princes Theatre, London	RG & his Indian Dancers & Musicians	Shevanti, Rajeshwar, Sarla, Leela, Kay Ambrose (talking)		Julian Braunsweg		

1947 November–December for one week (no date)	Princes Theatre, London	RG and his Indian Ballet Company	Shevanti, Rajeshwar, Sarla, Leela, Banumati, Anura, Jaron Yaltan, Nataraj	Dir: Rajani Lakhia Babu Rae & others	By arrangement with Bertram Montague Julian Braunsweg (for United Ballet Foundation)	Michael Rouse, Benn Toff, Frank Shelly, Kay Ambrose	
1948 February 13–25	Théâtre des Champs-Elysées, Paris	RG et son Ballet Hindou		Dir: Rajani Lakhia & Dipali Nag	Roger Eudes and Julian Braunsweg	Michael Rouse, Benn Toff, Kay Ambrose	Words describing Bharata Natya in programme, as well as K, KK & Manipuri
1948 March 2 extended to April 3	Saville Theatre, London	RG & his Indian Dancers & Musicians	Anura, Shevanti, Rajeswar, Leela, Bhanumati, Yaltan	Dir: Rajani Lakhia & Dipali Nag	By arrangement with Bernard Delfont and Julian Braunsweg – Music, Art & Drama Society	Michael Rouse, Benn Toff, Kay Ambrose	
1948 April 7–10?	Usher Hall, Edinburgh						
1948 April 15–17?	The Arts Theatre, Cambridge	Ram Gopal and his Indian Ballet					
1948 April 19–21	De Montfort Hall, Leicester	Ram Gopal and his Indian Ballet	As above				
1948 April 23 for two weeks	Copenhagen,	RG with his Hindu Dancers & Musicians			Braunsweg & Bengt Häger	Michael Rouse, Benn Toff, Kay Ambrose	

(*Continued*)

Dates	Venue	Title of show	Dancers	Musicians	Management 1	Management 2	Description/ info
1948 May 4	Cirkus Theatre Stockholm,	RG with his Hindu Dancers & Musicians			Braunsweg & Bengt Häger	Michael Rouse, Benn Toff, Kay Ambrose	
1948 May	Oslo	RG with his Hindu Dancers & Musicians			Braunsweg & Bengt Häger	Michael Rouse, Benn Toff, Kay Ambrose	
1948 June (extended to mid-June)	Gottenburg, and Stockholm	RG with his Hindu Dancers & Musicians			Braunsweg & Bengt Häger	Michael Rouse, Benn Toff, Kay Ambrose	
1948 June 21–6	Wimbledon Theatre, London	Ram Gopal's Indian Ballet					
1948 June 28–July 3?	Theatre Royal, Bath						
1948 July 5–10	Prince of Wales Theatre, Cardiff	RG and his Dancers & Musicians			Braunsweg		
1948 July 12–13	Opera House, Buxton	Ram Gopal Indian Ballet					
1948 July 14–17	Liverpool, Picton Hall						
1948 July 19–24	Royal Hippodrome, Belfast						

1948 July 26 for one week	Opera House, Leicester						
1948 August 2	New Theatre, Hull	Ram Gopal Ballet					
1948 August 12–28	Princes Theatre, London	RG & his Indian Dancers & Musicians	Kumudini, Lilavati & others		Bertram Montague in association with Julian Braunsweg (for Terpsichore Ltd)		
1948 August 30–September 11	Berne, Zurich, Basle, Geneva & Lausanne						
1948 September 30, October 1–3	New York City Center, New York	New York Golden Anniversary International Dance Festival	Featured Gopal and Paris Opera Ballet		Julian Braunsweg & Sol Hurok	Celebrating the Golden Jubilee of the City of New York	Requested by Nehru to represent India
1948 October 13–24 for twelve days	Century Theatre, New York	Ram Gopal and his Hindu Ballet Company	**CANCELLED!**		Sol Hurok		
1949 January 15	Imperial Institute, Film Theatre, London	Private recital	RG		Royal India and Pakistan Society		
1949 January 26–27	Victoria Hall, Hanley, Staffs	'Rhapsodie Espagnole' music & dance from Spain	RG part of mixed programme		Braunsweg and Leon Hepner		

(*Continued*)

Dates	Venue	Title of show	Dancers	Musicians	Management 1	Management 2	Description/ info
1949 15 February–March 3	Stockholm				Privately sponsored?		
1949 March 10	Helsingborgs Konserthus,						
1949 June/July?	South India, Ceylon						Sees Bala dance with Beryl de Zoete
1949 November	Stockholm						
1949	Istanbul & Ankara						
1950 March 7	Imperial Institute Cinema, V&A, London	East and West lecture demonstration	RG and Celia Franca		Under the Patronage of the Royal India, Pakistan and Ceylon Society		Kay Ambrose chaired
1950 April for one week) & May 8	Watergate Theatre, London	Series of lecture/ demonstration	Gopal, Janaki, Leela				

1950 October 16 for two weeks	Adelphi Theatre, London	RG with his Indian Dancers & Musicians	Kumudini, Sesha, Mrinalini, Jaron Yaltan, Janaki, Manil, Zan, Shanta, Sushila	Rajani Lakhia – musical director Kumar – sitar and sarod Sirisena – Bera, Madalan and Khol Razdan – sitar, Suresh Store – sitar, Lakshmi & Ragini – tambura and song	By arrangement with Jack Hylton. Eugene Iskoldoff in arrang with Lynford-Joel Promotions, Ltd. Under the Patronage of the Royal India, Pakistan and Ceylon Society	M. Rouse – co manager; William Jay – stage manager; Kate Austen – lighting
1950 October 30 for one week	Wimbledon Theatre, London	RG with his Indian Dancers & Musicians	Anura, Kumudini, Sesha, Mrinalini, Jaron Yaltan, Janaki, Manil, Shanta, Nandawathi,	Rajani Lakhia– musical director Kumar – sitar and sarod Sirisena – Bera, Madalan and Khol Razdan – sitar	Eugene Iskoldoff in arrangement with Lynford-Joel Promotions, Ltd.	
1950 December 11 for one week	Theatre Royal, Brighton	RG with his Indian Dancers & Musicians	Anura, Kumudini, Sesha, Manil, Nandawathi, Mrinalini, Jaron Yaltan	Rajani Lakhia – musical director Kumar – sitar and sarod Anura – drums and percussion Sirisena – Bera, Madalan and Khol	U.M.A. Production (London) Ltd in association with Lynford-Joel Promotions Ltd	M. Rouse – co manager; William Jay – stage manager

(*Continued*)

Dates	Venue	Title of show	Dancers	Musicians	Management 1	Management 2	Description/ info
1951 January 1 for one week	White Rock Pavilion, Hastings	RG & his Indian Dancers & Musicians	Anura, Kumudini, Sesha, Lalita, Nandawathi, Mrinalini, Jaron Yaltan	Rajani Lakhia – musical director Kumar – sitar and sarod Anura – drums and percussion Sirisena – Bera, Madalan and Khol	U.M.A. Production (London) Ltd in association with Lynford-Joel Promotions Ltd	M. Rouse – co manager; William Jay – stage manager	
1951 January 8	Watergate Theatre, London						
1951 January 9 for two weeks	Cambridge Theatre, London	As below	As below	As below			
1951 January 29	Prince of Wales Theatre, Cardiff	RG with his Indian Dancers & Musicians	As below	Rajani Lakhia – musical director Kumar – sitar and sarod Anura – drums and percussion Sirisena – Bera, Madalan and Khol Suresh Store – sitar	Barry O'Brien in association with U.M.A. Productions		

1951 February 5 for two weeks	King's Theatre, London	RG with his Indian Dancers & Musicians	Sesha, Kumudini, Anura, Mrinalini, Damayanti, Nandawathi, Jaron Yaltan	Rajani Lakhia – musical director Kumar – sitar and sarod Anura – drums and percussion Sirisena – Bera, Madalan and Khol Suresh Store – sitar	Barry O'Brien in association with U.M.A. Productions, Under the Patronage of the Royal India, Pakistan and Ceylon Society	M. Rouse – co manager; William Jay – stage manager; business manager –Otto Gregory	
1951 June 25 for one week	The Opera House, Manchester	Ram Gopal with his Indian Ballet and Orchestra	As below		U.M.A. Productions		
1951 July 23	Gaiety Theatre, Dublin						
1951 July	Llangollen Eisteddfod, Wales						
1951 November 20 +	Stockholm						
1952 February 20	V&A Museum, London	Illustrated Lecture by W. G. Archer accompanied by Gopal and dancers	No names of dancers	No names of musicians			Lecture titled 'Romance and Religion in Indian Painting and Dancing'

(*Continued*)

Dates	Venue	Title of show	Dancers	Musicians	Management 1	Management 2	Description/ info
1952 August 4	Leeds						
1952 August	Gaiety Theatre, Dublin						
1952 September 1	Berlin Cultural Festival, Berlin						
1952 September 28, 29	Stockholm						
1952 November 23 for three weeks	King's Theatre, London	RG & his Indian Dancers & Musicians	Kumudini, Govinda, Rekha, Anura, Tara Devi	Lakhia & musicians	Peter Daubney Presentations Ltd in association with H.E., the High Commissioner for India	Michael Rouse & William Jay	
1953 July 12 (festival was from June 15 to July 15)	Studsschuowburg, Amsterdam,	RG & his Indian Dancers & Musicians			Holland Festival		
1953 October	New York	?	?				
1954 May 12	India House, London	Spring Festival reception	Gopal, Anura, Amala, Chitra	N. N. Razdan & musicians			

1954 August 11–14 & September 3–4	Jacob's Pillow Dance Festival, Massachusetts (13th season)	Ram Gopal & the Celtic Ballet of Scotland (mixed bill)	RG	Percussion for Garuda – Eyrick Darby	Ted Shawn	?	No description of style (except *Rajput Serenade* (Kathak) but end of programme has Bharata Natya costumes and Kathak costumes by …
1954 August 16	Jacob's Pillow Dance Festival, Massachusetts	Ram Gopal and the Dance of India	RG Lecture/ demo	?	Ted Shawn	?	
1954 September	United Nations headquarters staff day, New York						
1954	Ceylon tour						
1955 January 15	Forbes House, Hyde Park, London	Diaghilev Exhibition. Gopal gives talk 'The Dance as Yoga'			The Observer		

(*Continued*)

Dates	Venue	Title of show	Dancers	Musicians	Management 1	Management 2	Description/ info
1955 January 23	Stoll Theatre, London	Charity performance Midnight Ballet honouring 25th anniversary of Pavlova's death	Gopal, Fonteyn, Somes, Markova, Dolin, Gilpin & others. De Valois gives talk on Pavlova		Gorlinsky		
1955 August	New York						
1955 November 16 8.00 p.m., & November 19, 2.30 & 8 p.m.	French Institute, London	Ram Gopal	Anura & company	?	Asian Music Circle	Stage manager – Charles Grey	
1956 September 3–7 (two different progs)	Edinburgh Festival, Edinburgh	RG and his new Indian Company 'Legend of Taj Mahal'	As below	As below	Sandor Gorlinsky		
1956 September 10–22 (two different progs)	Royal Festival Hall, London	RG and his new Indian Company	As below	As below	LCC with S. A Gorlinsky	Wardrobe David Henshaw	

1956 October 8 for three weeks (two different progs)	London Hippodrome	RG and his new Indian Company Legend of Taj Mahal	Shevanti, Kumudini, Satyavati, Anura, Namboodri, Surendra Sinha, Satyavan, Sukendu Dutt, Raman Lal	Rajani Lakhia – musical director	S. A. Gorlinksy for CONTINENTAL OPERA & BALLET ENTERTAINMENTS LTD		
1956 December 2	St Pancras Town Hall, London	Classical & Folk dances by dancers and musicians of Ram Gopal Company			Asian Music Circle		
1956 December	Théâtre des Champs-Elysées, Paris	RG and his new Indian Company	Kumdhini, Shevanti, Kamal, Satyavati, Namboodri	Lakhia + others	S. A. Gorlinsky	AD Doris Barry; William Jay – stage manager	Words describing Bharata Natya in programme, as well as K, KK & Manipuri
1957 January	Paris						
1957 June 14	Rembrandt Hotel, London	Ram Gopal one of several speakers			College of Psychic Science dinner		
1957 August	Edinburgh Festival, Edinburgh						

(*Continued*)

Dates	Venue	Title of show	Dancers	Musicians	Management 1	Management 2	Description/ info
1958 July 15–19	Jacob's Pillow Dance Festival, Massachusetts (26th season)	Ram Gopal (mixed bill)	RG	Sri Ramanlal – tabla for Kathak dance (kathak teacher and dancer)	Ted Shawn	Stage manager Judy Rutherford	Mention of Kathak in prog
1958 November 4, 6, 9	Trinidad. (three different theatres)		With La Meri & Smt Gina (Gina Blau)				
1959 May 3, 6, 9	Mahatma Gandhi Hall, London	Dances of India with Ram Gopal			Asian Music Circle		
1959 May 25 for one week	Royal Court Theatre, Liverpool	'Trio de Ballet'	RG, Marina Svetlova, Alexis Rassine				RG – India & Asia's finest dancer
1959 June 1 for one week	Kings Theatre, Edinburgh	'Trio de Ballet'	RG, Marina Svetlova, Alexis Rassine				RG – India & Asia's finest dancer
1959 June 8 for one week	Kings Theatre, Glasgow	'Trio de Ballet'	RG, Marina Svetlova, Alexis Rassine				RG – India & Asia's finest dancer
1959 June 15 for one week	Theatre Royal, Newcastle	'Trio de Ballet'	RG, Marina Svetlana, Alex Rassine				RG – India & Asia's finest dancer [NB. photo in Dublin City archives]

1959 June 24–July 5	The Playhouse, Oxford	Ram Gopal				
1959 August 28–September 1	Stockholm					
1959 October 20	Kenya	'Trio de Ballet'	RG, Marina Svetlana, Alex Rassine			
1959 December 3	Kampala	Opening of Uganda National Theatre	Ram Gopal			
1960 February 29–March 2	St Pancras Town Hall (as part of St Pancras Arts Festival), London	RG and a Troupe of Indian and Kandayan musicians and dancers	Nirmala, Shamin Mahal, Vibha Naik, Praful Patel. Sesha Palihakkara, Anura	Malti Jain – sitar Y. G. Srimati –veena Kishen Khare – tabla Shankar Angadi – tamboura	Asian Music Circle in association with St Pancras Public Libraries Committee	
1960 March 7–21	Princes Theatre, London	RG and his Indian Company, with Special Guest MARKOVA			By arrangement with Jack Harlton, presented by Barry O'Brien	SM Billy Jay Representing Markova, Dora Barry
1960 May 1?	Manchester Lesser Free Trade Hall, Manchester					

(*Continued*)

Dates	Venue	Title of show	Dancers	Musicians	Management 1	Management 2	Description/ info
1960 July 5	Llangollen, Eisteddfod, Wales	RG and his Indian Dancers					
1960 July?	Nervi International Ballet Festival, Genoa						
1960 August **1960** November 5	Edinburgh Festival, Edinburgh Jerusalem, Israel	RG and his Indian Company					
1962 March 18?	Trinidad						
1962 October 1	French Institute, London	Short programme of Gopal and his dancers, and Flamenco dancers	Gopal, Shala, Malika Devi		Organized by the Royal India, Pakistan & Ceylon Society		
1963 January 8	RMS Amazon (ship – Royal Mail Lines)	Ram Gopal and his Indian Dancers					

1965 March 8 for two weeks	Queens Theatre, London	Ram Gopal and his Dancers and Musicians	Malika Devi, Zohra Segal, Manjulika Bhandari, Tazi Sheharazad, Anura, Kiran Segal (daughter) + Bhangra group	Master Chikkoo, Baba Sen, Oliver Davis, Surindar Sandhi, Jasbinder Sandhu, Darshan Singh	Douglas Proudley & John Brason for Theatreways Ltd present RG, by arrangement with H. M. Tennant, Ltd	India and Asia's Greatest Dancer
1965 August 26	Commonwealth Institute, London	Gopal introduces Yamini Krishnamurti	Also gives talk and performances			
1965 September 20–22	Scala Theatre, London	Ram Gopal and Yamini Krishnamurti. Indian Classical Dancing				India's Greatest Dancer
1966 March 29–April 2	Commonwealth Institute, London					

Appendix 2: Gopal in commercial feature films and TV film

Hindustan Hamara [Our India] was a patriotic Hindi film made by the Documentary Film Corporation of India in 1940 in black and white and which ran for 139 minutes. Directed by Ram Daryani, the story covered a feudal melodrama. There is, however, very little information about this film or what part Gopal played. In ***The Planter's Wife***, a story of rubber plantation owner with a marriage at breaking point, Gopal is a hero called Nair. The film was directed by Ken Annakin and premiered on 16 September at Leicester Square cinema in London 1952 (see Chapter 4). It was featured in the same month's issue of *The World of Cinema* with an accompanying photo. Its international release in Hollywood on 6 December was announced *The Los Angeles Times*, 1952. Much later, in July 1996, the film was broadcast on British television. The British film kept the original title but the American version became ***Outpost in Malaya***. Filmed in Sri Lanka and at Pinewood Studios in Britain in black and white, the film ran for ninety minutes with a score arranged by Gopal's musical director Rajani Lakhia. Production company was J. Arthur Rank Organisation and Pinnacle Productions.

The Purple Plain starred Gregory Peck and was also filmed in Sri Lanka, at Elephant Pass, Sigirya Rock, and at the British Pinewood Studios. The director was Robert Parrish. Telling the story of a Canadian Second World War airman in Burma with the theme taken from a novel by H. E. Bates, Gopal plays the supporting role of one of the heroes, Mr Phang. Distributed first in London on 14 September 1954, then internationally, it was produced by Two Cities Film and ran for 100 minutes. In April 1955, prominent newspaper publicity announced the film's July showing in San Francisco and in Los Angeles.[1] Gopal's close friend Pamela Cullen was instrumental in getting him a part in the film and some small walk-ons for other friends.

In the film ***Elephant Walk***, released the same year (1954) and which starred Elizabeth Taylor and Peter Finch, Gopal does not act or dance but is credited

[1] See *The San Francisco Examiner*, 5 April 1955, page 31, and 7 April 1955, page 37; also the *Santa Cruz Sentinel*, 31 July 1955, page 11 which is mentioned briefly in Chapter 4.

with the choreography of the featured Kandyan dances. Filmed in Sri Lanka and directed by William Dieterle, the story is of a tea plantation owner who owns a house called Elephant Walk. Made by Paramount Pictures in colour, and running for 100 minutes, it was circulated first in the United States in April and later in Britain in August of 1954. The following year in 1955, ***Navy Heroes*** (alternative titles *The Blue Peter, School for Adventure*) was released in November in Britain and a month later in the United States. Directed by Wolf Rilla, it features a Merchant Navy officer returning to Britain after time spent in a Korean POW camp with Gopal playing the character of Dr Tigara. Filmed in Aberdovey, Wales, at the Outward Bound Sea School and Yacht Club, it runs for ninety minutes. Finally, in ***Leave to Die***, a British TV film, Gopal plays the part of Daya Ram. This is listed at the British Film Institute (BFI) and is one episode in a TV series titled *Rheingold Theatre*, an anthology series narrated, produced and starring Douglas Fairbanks Jr, and directed by Derek Twist. It was shown again on Yorkshire TV, UK, in May 1972. The rest of Gopal's TV appearances are discussed in Chapter 5.

Complete list of Gopal's films as a dancer and actor, plus TV appearances

1938 (Dir) 'The Dancer Ram Gopal'. Dir. D'Aguiar. [Restored by Ayisha Abraham, 2010.]

1939 'Ram Gopal and His Hindu Dancers and Musicians'. London TV.

1940 'Hindustan Hamara'. Dir. Paul Zils.

1944 'Draupadi', New Huns Picture. Dir. Baburao Patel. Gopal danced with Janaki and composed four-minute group dance.

1947 British Pathé newsreel. Gopal dancing at opening of new gallery at the V&A, London [silent].

1948 'Ram Gopal and Shevanti'. BBC TV. 27 November 1948. 9.30 p.m. in a programme of Indian dances including *Golden Eagle, Ajanta Frescoes* and *Rajput Serenade of Love. Drum Dance* by Anura and classical Indian music played by Ram Gopal's own company of Indian musicians. Presented by Christian Simpson.

1948 'Lord Shiva Danced'. Dir. Sarah Erulkar. India & UK. Shell Film Unit.

1955 'The Commonwealth Show'. BBC TV.

1952 'The Planter's Wife'. Dir. Ken Annakin (alternative US title 'Outpost in Malaya'). Gopal plays Nair. Pinnacle Productions.

1954 'Elephant Walk'. Dir. William Dieterle. Gopal choreographer. Paramount Picture Corporation.

1954 'The Purple Plain'. Dir. Robert Parrish. Gopal plays Mr Phang (hero). Two Cities Films.

1954 'Ram Gopal'. Dir. Carol Lynn. Filmed danced performance at Jacob's Pillow, USA.

1955 'We Do It Differently'. Prod. Joan Kemp-Welch. British TV film.

1955 'Navy Heroes'. Dir. Wolf Rilla (alternative titles: 'The Blue Peter', 'School for Adventure'). Gopal plays Dr Tigara. British Lion Film Corporation and Distributors Corporation of America.

1956 'Russian Ballet'. Dir. John de Vere Loder. UK documentary. Gopal contributor.

1956 'Leave to Die'. Dir. Derek Twist. Gopal plays Daya Ram. TV film, UK.

1957 'Chelsea at Nine'. Weekly TV cabaret show, Granda TV. Dir. Corby Ruskin.

1957 'Alan Melville Takes You from A-Z'. BBC TV. Hosted by Alan Melville.

1957 'McCreary Moves'. Gopal appeared as dancer.

1970 'Aum Shiva'. Dir. Claude Lamorisse. 2.5 hours. Screening at Commonwealth Institute, London.

1973 'Nataraja: King of Dance'. Dir. Claude Lamorisse.

1973 'WIB-Schaukel'. German TV chat show, hosted by Margret Dünser.

1989 'Bandung File: Ram Gopal, Dancing to the Music of Time'. TV documentary.

2012 'I Saw a God Dance'. Dir. Ayisha Abraham. Bangalore, India. Film Tales.

2016 'Remembering Ram Gopal, a Documentary'. Made by South Asian Diaspora Arts Archive (SADAA).

Bibliography

Abraham, Ayisha (2008), 'Deteriorating Memories: Blurring Fact and Fiction in Home Movies in India' in Karen L. Ishizuka & Patricia R. Zimmermann (eds), *Mining the Home Movie. Excavations in Histories and Memories*, 168–84, Los Angeles, London: University of California Press.

Abraham, Ayisha (2013), 'From the Rooftop into the Mine', *New Cinemas: Journal of Contemporary Film*, 11 (2/3): 169–82.

Abrams, Lynn (2016), *Oral History Theory*, London, New York: Routledge.

Ackerley, Joe Randolph (1952 [1932]), *Hindoo Holiday*, London: Chatto & Windus.

Akademi (2000), 'Coming of Age', https://akademi.co.uk/performance/coming-of-age-description. Accessed 24.08.20.

Allen, Matthew Harp (2010 [1997]), 'Rewriting the Script for South Indian Dance' in Davesh Soneji (ed.), *Bharatanatyam: A Reader*, New Delhi, 205–45, Oxford: Oxford University Press.

Alter, Joseph (1994), 'Celibacy, Sexuality and the Transformation of Gender into Nationalism in North India', *Journal of Asian Studies*, 53 (1): 45–66.

Ambrose, Kay (1941), *Balletomane's Sketch-Book*, London: Adam & Charles Black.

Ambrose, Kay (1943), *The Ballet-Lover's Pocket-Book*, London: Adam & Charles Black.

Ambrose, Kay (1950), *Classical Dances & Costumes of India*, London: Adam & Charles Black.

Ambrose, Kay (1951a), *The Ballet Lover's Companion*, London: Adam & Charles Black.

Ambrose, Kay (1951b), *The Story of Ram Gopal*, London: John Dilworth Ltd.

Anthony, Gordon (1953 [1952]), *Dancers of the World in Colour*, London: Phoenix House Ltd.

Appadurai, Arjun (1991), 'Global Ethnoscapes: Notes and Queries for a Transnational Anthropology' in Richard G. Fox (ed.), *Recapturing Anthropology: Working in the Present*, 191–210, Santa Fe: School of American Research Press.

Appiah, Kwame Anthony (1997), 'Cosmopolitan Patriots', *Critical Inquiry*, 23: 617–39.

Atkinson, Paul et al., eds. (2001), *Handbook of Ethnography*, London: Sage Publications.

Baas, Michiel (2015), 'The New Indian Male. Muscles, Masculinity and Middle Classness' in Knut A. Jacobsen (ed.), *Routledge Handbook of Contemporary India*, 444–56, Oxford, New York: Routledge.

Balaji, Murali & Khadeem Hughson (2014), '(Re)producing Borders and Bodies: Masculinity and Nationalism in Indian Cultural Texts', *Asian Journal of Communication*, 24 (3): 207–21.

Balchin, Marianne (2000), Interview with author, June.

Balme, Christopher & Berenika Szymanski-Düll (2017), 'Introduction' in Christopher Balme & Berenika Szymanski-Düll (eds), *Theatre, Globalization and the Cold War*, 1–22, Basingstoke, Hants: Palgrave Macmillan.

Banerjee, Sikita (2005), *Make Me a Man! Masculinity, Hinduism and Nationalism in India*, Albany, New York: State University of New York Press.

Banerjee, Sikita (2012), *Muscular Nationalism: Gender, Violence, and Empire in Indian and Ireland, 1914–2004*, New York: New York University Press.

Baron (1950), *Baron at the Ballet*, St James's Place, London: Collins.

Barthes, Roland (1975), *The Pleasure of the Text*, trans. R. Miller, New York: Hill & Wang.

Bharucha, Rustom (2003), *Rajasthan, an Oral History. Conversations with Komal Kothari*, New Delhi: Penguin Books India.

Basavarajaiah, Veena (2018), 'Corporatization of Dance. Changing Landscape in Choreography and Patronage since Economic Liberalization on Bengaluru' in Pallabi Chakravorty & Nilanjana Gupta (eds), *Dance Matters Too. Markets, Memories, Identities*, 95–106, New York, London: Routledge.

Beaton, Cecil (1991 [1945]), *Indian Diary and Album*, Oxford: Oxford University Press.

Beaton, Cecil (1951), *Ballet*, London: Wingate.

Beaumont, Cyril (1950), 'Review', *Sunday Times*, 22 October, n.p.

Beaumont, Cyril (1956), 'Ram Gopal Programme Note', Royal Festival Hall, London, September, n.p.

Beltz, Johannes (2011), 'The Dancing Shiva: South Indian Processional Bronze, Museum Artwork, and Universal Icon', *Journal of Religion in Europe*, 4: 204–22.

Bharatamuni (1986), The *Natya Sastra* [transl. Board of Scholars], Delhi: Sri Satguru Publications.

Bhattacharjya, Nilanjana (2011), 'A Productive Distance from the Nation: Uday Shankar and the Defining of Indian Modern Dance', *South Asian History and Culture*, 2 (4): 482–501.

Bollen, Jonathan (2002), 'The Morality of Movement: Intercorporeality at a Male Dance Festival', http://jonathanbollen.net/movement-and-matter/the-morality-of-movement/ Accessed 26.6.16.

Bollen, Jonathan (2020), *Touring Variety in the Asian-Pacific Region, 1946–1975*, Basingstoke: Palgrave Macmillan.

Bourdieu, Pierre (2004 [1986]), 'L'illusion biographique' trans. Yves Winkin & Wendy Leeds-Hurwitz in Paul Du Gay, Jessica Evans & Paul Redman (eds), *Identity: A Reader*, 299–305, London: Sage Publications.

Bradley, Lionel (1939), 'Ballet Bulletin', unpublished notebooks, V&A archive, London.

Braunsweg, Julian (1977 [1973]), *Ballet Scandals*, London: George Allen & Unwin Ltd.

Brenscheidt, Diana (2011), *Shiva Onstage. Uday Shankar's Company of Hindu Dancers and Musicians in Europe and the United States, 1931–38*, Zurich: Lit Verlag.

Brettell, Caroline B., ed. (1993), *When They Read What We Write: The Politics of Ethnography*, Westport, Connecticut: Bergin & Garvey.

Buckland, Theresa J. (1983), 'Definitions of Folk Dance: Some Explorations', *Folk Music Journal*, IV (4): 315–32.

Buckland, Theresa J. (1999), *Dance in the Field: Theory, Methods and Issues in Dance Ethnography*, Basingstoke, UK: Macmillan Press.

Buckle, Richard (1951), 'Review', *Observer*, 21 January, 6.

Burt, Ramsey (1995), *The Male Dancer. Bodies, Spectacle, Sexualities*, London, New York: Routledge.

Burt, Ramsey & Michael Huxley (2019), *Dance, Modernism and Modernity*, London: Routledge.

Butler, Judith (1993), *Bodies That Matter: On the Discursive Limits of 'Sex'*, London: Routledge.

Cannadine, David (2001), *Ornamentalism: How the British Saw Their Empire*, London: Penguin Press.

Carter, Alexandra (2018), 'Destabilising the Discipline: Critical Debates about History and Their Impact on the Study of Dance' in Geraldine Morris & Larraine Nicholas (eds), *Rethinking Dance History, Issues and Methodologies*, 114–22, London, New York: Routledge.

Cashmore, Ellis (2006), *Celebrity/Culture*, Oxford: Routledge.

Casperson, Jenny Levy (2016a), Interview, 'Remembering Ram Gopal, a Documentary', SADAA.

Casperson, Jenny Levy (2016b), Interview with author, August.

CERN, https://cds.cern.ch/record/745737?ln=en Accessed 7.8.20.

Chakravorty, Pallabi (2008), *Bells of Change. Kathak Dance, Women and Modernity in India*, Calcutta, London, New York: Seagull Books.

Chatterji, Joya (2018), 'From Imperial Subjects to National Citizens: South Asians and the International Migration Regime since 1947' in Joya Chatterji & David Washbrook (eds), *Routledge Handbook of the South Asian Diaspora*, 183–97, London, New York: Routledge.

Chattopadhyay, Saayan (2011), 'Bengali Masculinity and the National-Masculine: Some Conjectures for Interpretation', *South Asia Research*, 31 (3): 265–79.

Chaudhary, Zahid (2004), 'Controlling the Ganymedes: The Colonial Gaze in J. R. Ackerleys' Hindoo Holiday' in Sanjay Srinastav (ed.), *Sexual Sites, Seminal Attitudes: Sexualities, Masculinities and Culture in South Asia*, 83–98, New Delhi, London: Sage Publications.

Cheesman, Nick (2014), 'Bodies on the Line in Burma's Law Reports, 1892–1922', in Melissa Crouch & Tim Lindsey (eds), *Law, Society and Transition in Myanmar*, 77–94, Oxford: Hart Publishing.

Clifford, James (1992), 'Traveling Cultures' in Lawrence Grossberg, et al. (eds), *Cultural Studies*, 96–116, New York: Routledge.

Cohen, Matthew (2011), *Performing Otherness. Java and Bali on International Stage, 1905–19*, London: Palgrave Macmillan.

Cohen, Mitchell (1992), 'Rooted Cosmopolitanism', *Dissent*, 39: 478–83.

Comaroff, John & Jean (1992), *Ethnography and the Historical Imagination*, Colorado: Westview Press.

Coolawarla, Uttara Asha (1992), 'Ruth St Denis and India's Dance Renaissance', *Dance Chronicle* 15 (2): 123–52.

Coolawarla, Uttara Asha (2002), 'Response to Dr A. Grau's "Dance and Cultural Identity"', *Animated*, Autumn, 30–3.

Coolawarla, Uttara Asha (2004), 'The Sanskritized Body', *Dance Research Journal*, 36 (2): 50–63.

Coomaraswamy, Ananda K. (2011 [1918]), *The Dance of Siva: Essays on Indian Art and Culture*, New York: Dover Publications Inc.

Counsell, Colin (2009), 'Introduction' in Colin Counsell & Roberta Mock (eds), *Performance, Embodiment and Cultural Memory*, 1–15, Newcastle, UK: Cambridge Scholars Publishing.

Craig, Maxine L. (2012), 'Racialized Bodies' in Bryan S. Turner (ed.), *The Routledge Handbook of Body Studies*, 321–32, London, New York: Routledge.

Crisp, Clement (2002), '"ICARE": Remembering Serge Lifar', *Dance Research*, 20 (2): 3–15.

Cullen, Pamela (2016), Interview, 'Remembering Ram Gopal, a Documentary', SADAA.

Cullen, Pamela (2015–20), Personal communication with author.

Dattani, Mahesh (2013 [1989]), *Dance Like a Man*, London: Penguin.

Daugherty, Diane (2000), 'Fifty Years On: Arts Funding in Kerala Today', *Asian Theatre Journal*, 17 (2): 237–52.

David, Ann R. (2001a), *Perceptions and Misconceptions: Ram Gopal's Challenge to Orientalism*, MA diss., University of Surrey, Guildford, UK.

David, Ann R. (2001b), 'Ram Gopal: A Challenge to Orientalism. Part 1', *Attendance. The Dance Annual of India*, 35–45, New Delhi: EKAH-Printways.

David, Ann R. (2001c), 'Ram Gopal: The Post-War Years Part II', *Attendance. The Dance Annual of India*, 46–53, New Delhi: EKAH-Printways.

David, Ann R. (2006), 'When the Body Becomes the Dance – The "Orientalist" Gaze and the Idealised Male Dancing Body: Ram Gopal in the UK', *Pulse Journal*, (6) (Spring): 13–15.

David, Ann R. (2007), 'Religious Dogma or Political Agenda? Bharatanatyam and Its Re-emergence in British Tamil Temples', *Journal for the Anthropological Study of Human Movement*, 14 (4), http://jashm.press.illinois.edu/.

David, Ann R. (2010a), 'Gendered Orientalism? Gazing on the Male South Asian Dancer', *Proceedings of the 26th Symposium of the ICTM Study Group on Ethnochoreology*, Trest, Czech Republic, 21–8.

David, Ann R. (2010b), 'Negotiating Identity: Dance and Religion in British Hindu Communities' in Pallabi Chakravorty & Nilanjana Gupta (eds), *Dance Matters: Performing India on Local and Global Stages*, 89–107, London, New York and New Delhi: Routledge.

David, Ann R. (2010c), 'Gendered Dynamics of the Divine: Trance and Possession Practices in Diasporic Hindu Sites in East London' in Andrew Dawson (ed.),

Summoning the Spirits: Possession and Invocation in Contemporary Religion, 74–90, London, New York: I.B. Tauris.

David, Ann R. (2012a), 'Sacralising the City: Sound, Space and Performance in Hindu Ritual Practices in London', *Culture and Religion*, 13 (4): 449–67.

David, Ann R. (2012b), 'Embodied Migration: Performance Practices of Diasporic Sri Lankan Tamil Communities in London', *Journal of Intercultural Studies*, 33 (4): 375–94.

David, Ann R. (2013), 'Change of an Era? The ISTD Classical Indian Dance Faculty Comes of Age', *ISTD DANCE Magazine*, 464: 58–9.

David, Ann R. (2015), 'King of Bollywood? The Construction of a Global Image in Shah Rukh Khan's Dance Choreography' in Rajinder Dudrah & Elke Mader (eds), *Shah Rukh Khan and Global Bollywood*, 279–207, Oxford, New Delhi: Oxford University Press India.

David, Ann R. (2021), 'The "Voice of the Body": Revisiting the Concept of Embodied Ethnography in the Anthropology of Dance' in Stephen Cottrell (ed.), *Music, Dance, Anthropology*, 95–120, Herefordshire: Sean Kingston Publishing.

Davies, Charlotte Aull (1999), *Reflexive Ethnography – A Guide to Researching Selves and Others*, London, New York: Routledge.

Day, Tony & Maya H. T. Liem, eds. (2018), *Cultures at War: The Cold War and Cultural Expression in Southeast Asia*, New York: Cornell University Press.

de Zoete, Beryl (1947a), 'Indian Dancing', *Spectator*, 26 December, n.p.

de Zoete, Beryl (1947b), 'Review', *New Statesman*, 13 December, 47.

Denis, Ruth St. (1939), *An Unfinished Life*, New York: Harper & Brothers.

Deshpande, Sudhanva (2005), 'The Consumable Hero of Globalised India', in Raminder Kaur & Ajay Sinha (eds), *Bollyworld. Popular Indian Cinema through a Transnational Lens*, 186–206, New Delhi, London: Sage Publications.

Desmond, Jane (2001), 'Dancing out the Difference: Cultural Imperialism and Ruth St Denis' "Radha" of 1906', *Signs*, 17 (1): 28–49.

Devlin, Graham (1989), *Stepping Forward. Some Suggestions for the Development of Dance in England during the 1990s*, London: Arts Council.

Dodds, Sherill (2001), *Dance on Screen: Genres and Media from Hollywood to Experimental Art*, Basingstoke: Palgrave Macmillan.

Dyer, Richard (2004 [1986]), *Heavenly Bodies. Film Stars and Society*, London, New York: Routledge.

Dytrych, Hanka (2009), 'In the Ram Gopal School', in Theresa Glazer et al. (eds), *Poles in India 1942–1948: Second World War Story*, 447–8, Beckenham, UK: Association of Poles in India.

Erdman, Joan L. (1983), 'Who Should Speak for the Performing Arts? The Case of the Delhi Dancers', *Pacific Affairs*, 56 (2): 247–69.

Erdman, Joan L. (1987), 'Performance as Translation: Uday Shankar in the West', *The Drama Review*, 31 (1): 64–88.

Erdman, Joan L. (1996), 'Dance Discourses: Rethinking the History of the "Oriental Dance"' in Gay Morris (ed.), *Moving Words. Rewriting Dance*, 288–305, London: Routledge.

Erdman, Joan L. (2008), 'A Comment of Dance Scholarship', *Dance Chronicle*, 31: 306–9.

Erdman, Joan L., ed. (1992), *Arts Patronage in India: Methods, Motives, and Markets*, New Delhi: Manohar Publications.

Farnell, Brenda (1999), 'It Goes without Saying – But Not Always' in Theresa J. Buckland (ed.), *Dance in the Field: Theory, Methods and Issues in Dance Ethnography*, 145–60, Basingstoke, UK: Macmillan Press.

Fischer-Lichte, Erika (2009), 'Interweaving Cultures in Performance: Different States of Being In-Between', *New Theatre Quarterly*, 25 (4): 391–401.

Fisher, Jennifer & Anthony Shay, eds. (2009), *When Men Dance. Choreographing Masculinities across Borders*, Oxford: Oxford University Press.

Foster, Susan L. (2008), 'Movement's Contagion: The Kinesthetic Impact of Performance' in Tracy C. Davis (ed.), *The Cambridge Companion to Performance Studies*, 46–59, Cambridge, New York: Cambridge University Press.

Gard, Michael (2006), *Men Who Dance: Aesthetics, Athletics and the Art of Masculinity*, New York: Peter Lang.

Gaston, Anne-Marie (1996), *Bharata Natyam – From Temple to Theatre*, New Delhi: Manohar.

Gaston, Anne-Marie (2011), 'Dance and Hinduism. A Personal Exploration' in Hillary P. Rodrigues, (ed), *Hinduism in Practice*, 75–86, London, New York: Routledge.

Gibert, Marie-Pierre (2007), 'The Intricacies of Being Israeli and Yemenite: An Ethnographic Study of Yemenite "Ethnic" Dance Companies in Israel', *Qualitative Sociology Review*, 3 (3): 100–12.

Gilbert, David (2005), 'Interrogating Mixed-Race: A Crisis of Ambiguity', *Social Identities*, 11 (1): 55–74.

Gilbert, Helen & Lo Jacqueline (2007), *Performance and Cosmopolitics: Cross-Cultural Transactions in Australasia*, London: Palgrave Macmillan.

Giurchescu, Anca (1994), 'Power and the Dance Symbol and Its Socio-Political Use' in Irene Loutzaki (ed.), *Proceedings of the 17th Symposium of the Study Group on Ethnochoreology*, 15–22, Nafplion, Greece: Peloponnesian Folklore Foundation.

Gopal, Ram (1947), 'An Introduction to Indian Dancing', *Ballet*, 4 (6): 37–44.

Gopal, Ram (1952), 'Hindu Themes Have Influenced European Ballet – And Dancers', *Ballet Today*, 25: 6–7.

Gopal, Ram (1957), *Rhythm in the Heavens. The Autobiography of Ram Gopal*, London: Secker & Warburg.

Gopal, Ram (1962), 'Eastern Dances for Western Dancers', *Dancing Times*, 16–17.

Gopal, Ram (1976), Audio interview with Adam Pinsker, London, 4 July 1976.

Gopal, Ram (2000–2003), Interviews with author.

Gopal, Ram & Serozh Dadachanji (1951), *Indian Dancing*, London: Phoenix House Ltd.

Gordziejko, Tessa, ed. (1996), *South Asian Dance in Schools: Teacher's Handbook*, Bradford: ADiTi.

Gorringe, Magdalen (2021), 'Towards a British Natyam. Creating a "British" Classical Indian Dance Profession', PhD Thesis, University of Roehampton, London.

Gorringe, Magdalen (2022), Personal communication with author, June.

Grau, Andrée (2001), 'Dance and Cultural Identity', *Animated*, 23–6.

Grau, Andrée (2002), *South Asian Dance in Britain: Negotiating Cultural Identity through Dance*, (SADiB report), Roehampton: University of Surrey.

Greenhalgh, Paul (1988), *Ephemeral Vistas: Great Exhibitions, Expositions Universelles and World's Fairs, 1851–1939*, Manchester: Manchester University Press.

Gregory, Barbara (2000), Personal communication with author, March.

Gregory, John (2013 [1996]), 'Ram Gopal', *Independent* obituary, 13 October, n.p.

Gupta, Charu (2007), 'Charu Gupta on Om Shanti Om and Saawariya', https://kafila.online/2007/12/19/charu-gupta-on-om-shanti-om-and-saawariya/ Accessed 6.5.20.

Gupta, Charu (2011), 'Anxious Hindu Masculinities in Colonial North India: Shuddhi and Sangathan Movements', *Crosscurrents*, December, 441–54.

Hall, Fernau (1956), 'As I See It', *Ballet Today*, July: 8, 21.

Hall, Stuart (1973), *Encoding and Decoding in the Television Discourse*, Birmingham: Centre for Cultural Studies, University of Birmingham.

Hammergren, Lena (2004), 'Many Sources, Many Voices' in Alexandra Carter (ed.), *Rethinking Dance History*, 20–31, London, New York: Routledge.

Hammergren, Lena (2009), 'The Power of Classification' in Susan Leigh Foster (ed.), *Worlding Dance*, 14–31, Basingstoke, Hants: Palgrave Macmillan.

Hanley, Elizabeth A. (2006), 'The Role of the Dance in the 1936 Berlin Olympic Games – Why Competition Became Festival and Art Became Competition', *Journal of Olympic History*, 14 (2): 38–42.

Harris, Oliver (2019), 'Archaeology and the Creation of Pasts', 2019 Curl Lecture, Royal Anthropological Institute AGM, 20 October.

Haskell, Arnold L. (1950), *Going to the Ballet*, Harmondsworth, Middx: Penguin Books.

Hastrup, Kirsten (1992), 'Anthropological Visions: Some Notes on Visual and Textural Authority' in Peter I. Crawford & David Turton (eds), *Film as Ethnography*, 8–25, Manchester: Manchester University Press.

Hayward, Chris & Máirtín Mac An Ghaill (2003), *Men and Masculinities: Theory, Research and Social Practice*, Buckingham: Open University Press.

Hewison, Robert (1997[1995]), *Culture & Consensus. England, Art and Politics since 1940*, London: Methuen.

'Hindu Dancing', *Dancing Times*, n.p.

Hodgson, John & Valerie Preston-Dunlop (1990), *Rudolf Laban: An Introduction to His Work and Influence*, Plymouth: Northcote House.

Holger, Hilda, www.hildaholger.com/bombay Accessed 5.9.18.

Hubel, Teresa (2010), 'The High Cost of Dancing. When the Indian Women's Movement Went after the Devadasis' in Davesh Soneji (ed.), *Bharatanatyam. A Reader*, 160–81, Oxford, New Delhi: Oxford University Press.

Hurok, Sol (1953), *S. Hurok Presents a Memoir of the Dance World*, New York: Hermitage House.

Imperial War Museum (2012), *Cecil Beaton. Theatre of War*, London: Jonathan Cape.

'Impressionable Hindu Dancing', *Dancing Times*, n.p.

'Indian Dance Spell', *Daily Herald*, 13 August, 1948.

Iyer, Alessandra, ed. (1997), *South Asian Dance – The British Experience* (Choreography and Dance), Amsterdam: Harwood Academic Publishers.

Jackson, II, L. Ronald & Murali Balaji (2014), 'Introduction. Conceptualizing Current Discourses and Writing New Ones' in Ronald L. Jackson II & Murali Balaji (eds), *Global Masculinities and Manhood*, 17–31, Chicago: University of Illinois Press.

Janta, Aleksander (1970), *Pamietnik Indyjski* [The Indian Diary], London: Oficyna Poetow I Malarzy.

Jarrett-Macauley, Delia (1997), *Review on South Asian Dance in England*, London: Arts Council.

Jayadev, U.K. (2002), Personal communication with author, August.

Johar, Navtej (2017), 'Indian Idealism. The Disenfranchised Body in Yoga, Dance and Urbanity' in Gabriele Brandstetter & Holger Hartung (eds), *Moving [across] Borders. Performing Translation, Intervention, Participation*, 151–68, Berlin: Transcript Verlag, Bielefeld.

Jones, Joy (2016–19), Interviews with author.

Jones, Kenneth W. (1976), *Arya Dharm: Hindu Consciousness in 19th Century Punjab*, Los Angeles: University of California Press.

Kamath, Harshita Mruthini (2019), *Impersonations. The Artifice of Brahmin Masculinity in South Indian Dance*, Oakland, California: University of California Press.

Kampe, Thomas (2013), 'Between Three Worlds: The Choreographer Hilde Holger' in Charmian Brinson & Richard Dove (eds), *German Speaking Exiles in the Performing Arts in Britain after 1933*, 187–206, Yearbook 14, Research Centre for German and Austrian Exile Studies, Rodopi, Amste: University of London.

Kant, Marion (2004), 'German Dance and Modernity: Don't Mention the Nazis' in Alexandra Carter (ed.), *Rethinking Dance History: A Reader*, 107–18, London, New York: Routledge.

Kant, Marion (2011), 'Death and the Maiden: Mary Wigman in the Weimar Republic' in Alexandra Kolb (ed.), *Dance and Politics*, 119–43, Oxford: Peter Lang.

Karina, Lilian & Marion Kant (2003), *Hitler's Dancers: German Modern Dance and the Third Reich*, trans. J. Steinberg, New York: Berghahn Books.

Katrak, Ketu H. (2011), *Contemporary Indian Dance: New Creative Choreography in India and the Diaspora*, Basingstoke, UK: Palgrave Macmillan.

Kaushik, Mira (2016), Interview, 'Remembering Ram Gopal, a Documentary', SADAA.

Kedhar, Anusha (2011), 'On the Move: Transnational South Asian Dancers and the "Flexible" Dancing Body', PhD thesis, University of California, Riverside.

Kedhar, Anusha (2014), 'Flexibility and Its Bodily Limits: Transnational South Asian Dancers in an Age of Neoliberalism', *Dance Research Journal*, 46 (1): 23–40.

Kerrigan, Finola, et al. (2004), *Arts Marketing*, Oxford: Elsevier.

Kersenboom, Saskia (2010), 'The Traditional Repertoire of the Tiruttani Temple Dancers' in Davesh Soneji (ed.), *Bharatanatyam. A Reader*, 53–68, New Delhi, Oxford: Oxford University Press.

Keshavan, Gayathri (2019), Personal communication with author, July.

Khan, Naseem (1976), *The Arts Britain Ignores. The Arts of Ethnic Minorities in Britain*, London: Commission for Racial Equality.

Khan, Naseem (1997), 'South Asian Dance in Britain 1960–1995' in Alessandra Iyer (ed.), *South Asian Dance: The British Experience* (Choreography and Dance), 25–30, Amsterdam: Harwood Academic Publishers.

Khan, Naseem (2003), 'Ram Gopal', *Guardian*, obituary, 13 October, n.p.

Khan, Naseem (2016), Interview, 'Remembering Ram Gopal, a Documentary', SADAA.

Khan, Naseem (2017a), *Everywhere Is Somewhere*, West Yorkshire: Bluemoose Books Ltd.

Khan, Naseem (2017b), Interview with Magdalen Gorringe, 13 February.

Khan, Yasmin (2016), *The Raj at War. A People's History of India's Second World War*, London: Penguin Books.

Khokar, Ashish Mohan (1998), 'Ram Gopal: The King of Classical Dance', *Attendance: The Dance Annual of India*, 64–71.

Khokar, Ashish Mohan (2003), 'Ram Gopal Obituary', http://www.narthaki.com/info/profiles/profil29.html Accessed 12.12.03.

Khokar, Ashish Mohan (2017), Personal communication with author, December.

Khokar, Ashish Mohan (2018), 'Pioneers of Indian Dance: Ram Gopal', https://www.sahapedia.org/ram-gopal-1912%E2%80%932003 Accessed 10.2.20.

Khoo, Mavin (2021), *Manch* UK talk online, 22 January, n.p. https://www.facebook.com/pg/manchukarts/videos/?ref=page_internal Accessed 22.1.21.

Kothari, Sunil (1991 [1984]), 'Ram Gopal Interview', *Sangeet Natak*, 101–2, July–December: 10–31.

Kothari, Sunil (2000), 'Ram Gopal: At Home Abroad', *Sruti Magazine*, 187, April, 21–8.

Kothari, Sunil (2017), 'Remembering Ram Gopal', https://narthaki.com/info/gtsk/gtsk164.html Accessed 5.2.18.

Kothari, Sunil (2020), Facebook Live interview on Ram Gopal, 1 August.

Kowal, Rebekah J. (2020), *Dancing the World Smaller. Staging Globalism in Mid-Century America*, New York: Oxford University Press.

Krishnan, Hari (2009), 'From Gynemimesis to Hypermasculinity: The Shifting Orientations of Male Performers of South Indian Court Dance' in Jennifer Fisher & Anthony Shay (eds), *When Men Dance. Choreographing Masculinities across Border*, 378–91, Oxford: Oxford University Press.

Krishnan, Hari (2023), Personal communication with author, April.

Kumar, Nand (2003), *Indian English Drama: A Study in Myth*, New Delhi: Sarup & Sons.

Lakhia, Kumudini (2012), Interview, *I Saw a God Dance* film, dir. Abraham.

Lakhia, Kumudini (2016), Interview, 'Remembering Ram Gopal, a Documentary', SADAA.

Lakhia, Kumudini (2017), Interview with author, December.

Lakhia, Kumudini (2020), Facebook Live interview on Ram Gopal, 1 August.

Layson, June (1995[1983]), 'Historical Perspectives in the Study of Dance' in Janet Adshead-Lansdale & June Layson (eds), *Dance History – An Introduction*, 3–17, London: Routledge.

Leonard, Maurice (1990), *Markova: The Legend*, London: Hodder & Stoughton.

Lifar, Serge (1938), 'Review', *Le Figaro*, 13 December, n.p.

Lightfoot, Mary Louise (2015), *Lightfoot Dancing: An Australian-Indian Affair*, Bermagui: New South Wales [E-book].

Loomba, Ania (1998), *Colonialism/Postcolonialism*, London: Routledge.

Lopez y Royo, Alessandra (2004), 'Dance in the British South Asian Diaspora: Redefining Classicism', *Postcolonial Text [online]*, 1 (1): 1–14.

Lowen, Sharon (1992), 'Patronage and Dance in India, or "You Think Learning to Dance Was Hard"' in Joan L. Erdman (ed.), *Arts Patronage in India: Methods, Motives, and Markets*, 225–38, New Delhi: Manohar Publications.

MacAloon, John J. (2006), 'Introduction: Muscular Christianity after 150 Years', *The International Journal of the History of Sport*, 23 (5): 687–700.

Macaulay, Thomas B. (1967 [1843]), *Macaulay: Prose and Poetry*, Cambridge, MA: Harvard University Press.

Mackrell, Judith (1989), 'Lord of the Dance', *The Independent*, 5 September, 17.

Manning, Susan (1993), *Ecstasy and the Demon: Feminism and Nationalism in the Dance of Mary Wigman*, Berkeley, LA: University of California Press.

Manning, Susan (1995), 'Modern Dance in the Third Reich: Six Positions and a Coda' in Susan Leigh Foster (ed.), *Choreographing History*, 165–76, Bloomington: Indiana University Press.

Manning, Susan (2018), 'Towards a Transnational History of Modern Dance', unpublished paper given at *Rewriting Dance Modernism* conference, Krakow, September.

Marks, Laura (2000), *The Skin of the Film. Intercultural Cinema, Embodiment, and the Senses*, Durham, London: Duke University Press.

Martin, John (1938), 'Ram Gopal Is Seen Here in Hindu Dances', *New York Times*, 1 May, 15.

Martin, John (1948), 'Boris Work Given by Ballet Russe. Quelque Fleurs Has Premiere at Metropolitan – Ram Gopal Bows at Dance Festival', *New York Times*, 1 October, 30.

Massey, Reginald (1969), 'India's Dances in London', *Dancing Times*, April, 369.

Massey, Reginald (2004), *India's Dances: Their History, Technique & Repertoire*, New Delhi: Abhinav Publications.

Matthews, Julie (2007), 'Eurasian Persuasions: Mixed Race, Performativity and Cosmopolitanism', *Journal of Intercultural Studies*, 28 (1): 41–54.

McGahan, Katy (2015), 'Obituary for Sarah Erulkar', *The Guardian*, https://www.theguardian.com/film/2015/jun/15/sarah-erulkar Accessed 4.7.20.

Meduri, Avanthi (1996), 'Nation, Woman, Representation: The Sutured History of the Devadasi and Her Dance', PhD thesis, New York University, NY.

Meduri, Avanthi (2004), 'Bharatanatyam as a Global Dance: Some Issues in Research, Teaching, and Practice', *Dance Research Journal*, 36 (2): 11–29.

Meduri, Avanthi (2008a), 'Labels, Histories, Politics: Indian/South Asian Dance on the Global Stage', *Dance Research*, 26 (2): 223–43.

Meduri, Avanthi (2008b), 'Temple Stage as Historical Allegory in Bharatanatyam. Rukmini Devi as Dancer-Historian' in Indira Viswanathan Peterson & Davesh Soneji (eds), *Performing Pasts. Reinventing the Arts in Modern South Asia*, 133–64, New Delhi: Oxford University Press.

Meduri, Avanthi, ed. (2005), *Rukmini Devi Arundale (1904–1986). A Visionary Architect of Indian Culture and the Performing Arts*, Delhi: Motilal Banarsidass Publishers.

Merchant, Hoshang & Akshaya K. Rath (2019), *Gay Icons of India*, New Delhi: Pan Macmillan Publishing.

Meri, La (1977), *Dance out the Answer*, New York: Marcel Dekker, Inc.

Merriman, Andy (2013), *Greaspaint & Cordite. How ENSA Entertained the Troops during World War II*, London: Aurum Press.

Mitra, Royona (2015), *Akram Khan. Dancing New Interculturalism*, Basingstoke, Hants: Palgrave Macmillan.

Moore, W. G. (1951), 'New Films for the Classroom. Ballet', *Look and Listen*, 5 (11): 257.

Morcom, Anna (2013), *Illicit Worlds of Indian Dance: Cultures of Exclusion*, London: Hurst.

Munsi, Urmimala Sarkar (2011), 'Imag(in)ing the Nation: Uday Shankar's Kalpana' in Urmimala Sarkar Munsi & Stephanie Burridge (eds), *Traversing Tradition: Celebrating Dance in India*, 124–50, Oxford, New Delhi: Routledge.

'Music Academy Conference Brochure', Madras, n.p.

Narayan, T. K. (2004), 'How I Met Ram Gopal', *Sruti*, February, 44–6.

'Nautch in SW7', *Illustrated London News*, 20 September, n.p.

Neilson, Brett (1999), 'On the New Cosmopolitanism', *Communal/Plural: Journal of Transnational and Cross-Cultural Studies*, 7 (1): 111–24.

Nicholas, Larraine (2007), *Dancing in Utopia. Dartington Hall and Its Dancers*, Hants, UK: Dance Books.

Nicholas, Larraine (2013), 'Dance and the Historical Imagination' in Jenny Bunker, Anna Pakes & Bonnie Rowell (eds), *Thinking through Dance. The Philosophy of Dance Performance and Practices*, 241–55, Hants, UK: Dance Books.

Oakley, George D. (1938), 'Ram Gopal Gives Farewell Recital at Dillingham Hall', *Honolulu Star Bulletin*, 3 February, 11.

Osanami Törngren, Sayaka & Yuna Sato (2021), 'Beyond Being Either-Or: Identification of Multiracial and Multiethnic Japanese Youth', *Journal of Ethnic and Migration Studies*, 47 (4): 802–20.

Osella, Caroline & Filippo Osella (2006), *Men and Masculinities in South India*, London, New York: Anthem Press.

O'Shea, Janet (2005), 'Rukmini Devi: Rethinking the Classical' in Avanthi Meduri (ed.), *Rukmini Devi Arundale (1904–1986). A Visionary Architect of Indian Culture and the Performing Arts*, 225–45, Delhi: Motilal Banarsidass Publishers.

O'Shea, Janet (2007), *At Home in the World. Bharata Natyam on the Global Stage*, Connecticut: Wesleyan University Press.

Owen, Norton (2002), 'Ted Shawn's Moving Images' in Judith Mitoma et al., (eds), *Envisioning Dance on Film and Video*, 61–5, New York, London: Routledge.

Ozturkmen, Arzu (1994), 'Folk Dance and Nationalism in Turkey' in Irene Loutzaki (ed.), *Proceedings of 17th Symposium of the Study Group on Ethnochoreology*, 83–6, Nafplion, Greece: Peloponnesian Folklore Foundation.

Parker, Peter (1990), *A Life of J. R. Ackerley*, London: Sphere Books.

Peacock, Bernard (1947), 'Ram Gopal. An Ambassador of Indian Art', *World Ballet News*, 6, 11 December, 5.

Pepper, Terence, et al. (2004), *Beaton Portraits*, London: National Portrait Gallery.

Peterson, Indira Visawanathan (1998), 'The Evolution of the Kuravanci Dance Drama in Tamil Nadu: Negotiating the "Folk" and the "Classical" in the Bharata Natyam Canon', *South Asia Research*, 18 (1): 39–72.

Pollock, Sheldon, et al. (2000), 'Cosmopolitanisms', *Public Culture*, 12 (3): 577–89.

Purkayastha, Prathana (2014), *Indian Modern Dance, Feminism and Transnationalism*, Hants, UK: Palgrave Macmillan.

Qureshi, Regula B. (2009), 'Sina ba Sina or "From Father to Son": Writing the Culture of Discipleship' in Richard K. Wolf (ed.), *Theorizing the Local. Music, Practice, and Experience in South Asia and Beyond*, 165–84, Oxford, New York: Oxford University Press.

Rabinow, Paul (1986), 'Representations Are Social Facts: Modernity and Postmodernity in Anthropology', in James Clifford & George E. Marcus (eds), *Writing Cultures: The Poetics and Politics of Ethnology*, 234–61, Berkeley: University of California Press.

Ramesh, Rajyashree (2017), Personal communication with author, August.

Ramgopal, ed. (1931), *Selections from Ingersoll, Vols 1 & 2*, Mysore: Joyser Press.

Ramgopal & P. R. Singarachan (1928), *Shakespeare. Othello*, Bangalore: Bright & Co.

Ramgopal & G.R. Joyser (1926), *Sociology, or The Law and Progress of Mankind and Their Institutions*, Bangalore: The Bangalore Press.

Ramgopal, Peter (2019), Interview with author, August 2019.

'Ram Gopal Obituary', *The Times*, 14 October, 31.

'Ram Gopal Obituary', *The Telegraph*, 24 October.

'Ram Gopal', *Stage*, 10 July 1948.

Ramphal, Vena (2021), Personal communication with author, December.

Rao, U.S. Krishna (2003), 'The Ram Gopal I Knew', *Sruti*, 230: 27–8.

Rao, U.S. Krishna (2004), 'Tributes to a Great Guru', *Nartanam*, 4 (1): 21–6.

Rashid, Abdur (1950), 'The Duties and Functions of the Amin', *Proceedings of the Indian History Congress*, 13: 193–6.

Reason, Matthew & Dee Reynolds (2010), 'Kinesthesia, Empathy, and Related Pleasures: An Inquiry into Audience Experiences of Watching Dance', *Dance Research Journal*, 42 (2): 49–75.

'Review', *Dancing Times*, May, 752–3.

'Review', *Los Angeles Times*.

'Review', *San Pedro News Pilot*.

'Review', *Cavalcade*, 5 August 1939.

'Review', *The Times*, n.p.

'Review', *The Daily Telegraph*, n.p.

'Review', *The Sunday Times*, 30 July 1939.

'Review', *Dancing Times*, 52.

'Review', *Dancing Times*, 450–1.

'Review', *The Daily Telegraph*.

'Review', *Musical Events*, May 1948.

'Review', *Radio Times*, 19 November, n.p.

'Review', *Spectator*, 18 March, n.p.

'Review', *India News*, 4.

'Review', *Scotsman*, 18 October, n.p.

'Review', *The Times*, n.p.

'Review', *The Times*, n.p.

'Review', *The Times*, n.p.

Robinson, Harlow (1994), *The Last Impresario: The Life, Times, and Legacy of Sol Hurok*, New York: Viking Adult.

Ruyter, Nancy Lee Chalfa (2019), *La Meri and Her Life in Dance: Performing the World*, Florida: University Press of Florida.

Sai, Veejay (2015), 'A Visual Tribute to Ram Gopal, India's Forgotten Dance Superstar', 23 January, https://scroll.in/article/689145/a-visual-tribute-to-ram-gopal-indias-forgotten-dance-superstar Accessed 4.6.16.

Salter, Mark B. (2003), *Rights of Passage. The Passport in International Relations*, Boulder, CO: Lynne Rienner.

Sarabhai, Mrinalini (2003), 'Remembering Ram Gopal', *Nartanam. A Quarterly Journal of Indian Dance*, 3 (4), Oct–Dec (special edition): 51–2.

Sarabhai, Mrinalini (2004), *The Voice of the Heart: An Autobiography*, New Delhi: HarperCollins.

Sarker, Bisakha (2020), 'Uday Shankar & Anna Pavlova, An Intercultural Dialogue in Dance', online webinar discussion, *Sampad*, South Asian Heritage Month, 7 August, n.p. https://www.sampad.org.uk/news/south-asian-heritage-month/ Accessed 7.8.20.

Saroja, M.K. (2017), Interview with author, December 2017.

Sarwal, Amit (2014), 'Louise Lightfoot and Rajkumar Priyagopal Singh: The First Manipuri Dance Tour of Australia, 1951', *South Asian Popular Culture*, 12 (2): 89–110.

Sarwal, Amit & David Walker (2015), 'Staging a Cultural Collaboration: Louise Lightfoot and Ananda Shivaram's First Indian Dance Tour of Australia, 1947–1949', *Dance Chronicle*, 38: 305–35.

Scolieri, Paul A. (2020a), 'Ted Shawn and the Defence of the Male Dancer', Talk given at Jacob's Pillow, MA, USA, 7 March 2020, https://danceinteractive.jacobspillow.org/themes-essays/men-in-dance/ted-shawn-defense-male-dancer/ Accessed 5.8.20.

Scolieri, Paul A. (2020b), *Ted Shawn: His Life, Writings, and Dances*, New York: Oxford University Press.

Segal, Zohra (2015[2010]), *Close-Up: Memoirs of a Life on Stage and Screen*, New Delhi: Women Unlimited.

Selth, Andrew (2016), 'The Road to Mandalay: Orientalism, "Burma Girls" and Western Music', *Journal of Research in Gender Studies*, 6 (1): 159–91.

Shah, Reena (2005), *Movement in Stills. The Dance and Life of Kumudini Lakhia*, Ahmedabad, India: Mapin Publishing.

Shambu, Shane (2022), Personal communication with author, June.

Shawn, Ted & Poole Gray (1979 [1960]), *One Thousand and One Night Stands*, Garden City: Doubleday.

Shay, Anthony (1999), 'Parallel Traditions: State Folk Dance Ensembles and Folk Dance in "The Field"', *Dance Research Journal*, 31 (1): 29–56.

Shay, Anthony (2009), 'Choreographing Masculinity. Hypermasculine Dance Styles as Invented Tradition in Egypt, Iran, and Uzbekistan' in Jennifer Fisher & Anthony Shay (eds), *When Men Dance. Choreographing Masculinities across Borders*, 287–308, Oxford: Oxford University Press.

Sheybal, Vladek, https://vladeksheybal.com Accessed 6.10.18.

Siddall, Jeanette (1999), 'The Evolution of Dance Management in Britain' in Linda Jasper & Jeanette Siddall (eds), *Managing Dance: Current Issues and Future Strategies*, Horndon, 5–24, Devon: Northcote House.

Sikand, Nandini (2017), *Languid Bodies, Grounded Stances. The Curving Pathway of Neoclassical Odissi Dance*, New York, Oxford: Berghahn Books.

Sims, Jennifer P. (2012), 'Beautiful Stereotypes: The Relationship Physical Attractiveness and Mixed Race Identity', *Identities*, 19 (1): 61–80.

Singh, J.P. (2010), *Globalized Arts. The Entertainment Economy and Cultural Identity*, New York: Columbia University Press.

Singh, Lata (2009), 'Foregrounding the Actresses' Questions: Bengal and Maharashtra' in Lata Singh (ed.), *Play-House of Power: Theatre in Colonial India*, 270–94, New Delhi: Oxford University Press.

Singha, Rena & Reginald Massey (1967), *Indian Dances – Their History and Growth*, London: Faber & Faber.

Sinha, Ajay (2017), 'Iconology of a Photograph', *Art and Vernacular Photographies in Asia*, 8, http://hdl.handle.net/2027/spo.7977573.0008.106 Accessed 20.4.19.

Sinha, Ajay (2022), *Photo-Attractions: An Indian Dancer, an American Photographer and a German Camera*, New Jersey: Rutgers University Press.

Sklar, Deirdre (1991), 'On Dance Ethnography', *Dance Research Journal*, 23: 6–10.

Snyder, Allegra Fuller (1980), 'Lord Shiva Danced' in Elizabeth May (ed.), *Music of Many Cultures. An Introduction*, 80, Los Angeles: University of California Press.

Soneji, Davesh (2008), 'Memory and the Recovery of Identity: Living Histories and the Kalavantulu of Coastal Andhra Pradesh' in Indira Viswanathan Peterson & Davesh Soneji (eds), *Performing Pasts. Reinventing the Arts in Modern South India*, 283–312, New Delhi, London: Oxford University Press.

Soneji, Davesh (2010), *Bharatanatyam: A Reader*, Oxford, New Delhi: Oxford University Press.

Soneji, Davesh (2012), *Unfinished Gestures. Devadasis, Memory, and Modernity in South India*, Chicago: University of Chicago Press.

Srinivasan, Amrit (1983), 'The Hindu Temple-Dancer: Prostitute or Nun?' *Cambridge Anthropology*, 8 (1): 73–99.

Srinivasan, Priya (2012), *Sweating Saris. Indian Dance as Transnational Labor*, Philadelphia: Temple University Press.

Stange, Wolfgang (2018), Personal communication with author, September.

Stebbins, Genevieve (1886), *Delsarte System of Dramatic Expression*, New York: Edgar S. Werner.

Stoneley, Peter (2006), *A Queer History of the Ballet*, London, New York: Routledge.

Stuart, Otis (1995), *Perpetual Motion. The Public and Private Lives of Rudolf Nureyev*, New York: Simon & Schuster.

Subrahmanyam, Padma (1988), *Introduction to Natyasastra*, Pennsylvania: Arsha Vidya Gurukulam.

Subrahmanyam, Padma (2021), Online talk given for *Pancham*, hosted by Centre for Indian Classical Dance, Leicester (CICD), 10 June. https://www.cicd.org.uk/index.php/cicd-s-40th-anniversary/cicd-s-40th-anniversary Accessed 10.6.21.

Subramanyam, Anusha (2022), Personal communication with author, June.

Sundaram, Chitra (2022), Personal communication with author, June.

Swierenga, Robert P. (1991), 'List upon List: Ship Passenger Records and Immigration Research', *Journal of American Ethnic History*, 10 (3): 42–53.

Taylor, Diana (2003), *The Archive and the Repertoire: Performing Cultural Memory in the Americas*, Durham, London: Duke University Press.

Terry, Walter (1976), *Ted Shawn, Father of American Dance: A Biography*, New York: Random House Publishing Group.

Thiagarajan, Premalatha (2012) *Performing Indian Dance in Malaysia*, PhD thesis, U.C Riverside.

Thobani, Sitara (2017), *Indian Classical Dance and the Making of Postcolonial National Identities: Dancing on Empire's Stage*, Oxford, New York: Routledge.

Thomas, Helen (2018), 'Reconstruction and Dance as Embodied Textual Practice' in Geraldine Morris & Larraine Nicholas (eds), *Rethinking Dance History, Issues and Methodologies*, 69–81, London, New York: Routledge.

Topolski, Dan (2010), 'Feliks Topolski: Eye Witness to the 20th Century', talk given at Gresham College, London, 22 March. https://www.gresham.ac.uk/lectures-and-events/feliks-topolski-eye-witness-to-the-20th-century Accessed 11.8.19.

Topolski, Feliks 'Feliks Topolski', https://culture.pl/en/artist/feliks-topolski Accessed 11.8.19.

Törngren, Sayaka Osanami & Yuna Sato (2019), 'Beyond Being Either-Or: Identification of Multiracial and Multiethnic Japanese', *Journal of Ethnic and Migration Studies*, 7

(4): 802–20, https://www.tandfonline.com/doi/full/10.1080/1369183X.2019.1654155 Accessed 10.3.20.

'Traditional Indian Dances', *Dancing Times*, March, 197–9.

Turner, Graeme (2006 [1998]), *Film as Social Practice*, London, New York: Routledge.

Turner, Pam (2000), Interview with author, May 2000.

Van Vechten, Carl (1938), 'Review', 8 May, n.p.

Vatsyayan, Kapila (1987), 'Nature, Tradition and Originality', Nandalal Bose Memorial Lecture 1985, Santiniketan: Tarunbikas Lahiri.

Venkatachalam, Govindraj (1947), *Dance in India*, Bombay: Nalanda Publications.

Venkataraman, Leela (2003), 'Ambassador of Indian Dance', *The Hindu*, 24 October, n.p.

Venkataraman, Leela (2005), 'Made History and Made by History: Rukmini Davi's Integrated Approach to Bharatanatam' in Avanthi Meduri (ed.), *Rukmini Devi Arundale (1904–1986). A Visionary Architect of Indian Culture and the Performing Arts*, 123–38, Delhi: Motilal Banarsidass Publishers.

Veroli, Patrizia (2014), 'Serge Lifar as a Dance Historian and the Myth of Russian Dance in "Zarubezhnaia Rossiia" (Russia Abroad) 1930–1940', *Dance Research*, 32 (2): 105–43.

Viswanathan, Lakshmi (1996), 'Indian Dance Went International with Him', *The Hindu*, 5 July, n.p.

Walker, Margaret E. (2014), *India's Kathak Dance in Historical Perspective*, Surrey: Ashgate.

Watson, Nick J., Stuart Weir & Stephen Friend (2005), 'The Development of Muscular Christianity in Victorian Britain and Beyond', *Journal of Religion and Society*, 7: 1–21.

Wells, Catharine (2001), *East with ENSA. Entertaining the Troops in the Second World War*, London, New York: The Radcliffe Press.

Wenzel, Lynn & Carol J. Binkowski (2016), *New Jersey's Remarkable Women: Daughters, Wives, Sisters, and Mothers Who Have Shaped History*, Connecticut: Rowman & Littlefield.

Werbner, Pnina, ed. (2008), *Anthropology and the New Cosmopolitanism: Rooted, Feminist and Vernacular Perspectives*, London: Bloomsbury Academic.

Westman, Nancy (2006), *Dans med Häger*, Stockholm: Lind & Co.

White, Edward (2014), *The Tastemaker. Carl Van Vechten and the Birth of Modern America*, New York: Farrar, Straus & Giroux.

White, John (2000), Interview with author, August 2000.

Wilcox, Emily (2017), 'When Place Matters. Provincializing the "Global"' in Geraldine Morris & Larraine Nicholas (eds), *Rethinking Dance History*, 160–72, London, New York: Routledge.

Williams, Linda, ed. (1995), *Viewing Positions: Ways of Seeing Film*, New Brunswick: Rutgers University Press.

Williams, Peter (1956), 'The Legend of the Taj Mahal', *Dance & Dancers*, November, 19.

Williams, Peter (1960), 'Review', *Dance & Dancers*, May, 13.

Woody, Regina J. (1956), *Janey and the Summer Dance Camp*, New York: Alfred A. Knopf.

Wright, Arnold, ed. (1910), *Twentieth Century Impressions of Burma: Its History, People, Commerce, Industries, and Resource*, London: Lloyd's Greater Britain Pub. Co.

Yadagudde, Prakash (2020), *Manch* UK talk online, 3 July.

Index